Miss Marlow's book . . . is a worthy successor to her study of Peterloo; she is making a place for herself in this corner of history. She has done her work thoroughly, with much diligent delving to check even the smallest of doubtful details, and has been able to rectify some misconceptions . . . It is well illustrated, and the narrative is in an easy conversational style' – *The Guardian*

'If one peels away the sentiment, little is generally known about the Martyrs and Joyce Marlow is to be applauded for providing more information and a deeper appreciation of the individual characters and their lives after transportation' – *Times Educational Supplement*

'She writes with zest, and she has an inquisitive eye which has led her to some original research. With the assistance of archivists and others in Australia and Canada she has added new touches to our knowledge of the experiences of the Dorset labourers during their years of transportation, and also of their lives in Canada after their emigration in 1844 and 1846. She has, in particular, filled out a few details on the most silent member of the Tolpuddle Six, James Hammett' – *Times Literary Supplement*

D0530784

JOYCE MARLOW

The Tolpuddle Martyrs

GRAFTON BOOKS

A Division of the Collins Publishing Group

LONDON GLASGOW
TORONTO SYDNEY AUCKLAND

Grafton Books
A Division of the Collins Publishing Group
8 Grafton Street, London W1X 3LA

Published by Grafton Books 1985

First published in Great Britain by
André Deutsch Ltd 1971

ISBN 0-586-03832-9

Printed and bound in Great Britain by
Collins, Glasgow

Set in Baskerville

For Carole Fries who was the original editor
of this book and remains a close friend

Contents

List of Illustrations

Foreword to the Revised Edition

What I have done in this revised edition is (a) to correct factual errors, (b) to amend a few judgements with which, fourteen years after the book was originally published, I no longer entirely agree, (c) to compress the last chapter and epilogue into one and to bring subsequent events up to date to include the 150th anniversary commemorations. The factual error I made was to state that James Hammett was not a Methodist. To this question I had given considerable time and thought and I reached the conclusion that he was *not*, mainly from the negative standpoint that I could find no firm evidence that he *was*. It was an error on which no critic or reviewer picked me up, but a retired Methodist minister did. I had a fruitful correspondence with the Reverend R. D. Moore who had done a considerable amount of research into the story of the Tolpuddle Martyrs, who had once considered writing about them himself – though he nicely said he was glad he had not, because my book was much better than his would have been – and who had been 'stationed' in the Dorchester area. The Reverend Moore convinced me that James Hammett had always been a Methodist and had remained faithful to John Wesley's creed unto death. He also suggested that my estimate of Hammett's character was in need of slight revision. In this instance his evidence was hearsay, based on close contacts with Hammett's descendants in Tolpuddle in the 1950s, notably with his granddaughter, Mrs Roberts. The reported conversations seemed to me as valid as most of the evidence about 'the silent Hammett', so I have amended my earlier assessment of his character.

In the original edition of the book there was a page of acknowledgements to those who had helped me during my research. Some of those mentioned I know have since retired, some I suspect will have died, but I should nevertheless like to reaffirm my thanks to them, or to their memories. I extended my general thanks to the staffs of the Public Records Offices both at Chancery Lane and Ashridge, Herts (as they then were); to the staff of the British Museum; the County Archivist of the County Records Office in Dorchester; the Senior Archivist of the Archives Authority of New South Wales in Sydney, who, as I was unable to afford to go to Australia, sent me masses of photocopied convict documents; similarly to the Senior Archivist of the Archives Office of Tasmania in Hobart; and to the Press Officers at Australia House in London. I went on to thank the following specific persons: Mr Brown, the then Librarian of the T.U.C. at Congress House in London; Mr Stan Hayward of the National Union of Agricultural Workers which has since become the Agricultural and Allied Workers National Trade Group, incorporated within the Transport and General Workers Union; Mr David Bull of the Department of Public Records and Archives in Toronto; Mr L. O. Bealing of Bournemouth who had made available to me his considerable genealogical work on the Tolpuddle men; Mr Deering who in 1970 owned Tudor Cottage, Greensted, Essex which had formerly been New House Farm; and to Richard Jenkins, barrister-at-law, who had taken pains to answer my general legal queries and to clarify aspects of 1834 procedure. My final thanks went to Messrs George Loveless, Leslie R. Gray, Allen Granger Talbot, and Walter C. Heine, all of whom then resided in London, Ontario, and had provided me with a good deal of information on the five 'martyrs' who emigrated to Canada.

Otherwise I re-present my narrative history of The Tolpuddle Martyrs with only a minor face-lift.

Joyce Marlow
St Albans 1985

Preface
by the Rt. Hon. Neil Kinnock MP

Like so many major historical landmarks the Tolpuddle martyrdom arose from no great design.

The six Dorset Labourers now honoured by democrats everywhere did not have their eye on posterity. They were profoundly moderate and pitifully honest. They did not seek martyrdom or self-glorification.

Their aims were as simple as they were justifiable. They sought the dignity of work, the decency of a fair wage, and the security of collective action for themselves, their families and their fellow workers. Their actions were a desperate response to the plain fact that – in George Loveless's words – 'it was impossible to live honestly on such scanty means'.

It is the simplicity of their case and the propriety and patience with which they put it as much as the elementary justice of their demands which has given strength and resonance to their message down the years.

Until recently, the respect for their sacrifice amongst those inside and outside the British Labour Movement was tempered with a certain nostalgic sentimentality. Not just because of the century and a half which separates us from Tolpuddle, but because of the changed circumstances in which we live and work. Distance lent enchantment and also bred complacency about the permanence of the conditions of liberty and prosperity which had been built since the 1830s.

The events of the last few years, however, have been proof of the impermanence of those conditions. It is a simple, sad fact that it is possible to say today in a way that would not have been plausible five years ago that the lessons of 1834 have direct relevance to our situation now.

It is not just that we have seen Trade Unions increasingly subjected to financial penalties, legal restrictions and ideological attack – though that has been a feature of the past five years.

It is something far more profound than that. It is that in

Britain the Government has used its power to promote perceptible change away from a confident consensus about the freedoms of institutions and individuals to a conflict about matters as diverse as the independence of the BBC, the autonomy of local councils, the opinions of bishops, the rights of benefit claimants and much else. The conditions of the 1830s are too deeply buried to return. But when obedience is demanded in place of loyalty, and deference in place of respect, then authoritarian attitudes are being resurrected from the past.

That is why it is well for rulers and ruled to remember not just the Martyrs of Tolpuddle but also the lessons which their experience taught.

First, they showed that their liberties as individuals could only be presented and sustained by acting collectively and that such collective activity, far from being antagonistic to personal freedom as we are repeatedly told, is essential to it for all but the most economically and politically opulent.

That is not a paradox. It is a matter of historical fact that the liberties most precious to our people have been attained by collective action and are sustained by collective agreement. It is a matter of material fact that for the overwhelming majority of people in this country – including the relatively well-off – private freedoms depend upon public provision, individual liberty depends upon collective contribution, the welfare of each of us is the responsibility of all of us. And it is a matter of practical fact that collective action has not diminished vitality, it has increased fitness and exposed and fostered talent, inventiveness and self confidence.

Second, the example of the Tolpuddle Martyrs provides a reminder that formal political freedoms mean little if they are constrained by economic inequality.

The right – for instance – of working people to organize in free Unions is not an assumed liberty if it means dismissals for those who choose to exercise that course of action or if it means bankruptcy for the Unions supporting them. The right to legal representation is neutralized if it can be brought by the rich, but is too costly for the poor. The right to speak can become nominal if access to the broadcasting and publishing media is limited by prohibitive cost or impeded by the interests which own and control those media. The right to take opportunities to learn or to work – and the status, security and self-fulfilment that goes with them – can be made meaningless for the individual if access to those opportunities is effectively limited because an individual is female or black or disabled. And personal economic poverty – from whatever cause – is obviously in itself a suspension of freedom no matter how libertarian the general political environment appears to be.

It is a mistake therefore for we who know advanced conditions of liberty to languish in self-satisfaction. Apart from the need for freedoms to be safeguarded and strengthened in western democracies like ours there is also a need to support others who are engaged in efforts to preserve or establish their basic rights in the numerous parts of the world where democracy is denied.

That is a third lesson of Tolpuddle – if freedom is to progress it must expand. Today the same excuses which were used 150 years ago to prevent the Tolpuddle Martyrs and their generation from securing justice are being paraded against the demands made by peoples outside the industrialized world. 'They are ignorant', we are told. 'They are not practised in Government.' 'They have no sense of responsibility' . . . 'Political rights and obligations would at best confuse them, at worst corrupt them.' And all the time we know that the real objection to economic and political emancipation comes from the economically and politically powerful who know that if they share their strength they will lose their strength. Throughout the third world there is a Tolpuddle every day in every continent and country ruled by a Squire Frampton or a Viscount Melbourne.

But such is the human condition that in the very act of persecution the bullies of the world germinate resistance. The taste for freedom is created by starving people of liberty, for the deprivation of political rights is always accompanied by the denial of economic rights. All ruling orders which constrict political democracy move – sometimes by accident, usually by design – toward reducing material security. And there has never been and there will never be a ruling order that will or can for any length of time provide economic plenty whilst prohibiting political democracy.

That too is a lesson from the Dorchester Assizes to be understood at all times.

And the final lesson to be taken and used comes directly in the words of the people of the Martyr's times.

A commentator on the parochial rebellions of the early 1830s wrote:

> we assign to political opinions properly so called only slight effect in producing the altered habits of the peasantry. They care little and know less about the questions of the franchise which vehemently agitate the inhabitants of manufacturing districts.
>
> But the vague notions of political and personal rights thus propagated have had considerable influence in generating and perpetuating a general dissatisfaction and a more active spirit of insubordination connected with no slight feeling of the power of the masses . . . A ringleader on trial emphatically whispered to a magistrate we have found the secret – *numbers will do it.*

A decade or so earlier in the wake of the Peterloo Massacre Shelley had written

> Rise like lions after slumber
> In unvanquishable number
> Strike your chains to earth like dew
> Which in sleep have fallen on you
> Ye are many – they are few

That is the message of majority which runs through the story of the Loveless brothers, Thomas and John Standfield, James Hammett and James Brine, the protests which their persecution aroused and the efforts which secured their freedom. And in faithful telling of that story Joyce Marlow breathes life into 'the watchword liberty' which remains the greatest of all human causes.

12

1: 'Respecting the Characters, etc., of the Six Men'

At day break of February 24th, 1834, in the small Dorset-shire village of Tolpuddle, a man left his cottage for his usual work as a labourer on a nearby farm. His name was George Loveless and he was thirty-seven years old. Tradition assumes that it was the sort of dank, cold day that bedevils the English winter with heavy grey skies merging into lifeless fields, thereby fitting the grimness of the weather to the events that overtook Loveless and his companions. In fact nobody who participated in the day's drama ever mentioned the elements, so later the sun could have risen, the skies have been blue, the air crisp and clear, in cheerful contrast to what took place.

Behind him in the cottage Loveless left his wife, Elizabeth, and three children. He was not to see them again in freedom for over three years, for he had not progressed far before the local constable, James Brine, accosted him. The following conversation ensued:

BRINE: I have a warrant for you, from the magistrates.
LOVELESS: What is its contents, sir?
BRINE: Take it yourself, you can read it as well as I can.

Loveless, who could almost certainly read far better than the constable, took the document. The charge was of having participated in the administration of an illegal oath. Brine then asked him, 'Are you willing to go to the magistrates with me?' to which Loveless replied, 'To any place wherever you wish me.' He and the constable proceeded to other cottages in the village, as the warrant contained five more names on the same charge of having participated in the administration of an illegal oath. The others thus named were George Loveless's youngest brother, James; Thomas Standfield and his eldest son, John; James Hammett and James Brine (no relation of the arresting constable; Brine happens to be a common Dorset name). All six men had been born and bred in and hardly strayed beyond the boundaries of Tolpuddle. All six were farm workers and members of the Friendly Society of Agricultural Labourers recently founded in Tolpuddle.

As the group approached James Hammett's cottage, local legend asserts that his young wife, Harriet, started to scream and wail and that her demented cries echoed through the village. Whether this was second sight, as Harriet Hammett was not to see her husband for more than five years, or whether the presence of the constable with the warrant was sufficient to induce the lamentations, legend does not record. However, Hammett obeyed the constable's instructions as willingly as did his companions, presumably watched by many of the villagers, because even if Mrs Hammett failed to scream like a banshee the constable's dawn activities must surely have aroused interest in a small, enclosed community. When the constable had visited the relevant cottages the six men, in his lone charge, set off calmly to walk the seven miles to the magistrates in Dorchester. Calmly? Perhaps they had inner fears and apprehensions but no outward alarm or doubt as to their speedy return was shown. Who were these six men? What manner of men were they who were to immortalize the comical name of Tolpuddle?

George Loveless was the leader of the group, as the constable's honouring him with the first arrest indicated. Perhaps the first thing to be said about Loveless is that he was a Methodist. Certainly he himself always believed that he had been victimized as much for his Methodism as for any other reason, including his membership of a trade union. It was a contention upheld by the *Morning Chronicle* when, six weeks after his arrest, it wrote of him as an object of persecution 'because he is a local preacher' and because 'persecution yet assails the poor Methodists of the country villages of the South and West of England'. Over the years many Nonconformists had been persecuted and in recent decades Methodism had, in the eyes of the Anglican hierarchy, frequently equalled sedition. The equation was not without justification because many of the Radical reformers were the products of a Methodist upbringing, fervently responding to the Methodist emphasis upon the individual stretching to the full the talents that God had given him. By 1834, in the new industrial towns that had spawned the Radical activity, the equation between Methodism and sedition had become blurred, partly because the whole spectrum of agitation had widened, partly because orthodox Methodists had been quick to demonstrate their loyalty to the State. For John Wesley had also preached that the State is ordained of God, therefore his followers should respect and honour their country's laws and government. In an area such as southeast Dorset, where the old-entrenched power structures remained at their most entrenched, where land-owning magistrates were Anglicans to a man, the equation was still valid. Merely by being Methodists the southern rural adherents of Wesley's creed demonstrated their difference, and in such difference lay the seeds of discontent which were to be firmly uprooted before they could flower into sedition.

Loveless was born in 1797 and as a Methodist he almost certainly learned the rudiments of literacy and numeracy at a Sunday School, but he was a mainly self-educated man. Despite the appallingly low agricultural wages – he was by trade a ploughman – he managed to acquire a small theological library, though at what cost in frugality and self-denial one can only guess. After long, hard hours labouring in the fields six days a week and without any statutory holidays, he studied at night, poring over his books by the light of a candle, until he had acquired a very

15

good standard of education, general and theological. For several years before his arrest Loveless had, as the *Morning Chronicle* observed, been a lay preacher; an attainment which indicates his above-average intelligence, application and determination, as well as the desire to teach and guide his fellow men. These characteristics were strongly in evidence in the actions which led to his arrest. Locally Loveless was known as a powerful, lucid Methodist orator who attracted good-sized crowds to his meetings, whether they were held in a chapel or in the open air. On Sundays he often preached in three different villages in the Weymouth circuit, walking twelve or more miles in the process, whatever the weather. The industry and self-denial he devoted to his religion may have been one of the reasons for the lateness of his marriage, which took place in 1824; for his class during this period, twenty-seven was a late age to go to the altar. His wife, his beloved Betsy, was born Elizabeth Snook Sprachlen in the nearby village of Dewlish, and by 1834 they had the three children whom Loveless left behind in his cottage when he set off to work on that February morning. In the years that lay ahead Betsy Loveless proved to be as stalwart, steadfast, and courageous as her husband, and all the available evidence points to theirs being a particularly close, loving, lifelong partnership.

Another reason for the comparatively late marriage could have been his sober, earnest temperament, for George Loveless reflected both sides of the Methodist coin; the orthodox one which urged its adherents dutifully to honour their King and Country, if not their country's established religion; and that which exhorted its followers to utilize the brains that God had given them. George Loveless had used his brains and his deliberations had led him to the conclusion that however hard he worked he could decreasingly support himself, his wife and his children on his wages; that this was unjust; that steps must be taken to remedy the injustice. Having reached a decision he acted, but the steps he took seemed to him reasonable and, above all, legal. Loveless was not an impulsive man who lightly undertook responsibility, nor did the God in Whom he believed countenance revolutionary action. It was, however, the interaction of character, temperament, and the teachings of Methodism that put him on the road to Dorchester and beyond on that morning of February 24th, 1834.

We have a clear picture of Loveless's physical appearance, assembled not only from the drawing that later appeared in *Cleave's Penny Gazette* but from the detailed examinations he was to undergo on the road that lay ahead from Dorchester. He was small of stature, being 5 feet 4½ inches – although it should be remembered that in 1834 the average Englishman was considerably more stunted than he is today. Loveless's hair was dark and his complexion swarthy, but his whiskers – shorn off by the time of the drawing but decorating his face in 1834 – were red. The determined chin that stares out from the drawing was in 1834 described as 'dimpled', and he possessed two scars, one on the upper lip, one on the left hand.

The Lovelesses were a large family. Thomas and Dinah Loveless had ten surviving adult children, including George and James. Generally they seem to have been spirited and independent-minded. When the local magistrate, James Frampton, later forwarded a list to the Home Office of those known to belong to the Friendly Society of Agricultural Labourers it contained, as he noted, 'no less than seven persons of the name of Loveless', that was in addition to George and James, all of whom the magistrate believed to be related.

George was the seventh child, while James was the youngest, being born in 1808 and therefore twenty-five at the time of the arrests. He, too, was married and had two children. He also devoutly followed the tenets of Methodism and, as was later said of both brothers, 'had, by dint of study and application, become so qualified in mental capacity as to be enabled to give lectures in the neighbourhood to their fellow labourers, and had been received into the Wesleyan Conference as preachers'. James had the same dark hair and swarthy complexion as George, but although he was tall for the period, being 5 feet 7½ inches, he was described as 'round shouldered'. Both brothers were regarded by the authorities as the ring-leaders in the formation of the Tolpuddle Friendly Society of Agricultural Labourers but to an extent James seems to have functioned in the shadow of George, as often happens when the older brother is the stronger character. However, if James originally applied himself to the tenets of Methodism, or joined the Society from hero-worship, he was to demonstrate some of the courage and determination of his brother. When they were separated by hundreds of miles, each without knowledge of what was happening to the other, James neither cracked nor lacked independence of spirit.

Another member of the large Loveless clan was involved in the group, and a heavy involvement it was, too. In 1812 Diana (or Dinniah, as it was often spelled) Loveless, the sister of George and James, had married Thomas Standfield. On that February morning in 1834 she was, therefore, to suffer the arrest of two brothers, her husband and her eldest son. Her husband Thomas was, at forty-four, the eldest of the group. He had dark hair flecked with grey, was swarthy of complexion and, like his brother-in-law George, was described as having 'a dimpled chin'. Again like his brothers-in-law he was a staunch Methodist, although not a lay preacher. After the Lovelesses he was the most committed to the Society's activities, many of their meetings, including the one that trapped them, being held in the upstairs room of his small thatched cottage in Tolpuddle High Street. John Standfield was the eldest of his six children, being born in 1813, and twenty-one at the time of the arrests. At 5 feet 8¼ inches John was the tallest of the group, dark and swarthy like his father, with the same 'dimpled chin'. He was subject to moles, having two round his right eye, one in the middle of his right cheek, and one below his lips. He was a bright, lively young man, full of spirit, fond of music and possessed of a good singing voice. He followed his father's religion of Methodism, was unmarried, and in the years that lay ahead was to prove himself a devoted son. After George Loveless he was probably the most intelligent of the group. Certainly he was to show courage, initiative and an ability to reason.

The two Lovelesses and the two Standfields formed a tight-knit group, bound by blood and marriage ties, and religion. For several years they also worked on the same farm, in the employment of a Mrs Northover who was later to supply them with excellent character references. With their common bonds, backgrounds and jobs they were a ready-made kernel, a pre-formed central committee when action seemed, or by George Loveless was deemed, necessary.

James Brine had no blood or current marriage links with either the Lovelesses or Standfields, although later he was to marry Elizabeth Standfield, the daughter of Thomas and the sister of John, and thus further tighten the bonds. Brine, who was born in 1813 but had not celebrated his twenty-first birthday when arrested, may already have been attracted to Elizabeth. She was then only fourteen but maturity came quickly in the harsh circumstances of rural life. He was 5 feet 5¾ inches tall, dark-haired like his companions but with a sallow rather than swarthy complexion. The Celtic strain is visible in the physical characteristics of the five men, there being nothing of the blue-eyed, fair-haired Anglo-Saxon about them. Brine was recorded as having 'a long nose' and the impression is of a bright, inquisitive personality, perhaps more emotional than the others – his later account of what befell him was by far the most dramatic. As Brine was not a Methodist but a member of the Church of England, it must have been temperament and personality (and perhaps Elizabeth) that drew him into the group.

Lastly there was James Hammett, born at the end of 1811, and therefore twenty-two when arrested. Five feet 7¼ inches tall, Hammett too was dark-haired but was more Anglo-Saxon in appearance, being blue-eyed and fair-complexioned. He had at some time survived the only too common disease of smallpox, having a pockmark on his right cheek. However, he seems to have been attractive to women as he had three marriages in all. In 1834 he had been married a couple of years, for the first time, and had a one-year-old baby son. Hammett is placed last in the group because he seems from the start to have been, and was later definitely to become, the odd man out. There were no blood or marriage links between him and the others. His sister, Elizabeth Hammett, was to marry Stephen Loveless, a nephew of George and James, but this did not occur until 1837 when the main drama was finished, and the marriage did not impinge upon the tight cohesion of the central Loveless/Standfield/Brine group. Among the character details of all six men forwarded to the Home Office by the most active local magistrate after their trial, neither he nor James Brine was listed as being a Methodist, whereas it was carefully noted that the two Standfields and the two Lovelesses were. Hammett was, however, a Methodist and remained a loyal member of that faith until his death. It was presumably the shared tenets of their yet persecuted religion that originally drew him into the Society.

But was James Hammett ever a member of the Friendly Society of Agricultural Labourers founded in Tolpuddle? Doubt has been cast upon this generally accepted and seemingly obvious proposition, arising in part from the substantiated fact that he was not present at the fatal meeting in Thomas Standfield's cottage that trapped the men, and that he accepted the responsibility of shielding his younger brother who was present. Mid-twentieth century research into Methodist registers showed that there were three James Hammetts probably alive in Tolpuddle in 1834, and it has been suggested that our Hammett not only shielded his brother, but also one of his namesakes. To accept responsibility for your own brother when you have been deeply involved in a society's activities is one thing; to shoulder the blame for two persons when you have never been connected with the society is a different matter. If Hammett indeed took the latter course it would indicate an uncommon nobility of character and would of course mean that one of the most celebrated of early trade unionists was not a member of a trade society (even though his brother definitely was). The action might also indicate a passively acquiescent nature bordering on idiocy; and that he was a slow-witted fellow who followed where George Loveless led has been suggested. The problem with Hammett is that he, unlike the other five men, said so little about the most traumatic years of his life. Unlike them he left no written account of his appalling experiences and later made only the briefest of public statements, which for years nobody bothered to check, preferring 'the silent Hammett' of legend. But James Hammett would have needed to have been mentally retarded not to have realized there was at least the possibility of trouble in following where George Loveless was leading. Furthermore, although Hammett himself later confirmed that he was not present at the fatal meeting, he never denied membership of the Society, nor explicitly did any of his companions. Certainly the most active magistrate was convinced that Hammett was not only a member of the Society, but one of the ring-leaders. The magistrate had no problem instructing Constable Brine *which* of the three James Hammetts to arrest. It would therefore seem, beyond that reasonable shadow of a doubt, that all six of the men who became 'the Tolpuddle martyrs' were actually members of the trade society which brought about their martyrdom. Hammett was not of the same intellectual calibre as George Loveless, but then neither were the others. He must have possessed sterling qualities that made him act, in the face of possible dangers, against the grain of the demoralization that held thousands of his fellow labourers throughout southern England in its apathetic grip. Had he not lived in a village where there was a George Loveless he may well not have acted of his own volition, but with such a man as a neighbour, Hammett himself had sufficient spirit to stand up and be counted.

One other fact set Hammett apart from his companions. He had a previous criminal record, of which the magistrates and their supporters later attempted to make much. His crime consisted of having been 'charged on oath on suspicion of having on or about the 28th day of February last, stolen three pieces of iron, the property of Mr William Brine of Tolpuddle'. (February last being 1829.) Whether or not he stole the iron we do not know because to be suspected and charged on the oath of a gentleman was sufficient for sentence to be effected which in his case it was – the existing records prove that Hammett served four months' hard labour at the House of Correction in Dorchester in the year 1829. His having had direct experience of early nineteenth-century English prisons would again seem to indicate that it was from character, not from sheep-like stupidity, that he joined the Friendly Society. He was the only one of the six men who had actually suffered the miseries of imprisonment and knew what current justice could entail. Not that any of them anticipated arrest or imprisonment when they formed their Friendly Society but they were aware of the strength and obduracy of the forces ranged against them and therefore of possible dangers.

George Loveless's self-taught literacy, the standard which he and his brother James had attained as lay preachers, has already been mentioned, but all six men could read and write, including Hammett, if not to the same high degree as the Lovelesses. At a time when schooling for village labourers was virtually non-existent and rural illiteracy was widespread[1] this emphasizes their above-average intelligence and independence of mind – the qualities that set them apart from so many of their fellow-labourers and led them to act.

On that morning of February 24th, 1834, George and James Loveless, John and Thomas Standfield, James Brine and James Hammett, bade what they thought was a temporary farewell to their wives, mothers and children. As they accompanied the constable on the rough road to Dorchester none of them knew what lay ahead. Each step past the familiar bare hedgerows, the stark lifeless trees, took them nearer a total deprivation of liberty, towards nightmare years that were to transport them thousands of miles across sea and land to countries and climates unimagined; during which they were to witness the depths of human degradation and to endure a form of slavery; from which they were to emerge not unscathed, but as triumphant survivors enshrined as 'martyrs'.

Before examining the complex framework of character and circumstance that led to the arrest of these six men on the charge of having participated in the administration of an illegal oath, the vast changes that had occurred in rural England, particularly southern England, need to be

[1] The 1840 literacy figures, from the earliest census taken, show that in fact Dorset emerged well. Only 30 per cent of the Dorset population was recorded as being illiterate, whereas in Bedfordshire it was 69 per cent, in Huntingdonshire 51 per cent, Essex 50 per cent and so on. But as E. J. Hobsbawm and George Rudé have pointed out, in *Captain Swing*, the returns were drawn from parish registers, and the ability to scrawl your name, rather than mark with an X, was no test of general literacy.

outlined. It was these that produced the circumstances that induced the Tolpuddle men to form their Friendly Society, and thus lift themselves from obscurity into the annals of English history.

2: 'How Do You Live upon Half a Crown a Week?'

By the 1830s an agrarian revolution had occurred to parallel the accompanying industrial revolution. Like the latter it was an evolutionary process, but again like the latter its effects were sufficiently traumatic and dramatic to justify the term 'revolution'. But unlike its industrial counterpart it was a revolution that few noticed. Nobody could fail to be aware of, even if they chose to ignore, the mushrooming growth of such towns as Manchester, Leeds, Sheffield, Birmingham, Glasgow, of the industrial developments that were changing the face and the economy of Britain. But to the majority of Englishmen rural England, with its picturesque villages and its happy peasantry, remained the beautiful, green land it had always been. There were one or two disturbers of this romantic vision, notably William Cobbett, that great journalist and champion of 'the Commons of England', but even Cobbett could not stir the nation's conscience virtually single-handed.

What had in fact happened in rural England was the Enclosure Acts, the majority of which occurred between 1770 and 1830 (some land was enclosed before 1770, and some after 1830, but these were the vital years). In that period six million acres of common land were enclosed. To see what this cold statistic meant in human terms, let us examine what life was like for the fathers and grandfathers of the Lovelesses, the Standfields, Brine and Hammett. They lived in a Tolpuddle that was, as were hundreds of villages throughout southern, western, eastern and central England, part of a complex and ancient economy. (The North never completely fitted into the pattern, it was too far away from the old centres of English life, and the rude northern barbarians were left to their own devices.) There was the Lord of the Manor, and other squires and landlords who already owned large tracts of land, which were their private property. But there were also the common lands on which the Lord of the Manor held the mineral and surface and sporting rights, but which belonged to the village and villagers. They were divided into arable, pasture and waste land, and village committees decided what should be sown. As the years went by, the management of the arable and pasture lands fell more and more into the hands of the local hierarchy influenced by the Lord of the Manor. However, each villager retained the ancient, apparently inviolable rights to graze his cattle on the common land, to gather brush-wood or turf for fuel from the waste land, to collect the gleanings from the community harvest which helped keep his family in bread for the winter months and to own a strip of common land on which he could grow what he chose. He also had some say in the management of the community land which meant he had a voice and status in the village life as a whole. Again, over the years, the labourers' voice in community affairs lessened while the landlords' and magistrates' acquired more stentorian tones. But the grandfathers of the Standfields, the Lovelesses, Brine and Hammett had an accepted position on the hierarchical village ladder.

It must be stressed that Grandfathers Loveless, Standfield, Brine and Hammett were by no means independent. The amount of land they owned, the extra gleanings they were allowed to gather, did not keep them. They always worked for the squires and large farmers as labourers on wages, and because of the vagaries of the English climate and recurring agricultural depressions they were always liable to be thrown out of employment. Life in general was always tough. The image that was later drawn in the post-Enclosure years (and to which William Cobbett to a degree contributed) of the sturdy, healthy, independent English peasant was partly myth. With reference to health, sanitation was of course non-existent and villages were regularly ravaged by disease (hence the pockmark on James

Hammett's face). The myth, like all good myths, has a basis of truth. The grandfathers had a minor independence. They were three-quarters employed labourers subject to the whims and character of their master, but they were one-quarter producer, with their allotted strip of land and their periphery rights. That one quarter made the difference between a subsistence level and starvation; more important, these ancient rights gave them a status in the village.

Then came Enclosure. Part of the impetus for Enclosure derived from the genuine desire to improve the output of English agriculture, particularly grain, because the expanding populations of the new industrial towns demanded their daily bread which grain provided. The system whereby thousands of acres of common land were farmed by hundreds of villages in small strips seemed wasteful and inefficient. Indeed it was, and in the Enclosure years the output of grain more than doubled. But the Enclosure impetus was also largely greed. Once the ball started rolling, the powerful and influential squires and large farmers found they could, without much difficulty, acquire common land and turn it into their own private property. It was a prospect few could resist. Virtually nobody considered what the effect would be on those suddenly deprived of their ancient rights to grow, to graze and to glean on the common lands.

Enclosure began with a petition to Parliament which propounded the inefficiencies of the present system, and the advantages to be gained from working large areas under a single management. In the Enclosure years literally thousands of individual petitions were presented to Parliament by the squires and landlords. Once they had been presented each individual Bill was introduced into Parliament and next referred to a committee which considered any counter-petitions against the proposed measures. Assuming there were none, or if they were considered invalid, the Bill was passed and finally received the Royal

Assent. Commissioners then descended and redistributed the common land in the villages. Following the redistribution up went the hedges. The patch-work quilt effect of the English countryside is now regarded as characteristic, but it occurred as a result of Enclosure.

A few villages, with a strong effective leader, successfully counter-petitioned against Enclosure. Even if they did not win the battle against the swallowing up of the common land, the villagers received some compensation for the loss of the allotted strips and the old periphery rights to graze their cattle and collect the gleanings (because they, of course, went too once the land was private property). But most villagers did not know what had occurred until after it had happened. They lived isolated lives, with no political rights, no vote and had little knowledge of what took place in the House of Commons. While they were still busy earning their daily bread, or considering how they could organize themselves against the landlords and stop the Enclosure of their common land, the Bill received the Royal Assent. The villagers received no compensation whatsoever for the loss of their land and previous rights.

By the time George and James Loveless, John and Thomas Standfield, James Hammett and James Brine were born, the agricultural labourers were possession-less, status-less beings, deprived of all previous rights. If they were lucky they lived in a cottage belonging to the farmer, without a garden or a strip of land to call their own; if they were unlucky they existed as nomads. In both cases they were totally and absolutely dependent upon the wages their employers could or would pay them. In a glutted labour market, the wages the farmers could or would pay were often at starvation level.

So what, as an agricultural labourer in a now Enclosed area – facing the stark fact that, labour from morn till night as you might, the rewards were insufficient to support your family – could you do? Did the State provide any aid?

To a minor degree it did, but the aid provided was yoked to the reason why, labour as you might, you could not achieve a subsistence wage. In 1834 the old Elizabethan Poor Law, whereby the State had taken over from the Church the duty of supporting the paupers of the parish from the rates, was still in existence. But in the old days the paupers had been a small section of the community – the decrepit, the dying, the bastard and orphaned, those absolutely unable to fend for themselves – and, at a low level, the rates had just about supported them.

With the advent of Enclosure hundreds of families were deprived of their old rights and means of subsistence, and were forced to apply for parish relief. Before the end of the eighteenth century the Elizabethan Poor Law was out of control. Thus, in 1795, the famous Speenhamland decision was reached. A group of magistrates, accepting the fact 'that the present state of the poor does require further assistance than has generally been given them,' met in the Berkshire village of Speenhamland (long a part of the town of Newbury), in an effort to raise wages and relieve the burden on the rates. Unfortunately, their efforts produced a result that was not only disastrous for the continuing state of the poor, but also increased the burden on the rates. For at Speenhamland what has been called 'the bread and children law' came into being. Instead of fixing a minimum wage, the magistrates decided that if the fluctuating price of bread rose to a certain level and/or a man had more than a certain number of children and his wages fell below another level, the difference was to be paid from the rates. Again, unfortunately, the scheme was adopted throughout the country.

The resulting situation was that farmers were encouraged to pay as little as possible because the difference had to be subsidized from the rates. It left the labourers in a hopeless predicament. If they complained about the wages they were, in the glutted labour market, immediately turned off.

Even without a complaint they were just as likely to be sacked due to an even more tortuous situation which had arisen, the dog-in-the-manger logic of which was explained by a farmer witness to the Poor Law Commission. If he, Farmer X, heard that Farmer Y had turned off twenty of his men, his reaction was to sack twenty too because he, X, as a ratepayer would have to subsidize Farmer Y's men on parish relief, so Y could subsidize the same number of his.

As an additional burden the agricultural labourers' right of movement had long been controlled by the Laws of Settlement. These laws had, in fact, been amended by 1834 but because the right to move had been legally abridged for so long the will was virtually non-existent. It was accepted that the labourer stayed in his own parish, where, only where – and this was another deterrent to movement – he had the right of relief.

Over the years the vicious circle of low wages and parish relief tightened. After Waterloo the already glutted market was further flooded by thousands of soldiers returning from the wars, and the spiral tightened. Also after 1815 there was a general agricultural depression. The long French Wars had produced unnatural boom years, but the farmers measured their current position against those years, and with the going tougher and the profits fewer, the inclination to pay a living wage lessened. More and more families needed parish relief, whether according to the Poor or Speenhamland laws. To cut the burden on the rates, or at least keep it level, farcical situations arose with one parish smuggling its poor into another. There were incessant law suits between parishes costing thousands of pounds per annum – more than the original demand on the rates would have been. The administration of relief became increasingly harsh and more humiliating, on the premise that if receiving it was made wellnigh intolerable fewer would ask. Slave auctions of fit men claiming relief were held on the village greens, paupers were forced to walk round the villages with bells round their necks proclaiming their desperate situations, men to tramp thirty miles a day to obtain their eightpence relief.

One cynical labourer summed up the post-Enclosure situation thus, addressing the hierarchy at large with eloquent rhetoric: 'For whom are they to be sober? For whom are they to save? For the parish? If I am diligent, shall I have leave to build a cottage? If I am sober, shall I have land for a cow? If I am frugal, shall I have half an acre of potatoes? You offer no motives; you have nothing but a parish officer and a workhouse! Bring me another pot!' Drowning your sorrows in as much drink as wages allowed was one answer to the miseries of rural life. Another answer, for those with independence of spirit, increasingly tended to be crime. William Cobbett asked a labourer:

'How do you live upon half a crown a week?'
'I don't live upon it,' said he.
'How do you live then?'
'Why', said he, 'I poach, it is better to be hanged than to be starved to death.'

As rural crime rates soared, particularly for poaching which was regarded as fair play – for had not unjust Game Laws and Enclosure Acts infringed upon earlier ancient game rights – so did the belief that 'nothing but the terror of human suffering can avail to prevent crime,' and the consequent severity of punishment. It was the hierarchy ignoring the causes and seeing only the symptoms of crime that helped produce such sentences as fourteen-year-old boys being hanged for stealing a sheep, and young men being transported for life for stealing a tablecloth. The peasantry had to be kept down, for the other road led to anarchy. And James Hammett's sentence of four months'

31

hard labour for perhaps stealing three pieces of iron was quite mild.

On all sides the village labourer was increasingly trapped and demoralized. However, apart from drink, crime or anarchy there was a course of action lying open to those who were not sunk in despair or apathy and that was a political one. In the towns this had been taken, not admittedly with great effect, but even in 1834 some concessions had been made to urban discontent. So why was none taken in, and therefore nothing given to, the country districts?

Concerted rural political action was almost a non-starter. So many factors were against it. Whereas the industrial towns had undergone a completely new experience, indeed were a new experience, that had shaken the existing structures from near-top to bottom, in the country it was a case of *plus ça change, plus c'est la même chose*. In the country there had been no disturbance of the hierarchy, no new classes had emerged, merely a loss of status of an existing one. In the country, power was still concentrated in the same few hands, in none more tightly than the magistrates'. The magistrate system dated back to the middle ages, to the days of Edward III, when Justices of the Peace were appointed throughout England to effect certain government orders and to keep the peace in their counties. Over the centuries more and more power devolved on to them. Any new duty became theirs, any old duty that was not functioning adequately passed under their jurisdiction, and they were the local eyes and ears and mouthpieces for the central government. In the absence of national law and order enforcement bodies – it was England's proud boast that she had no standing army and there was, of course, no national police force – they wielded immense power in both town and country districts. On the whole it is a testimony to the energy and integrity of the magistrates that the ramshackle system functioned as well as it did, without collapsing into total repression or boiling into revolution. As the nineteenth century progressed, their power was increasingly eroded in the face of organized resistance until the system could no longer function adequately in the towns. In the country, magistrates remained landlords, employers, the link between local activity and central government, the keepers of the peace empowered to arrest, to try, to sentence or to commit to the Assizes those who fell foul of them. The six Tolpuddle men were to become aware of the width and scope of the magistrates' powers.

In the country there was also the question of proximity, human and geographical. Thousands of people herded into factories offered a better breeding-ground for organized discontent than thousands of farm labourers doing their individual jobs on hundreds of farms. The labourers could – as the Lovelesses, Standfields, Hammett and Brine did – get together in the evening, but it was much easier to assemble a larger number from a factory. There was the closeness of village life. Anonymity had to a degree arrived in the towns, but in the village there was no such comforting cloak. Squires and magistrates soon knew of people's activities. There was the question of distance and speed of communication. Rural England remained very isolated. The better roads, the new railway tracks, linked the industrial towns. What could now be communicated and expedited between towns by mechanical transport, had to be organized on foot or horseback in the country.

Because the unrest was in the towns, the focus was on the towns, and vice versa. Because there was no apparent acclaim or parliamentary gain or personal glory, nor so obvious an easing of social conscience to be obtained from the torpid, dispirited countryside, nobody bothered to organize it. The agricultural labourer was enmeshed in another vicious circle. The Radical newspapers and orators thundered about the horrors and injustices of life in the industrial towns, but there was scarcely a murmur about the horrors or injustices of rural life. The new industrial masses had a hundred champions to the village labourer's handful. If God and government helps those who help themselves, the same was true of the Radicals and the village labourers. By the end of the 1820s the situation in southern and central England, in those grain-producing areas most affected by Enclosure, was desperate. Men simply could not support their families however hard they worked. The children were crying with hunger. They were subjected to dire humiliations by overseers of parish relief. Every ounce of pride and self-respect had been taken from them. Nobody apparently cared, despite William Cobbett's attempts to make people care with descriptions such as the following:

> Their dwellings are little better than pig-beds, and their looks indicate that their food is not nearly equal to that of a pig. Those wretched hovels are stuck upon little beds of ground on the roadside where the spade had been wider than the road demanded . . . In my whole life I never saw human wretchedness equal to this; no, not even amongst the free negroes in America.

Finally, in the autumn and winter months of 1830, the agricultural labourers tried to help themselves by erupting into rebellion. What has been called the last 'Peasants' Revolt' of those autumn and winter months was supposed to have been led by 'Captain Swing', a wild, romantic figure riding the southern counties at night and stirring the peasantry into insurrection – but unfortunately Captain Swing did not exist. The revolt had no leader. It was a disorganized, spontaneous upsurge born of desperation as both *The Times* and a magistrate agreed. *The Times* said: 'There is no ground for concluding there had been any extensive concert among them. Each parish, generally speaking, has risen per se.' The magistrate said: 'The insurrectionary movement seems to be directed by no plan or system, but merely actuated by the spontaneous feelings of the peasants, quite at random.'

The spontaneous combustion started in Kent at the end of August 1830. It has been suggested it began there because of Kent's proximity to London, and because news of Radical and trade unionist activities in the North of England had percolated via the metropolis. But Kent was also close to France where Charles X had just been deposed and a contemporary Dorset diarist expressed her opinion of this event and its likely repercussions thus: 'The month of August, 1830, was distinguished by the final folly of the King of France . . . which will probably entail disturbances and discontent by again executing a revolutionary spirit, not only throughout his own Kingdom, but also through Europe.'

Revolution, in the sense of overthrowing the régime, was certainly not in the minds of the 'Swing' participants. They were appealing to the government in whom (despite the evidence of the thousands of Enclosure Bills) they seemed to have retained a touching faith. They were asking the government to take note of their conditions and introduce legislation to improve them. A legal minimum wage was what they really wanted, although so disorganized was the revolt that no proper, clear-cut demands were made. Printed handbills were circulated in some areas, with simple and pathetic demands – 'All we ask, then, is that our wages may be advanced to such a degree as will enable us to provide for ourselves and families without being driven to the overseer.' A labourer told Henry Hunt, the once great Radical hero from the days of the 'Peterloo Massacre', 'We don't want to do any mischief, but we want the poor children when they go to bed should have a belly full of tatoes instead of crying with half a belly full.'

The rioting spread quickly from Kent into Sussex, leap-frogging most of Surrey, then into Hampshire, Wiltshire and parts of Dorset. Significantly it was strongest in those grain-producing areas most heavily affected by Enclosure. In each village that had risen there were countless meetings. The villagers either marched on the homes of the local vicars, squires and farmers, or demanded that the hierarchy meet them at an appointed place where they submitted their requests for a decent living wage. To implement the requests, in some areas ricks were burnt and in others machinery was wrecked. Hundreds of letters were delivered to the various members of the local hierarchies, signed 'Captain Swing' (in whom everybody believed, though not one person ever actually claimed to have seen him). The letters were of a threatening nature – either you accede to our demands or your house will be burnt or your crops destroyed or something nasty will happen to you – but very few of the threats were carried into effect. The only people who were roughly treated were the overseers and administrators of parish relief. Some of them were put in carts with bells round *their* necks and wheeled out of the parish.

But the rebellion lacked central leadership – it could have done with a real Captain Swing. It lacked a clear-cut aim – 'all we asked' was much too vague. It lacked violence, the sad key to so many successful revolutions – 'the conduct of the peasantry had been admirable,' said *The Times*. It was consequently doomed and by the end of 1830 it was virtually finished, each parish subsiding into bewildered acquiescence as before it had risen into desperate rebellion. 'The Swing' movements – agricultural labourers withdrawing their labour, marching around the place, holding meetings, demanding higher wages and better conditions of employment, stepping from their accustomed servility, taking the initiative – had occasioned great panic in the affected areas. In many establishment minds it had French

Revolutionary echoes – because that terrible event had started with the peasants' rioting. But very little property was attacked, no lives were lost, and there were hardly any casualties. Considering it lasted four months, and spread over half southern England, those were remarkable facts which could hardly be termed revolutionary. However, the government reacted as if most of the great houses of southern England had been destroyed and hundreds of people killed. Special Commissions were hastily assembled to deal with the 'Swing' participants. Before them were indicted hundreds of bewildered young men, some of whom had done no more than attend a meeting. The sentences passed by these Special Commissions were as remarkably severe as the insurrection had been remarkably free from violence. Two hundred and fifty people were sentenced to death (nine actually executed), over five hundred to transportation across His Majesty's high seas and over six hundred to prison in England. *The Times* reported on the scene at the Wiltshire Special Commission: 'The cart for the removal of the prisoners was at the back entrance to the court-house and was surrounded by a crowd of mothers, wives, sisters and children . . . The weeping and wailing of the different parties . . . was truly heartrending. We never saw so distressing a spectacle before, and trust the restored tranquillity of the country will prevent us from seeing anything like it again.'

No other protest movement – the Luddite Riots (whose pattern 'Swing' closely, if much less violently, followed), early Trade Unionist or later Chartist – was so fiercely punished as was this last 'Peasants' Revolt'. The reason for the severity of the punishment was because it was a southern rural insurrection. The unrest was in the towns and most Radical and trade union activity was in the northern industrial areas. Although the government was doing all it could to nip the agitation in the bud, to a degree the unrest in the industrial North was accepted. It was an unpalatable fact of political life, which with luck and stern measures might be checked. The idea of pastoral, rural southern England, the heart of all that mattered and had long been best in English life, organizing itself against its masters was too horrifying to contemplate. Such organization must be dug out by the roots before it even began to bud. The government comforted itself with the thought that the insurrection must have been influenced by outsiders. Papist plots, revolutionary ideas or agitators from France were vaguely suggested and then there were those faithful standbys, the English Radicals, always bent on anarchy. The fact that Cobbett happened to have been on a lecture tour in Kent when the insurrection started, and that Henry Hunt was present in Hampshire during the troubles, was viewed with great suspicion (Hunt lived in Hampshire so it wasn't surprising that he should be there). Lord Grey admitted in Parliament that although the government had a duty to suppress the rebellion, it also had a duty to find a remedy for the distresses of the labourers. It was a duty quickly and conveniently forgotten. What was not forgotten was that the southern rural areas had rebelled – an occurrence that must not be allowed to happen again. The 'Captain Swing' revolt was also played against a backcloth of mounting agitation for parliamentary reform which did not help it. The Whigs had finally accepted that some measure of parliamentary reform was inevitable and that it was their task as the old custodians of English liberty to effect it. Again the reform agitation was urban and largely northern based, and again the canker must not be allowed to spread into the southern agricultural areas. While bending to the forces of the left on the one hand, on the other the government felt it must stamp even harder on the incipient rural radicalism as evinced by the 'Swing' activities.

'Swing' was a vital overture to the drama of the Tolpuddle men. There is no evidence that any of them were involved in the insurrection, although the magistrates tried hard in 1834 to produce some. George Loveless said flatly that they were not, and his temperament – earnest, cautious and law-abiding – would seem to have been against involvement because even if it was disorganized 'Swing' was a subversive movement and Methodism did not countenance subversion. However, Tolpuddle came into the grain-producing area of Dorset affected by 'Swing' activities. There were several disturbances in the immediate vicinity during the autumn months of 1830, and demands were presented to the farmers for higher wages. Tolpuddle also came under the jurisdiction of a magistrate, James Frampton, who took swift, firm action in 1830, whereas the attitude of many magistrates, certainly in the beginning, was ambivalent. Many shared the view expressed by one of their brethren that 'The poor in the Parishes of the South of England ... have been ground into the dust in many instances by the Poor Laws ... Instead of happy peasants, they are made miserable and sour-tempered paupers ... Should you wonder they are dissatisfied?'

During the 'Swing' trials before the Special Commissions, *The Times* delivered a homily to the landlords: 'Let the rich be taught that Providence will not suffer them to oppress their fellow creatures with impunity. Here are tens of thousands of Englishmen, industrious, kind-hearted but broken-hearted beings, exasperated into madness by insufficient food and clothing, by utter want of the necessaries for themselves and their unfortunate families.' But in an earlier report, *The Times* had spoken of the insurrection as 'a dangerous precedent'. In the mind of no one did the danger of the precedent lodge more firmly than in that of the Tolpuddle magistrate James Frampton.

3: 'A Kind of Agricultural Savings Bank'

The swift reprisals taken against 'Swing' movements left the southern counties shattered. Too many families were left without their fathers, too many villages lost their brightest and ablest spirits, in too many districts the sad song echoed:

> We labour hard from morn to night, until our bones do ache,
> Then everyone they must obey, their mouldy beds must make.
> We often wish, when we lay down we ne'er may rise no more
> To meet our savage Governors upon Van Diemen's shore.[1]

But not all spirits were broken. In some areas the doomed revolt even produced the desired effect, the more sympathetic or sensible of masters slightly raising wages. The Tolpuddle area was not amongst them and George Loveless set about remedying this injustice.

His initial moves, in 1832, were in concert with most of the Tolpuddle villagers. There was a meeting between farmers and men at which it was agreed that the masters would advance wages to parity with other districts, and after which, to quote Loveless, 'the whole of the men went to their work, and the time that was spent in the affair did not exceed two hours'. Loveless also stated that the agreement was witnessed by the local vicar, Doctor Warren, who swore that, 'If you will go quietly to your work, you shall receive as much for your labour as any

[1] Van Diemen's Land, now Tasmania.

men in the district; and if your masters should attempt to run from their word, I will undertake to see you righted, so help me God!'

The masters did not keep to their word. Wages in other parts of Dorset were ten shillings a week, but the Tolpuddle men never received more than nine shillings and by the end of 1832 they had been reduced to eight shillings which, as Loveless recorded, 'caused great dissatisfaction'. Further village meetings were called, and all the labourers 'with the exception of two or three invalids', as Loveless scrupulously noted, repaired to the house of the nearest local magistrate, William Morden Pitt, to ask his advice. Pitt recommended a further meeting with the masters to be held under the auspices of a local magistrate, a recommendation willingly accepted by the villagers. Their willingness stemmed from the misapprehension held by many village labourers that magistrates still retained the powers they had once possessed to arbitrate in such disputes and impose a local minimum wage. A meeting was convened by Pitt in the County Hall in Dorchester, and the magistrate who officiated was James Frampton, the presiding magistrate of the Dorchester division. For George Loveless, elected by the Tolpuddle villagers as one of their representatives, it was his first encounter with a man who was to play a vital role in his life. At this semi-official though informal session in the County Hall, George Loveless (if the narrative he wrote later is to be believed) acted as the chief spokesman, and it seems a reasonable proposition that the lay preacher, a man accustomed to public speaking, should assume this role. Even with so able a spokesman as Loveless, with his considerable talent for marshalling argument and stating a case both clearly and reasonably, the hearing proved totally unsatisfactory. The Tolpuddle deputation was informed by James Frampton and the assembled masters that the magistrates had no power to fix wages, indeed there was no law in the land to compel the masters to pay a minimum sum and that consequently farm labourers must work for whatever wages their masters chose to pay. When Loveless remonstrated that they had neither sought Mr Pitt's advice nor attended this session in order to try to force new terms from their masters, but were endeavouring to uphold an agreement already made between them and their masters, he was told no such agreement had taken place. Doctor Warren, the Tolpuddle vicar, who had sworn to see the men 'righted', was then cited as the solemn witness to the agreement, but when taxed the vicar denied having made any statement. The denial did not increase the low esteem in which Loveless held Church of England vicars whom he regarded as much a part of the unjust system as were the squires and magistrates. They had forgotten God (if they had ever known Him) and their parishioners, and owed their allegiance to the State and the status quo.

The result of the meeting was that the men were back at work on eight shillings a week. How that was regarded a few verses from a contemporary folk song will illustrate:

Come all ye bold Britons, where'er you may be,
I pray give attention and listen to me
There once was good times, but they've gone complete
For a poor man lives now on Eight Shillings a week.

Such times in old England there never was seen,
As the present ones now, but much better have been,
A poor man's condemned and looked on as a thief,
And compelled to work hard for Eight Shillings a week.

The 'Nobs of Old England' of shameful renown
Are striving to crush the poor man to the ground,
They'll beat down their wages and starve them complete
And make them work hard for Eight Shillings a week.

A poor man to labour (believe me 'tis so),

To maintain his family is willing to go
Either hedging or ditching, to plough or to reap,
But how does he live on Eight Shillings a week?

The answer was that he could not. But the labourers around Tolpuddle were being asked to live on seven shillings, and then six shillings, for shortly after the Dorchester meeting wages were reduced. The explanation offered by the masters was that times were bad for them, too, and they could not afford to pay more than seven, and then six, shillings a week. It seems more than a coincidence that the two reductions followed hard upon the heels of a minor but organized protest.

Loveless said that all the labouring men then consulted as to what should be their next move, as 'it was impossible to live *honestly* on such scanty means'. (The italics are mine, underlining the frequent recourse to poaching and crime by basically honest men.) If it was from the Dorchester meeting that George Loveless emerged as a natural leader, it was from this juncture in mid-1833 that the ready-made caucus of the Lovelesses and Standfields asserted itself. Tradition places their meetings under the sycamore tree on Tolpuddle village green, where they assembled after a hard day in the fields, engaging in earnest discussion as the long summer evenings gathered into night.[2] Redress from the magistrates and parsons was, as they had learned, out of the question. Revolutionary action was not of their nature and the example of 'Swing' was not an encouraging one, but something had to be done. They could not continue to live on such low wages, with their children suffering from lack of food. In any case they were as men, as human beings, entitled to a decent living wage. It was George

[2] The sycamore tree still stands on the village green, long renowned as 'the martyrs' tree'. It is suffering from old age and has to be supported by stout props.

Loveless, the reader, the thinker, the most educated amongst them, who came up with the next move. He had, as he later recorded, 'seen at different times accounts of Trade Societies'.

By 1833 trade unionism was legal and had been since 1824. In that year the previous Statutes, notably the Combination Acts of 1799 and 1800, which had made illegal the organization of working men into societies or combinations for any purpose whatsoever, had been repealed. The Bill had, as Francis Place, the indefatigable architect of repeal wrote, passed through Parliament 'almost without notice of members within, or newspapers without'. But it had not passed without the notice of trade unionists, thousands of whom already existed despite the previous illegality of combination. There was an immediate burst of now legal militancy – strikes, demands for higher wages and better conditions – in the stronghold of trade unionism, the industrial North of England. By 1825 Parliament had awoken to the implications of the Bill that had slipped past while it was half asleep, and the 1824 repeal of the Combination Acts was amended. However, even under the 1825 amendment, a limited protection under common law remained for trade unions. The right of working men to combine together into unions or societies and to bargain collectively with their masters in connection with hours and wages was established. By 1833 the Grand National Consolidated Trades Union had been founded in London by Robert Owen. This was not the first attempt at a general union of trades to present a solid bargaining face to the masters. Several earlier attempts had been made in the North of England, some pre-dating the legality of unions. Notably, John Doherty had formed a General Union of Spinners which had held a conference on the Isle of Man in 1829, but it had collapsed by 1831. Owen's Grand National Consolidated was the first London-based attempt at general union, the first whose ripples were likely to affect the southern agricultural areas.

Thus what George Loveless set out to do as a result of those earnest discussions under the sycamore tree, to found a Friendly Society of Agricultural Labourers in Tolpuddle, was legal – dozens of unions existed in the North of England, and Owen's Grand National Consolidated was active in the metropolis. In collecting information about Friendly Societies, Loveless was assisted by other members of his large family. After the arrests in February 1834, in addition to the list which showed that 'no less than seven persons of the name of Loveless' belonged to the Society, a copy of 'printed paper headed Flax and Hemp trade of Great Britain' was found in his cottage, and, according to the presiding magistrate, James Frampton, it had been obtained from the Flax Dressers Trades Union in Leeds by George's brother, John, who was a flaxdresser living in nearby Bridport. George himself later spoke of another relation, Robert Loveless who lived in London, 'who sent word to me and the others he thought the Society would be a good thing'. Although various members of the Loveless clan were involved in the initial enquiries, the driving force, the man who provided and sustained the impetus, was undoubtedly George Loveless. 'The others' of whom he spoke were his own family, the Standfields, and a small group of tried and trusted friends. It should be noted that none of the men was a political animal as such, and of political motive none was accused. Trade unionism may now be associated with a political bias, but in 1833 it was an economic movement. A certain over-lapping between Radicals and trade unionists was inevitable, but by no means all Radicals were in favour of the unions, and certainly most who joined the unions did so from an economic motive, for a more just share of the cake. Few were aware of the political implications of the larger share.

By the end of October 1833 George Loveless had made

contact, assisted by his relation Robert in London, with Owen's Grand National Consolidated Trades Union. As a result of this contact a meeting was organized in Tolpuddle. Among those who attended – the selected venue was Thomas Standfield's cottage – were forty labourers from the area, including George and James Loveless, John and Thomas Standfield, James Brine and, one assumes, James Hammett because nobody ever said he was *not* there, together with two delegates from the Grand National Consolidated who had travelled down from London. At the time of the first official census in 1841, the male population of Tolpuddle was 175 of whom more than half were children. Assuming a reasonably steady population figure, this means that a good proportion of the adult males attended the October 1833 meeting in Thomas Standfield's cottage. Not all those present actually came from Tolpuddle. The man who became the Society's corresponding secretary, for example, George Romaine, came from nearby Bere, but the number of forty, as given by George Loveless, shows that there was considerable support for concerted action within the village.

A clear-cut set of general union laws, rules and regulations was already in existence, based on the North Country trial, error and experience of trade unionism (hence James Frampton's assertion that the information about trade societies was obtained from Leeds). At the meeting in Standfield's cottage, the rules were read out by the delegates to the assembled company. The general laws outlined the administration of the Society. A grand committee of management should be appointed, of not less than seven men, including a corresponding secretary. One-half of this committee was to be democratically elected every three months by the members of the local lodges which were, hopefully, to be appointed in every parish and district. Each lodge was to have a president, vice-president, secretary, treasurer, conductor, warden, outside and inside guardian – the guardians being literally to guard the lodge from intruders or spies. As further protection against spies, each lodge had a password. (For Tolpuddle it was 'Either Hand or Heart'.)

Financial matters were also included in the general laws. Each new member was to pay a shilling entrance fee and a penny per week thereafter, with the grand committee possessing the power to raise the weekly subscription in times of emergency. Accounts were to be done once a month, and any member not paid up was liable to a fine of eightpence. However, no member should be required to pay his weekly subscription when sick or out of employment. The actual aim of trade unionism – the advancement of wages and improvement of conditions – was not stated in the general laws; but what should be done if any master (a) attempted to reduce wages and (b) to 'stand off' a man solely for belonging to a union, was. In the first instance the member should immediately communicate with the corresponding secretary of the grand lodge, and all members should finish whatever work they had in hand and leave together. In the second instance, the whole body of men should immediately leave, and no member of the lodge would be allowed to work there until the matter had been satisfactorily settled. While being 'stood off' the members would, again hopefully, be supported by other members and the general funds. The grand committee of the grand lodge would have final and binding sanction over all the actions of all the lodges, whether concerned with withdrawal of labour, standing or being stood off, or working with non-union members.

The penultimate rule stated 'that the object of this society can never be promoted by any act or acts of violence, but, on the contrary, all such proceedings must tend to injure the cause and destroy the society itself. This order therefore will not countenance any violation of the laws.' Throughout the general laws and by-laws a high moral tone can be detected. No obscenity was to be tolerated in song or toast. No member was to be allowed to smoke during the initiation of a fellow member (or maybe this was a practical fire precaution). No member was to be allowed to eat, read, sleep, swear or bet wagers or use any absurd language during lodge hours. Any member who brought the Society's good name into disrepute by ill-behaviour outside was to be dismissed. Underlining the non-political aspect of trade unionism, and its would-be inter-denominational appeal, no political or religious subjects were to be discussed during lodge hours.

To these lengthy, detailed rules, George Loveless and the other thirty-nine men listened attentively. When the reading was finished there was doubtless much discussion. The delegates offered further practical advice on the formation of the Society, and, it is to be hoped, warned them of the difficulties that lay ahead. Promulgating rules about men sticking together, withdrawing their labour in concert, refusing to return to work until the masters agreed to decent wages and conditions, was one thing. Putting them into practice in the face of a glutted labour market, with hundreds of unemployed men and their starving families ready to leap into any vacancy, or when your own family was starving, was another. In the rural areas there were the added difficulties that the magistrates who had the power to arrest were also the farmers to whom the demands for better wages would be submitted and from whom labour would be withdrawn if necessary; the cottages in which the would-be unionists lived went with their jobs; and the farmers and landlords had the absolute right to evict anybody they chose to. (Housing tied to factories was also a deterrent factor in the towns, but less directly so than in the country. The landlords in the slum areas of the towns were not necessarily the factory owners, whereas in the country the farmer for whom the labourer worked always owned the cottage in which he lived. This was also a potent factor in the miners' bitter struggle with the coal-owners, for their cottages were also always tied to the job.) Having been clearly warned, it is hoped, that trade unionism offered no easy road to the improvement of wages and conditions, the men decided it was the sober, earnest, logical answer to the combined power of the masters. George Loveless was particularly impressed by the sobriety and earnestness of the proceedings. He later said, 'The names of God and Jesus Christ were introduced into the Declaration ... it was a sort of form of Prayer, calling upon God to keep us steadfast in what we had engaged.' He was also impressed by the delegates themselves who 'appeared to be of the better sort of people'. Most important, the formation of a trade society seemed the legal answer to their problems. As a result of this meeting in Thomas Standfield's cottage it was decided to start a Friendly Society of Agricultural Labourers in Tolpuddle as, optimistically, the grand lodge of a surrounding Dorset network which would, in due course, be incorporated into the framework of the Grand National Consolidated Trades Union.

However, one aspect of 1830s trade unionism has been omitted – the ritual of initiating the member into the union. In the general laws it was skimmed over by the phrase 'on his initiation'. It was this ritual, and what was entailed therein, that was to prove the magisterial and governmental trap that snapped on Loveless and his friends. The initiation ceremony was already regarded by some union leaders, such as Robert Owen himself, as a relic of ill-befitting barbarism. However, it dated back to the days, not so long ago, when trade unions were illegal, when the serious nature and real dangers of combination and the need for secrecy had to be impressed upon the new member.

Before the end of 1833, the Lovelesses and Standfields, Hammett and Brine had initiated themselves and the other founders into the Tolpuddle Friendly Society and were casting the net wider. It was on December 9th, 1833, that the fatal initiations were held in the same upper room of Thomas Standfield's cottage in which the decision to start the Society had been taken a few weeks earlier. They were attended by a labourer called Edward Legg who turned informer and another man called John Lock who gave evidence at the trial. What exactly happened in that upper room is not known, as neither Legg nor Lock made clear statements at the trial, none of the prisoners could give evidence in his own defence, nor did any of them later record the details of the Tolpuddle initiation ceremony. From such evidence as was presented a reasonable picture emerges and it was, as Robert Owen suggested, wrapped in relics of barbarism.

The initiates, including Edward Legg and John Lock, were led upstairs in the presence of John Standfield, and George and James Loveless. At the entrance to the upper room they were told to blindfold themselves with their handkerchiefs before being led in. Once inside they were instructed to kneel down and a few words were read. 'I don't know what it was about,' said John Lock later, 'it seemed to be out of some part of the Bible.' After the reading, the initiates were told to stand up and remove their blindfolds. In the corner of the room, overshadowing them, was a painting. There was some confusion at the trial as to whether there were two paintings, and whether they were of Death the reaper with a scythe in his hand, or Father Time as a skeleton with a scythe in his hand, or both. But certainly there was an awesome painting, standing six feet high. To emphasize the solemn nature of what the initiates were undertaking, James Loveless pointed to the painting(s) and intoned 'Remember thine end'. Both the Lovelesses were described as being in white dresses 'more like a surplice than a smock frock'. The religious nature of the ceremony, as indicated by the Bible and surplices, was deliberate. Men were then practising, believing Christians, and the quasi-religious note was further to impress upon them the binding solemnity of the occasion. After contemplating Death and/or Father Time, the initiates were instructed to kneel again and their eyes were rebandaged. Someone again read something, though neither witness knew who or what, and they were requested to kiss the Bible. Without doubt this was the moment when the initiates took their oath, as then practised by all trade unions, an oath not to reveal the members or the activities of the Society they were joining. Having kissed the Bible, the blindfolds were removed, and the practical rules of the Society were fully explained – having to pay one shilling to join and a penny a week thereafter, supporting men who were standing off from work, lodge meetings, etc. – and there was a homily about them all being brothers, almost certainly delivered by George Loveless. At the initiation ceremony James Hammett was not present, as already indicated. Why he silently allowed himself to be indicted we shall soon see.

By the end of 1833, on account of this meeting in the upper room of Thomas Standfield's cottage, the fate of the six men was sealed. However, they were allowed to go about their work and the business of further organizing a Dorset network until the early morning of February 24th, unaware of the fusion of circumstances and personalities that had already started to trap them.

4: 'The Nobs of Old England'

The circumstances conspiring against the Tolpuddle men were the recent 'Swing' insurrection, the alarm it had occasioned and the consequent watchfulness for further signs of southern agricultural unrest. However, by starting their Friendly Society they alighted upon the greatest fear of the day, the fear of trade unions. Against the evils of unionism, Whig and Tory newspapers and innumerable pamphlets fulminated week by week and month by month.

A few extracts from one such pamphlet entitled *A Voice of Friendly Warning Addressed to the Labouring Classes who have been and are tempted to become Members of an Illegal Union*, by a clergyman, will demonstrate the lurid quality of the opposition and the basic nature of the fears. (By an 'illegal' union, the reverend gentleman meant any trade union.) He urged his readers 'to shun those wicked and vicious companions who are tempting you to your eternal ruin'. Unionists were patently wicked and vicious for why otherwise should their societies be shrouded in secrecy or extort money from members? The object of human existence was 'the glory of God, the welfare, the true happiness of man'. This object could never be achieved by unionism, for it went against the structure which God Himself had ordained, and was therefore 'a crime of the deepest dye, a crime against God'. Did men expect to force upon their country their 'own crude and ignorant schemes for the improvement of conditions'? They were crude and ignorant because they upset the balance of the greater scheme arranged by God and comprehended by persons such as the vicar. If men valued their immortal souls they must, therefore, withdraw from the unions for they were 'a foul blot upon an Englishman, upon your own manhood, on your profession as Christian'. Having eschewed the foul blot, the reader was exhorted to 'Be religious, and you cannot do wrong! Serve God and you must be happy. Honour and obey the King. Love your country. Revere the constitution. Maintain the laws. Be content in that station which it has pleased an all-wise Providence to place you. Observe the religion of your Fathers, the pure doctrine of the Established Protestant Episcopal Church of England and Ireland.'

Accepting your lot in life, and being content to be rewarded in the life hereafter was an old cry and one much favoured by Church of England vicars. Many people believed that the lower classes were incapable of arranging their own affairs; that in human life there must always be masters and men, governors and governed because we are not all born with equal capacities. What they failed to grasp was that human life does not stand still; that an industrial and agricultural revolution had overtaken England; that thousands of people were living in poverty and desperation; that ameliorative action had to be taken, if not for, then by these people. The equation between being born with unequal capacities and being equal in the sight of God and therefore entitled to some equal basic rights, was impossible to balance, while the idea of society's political collective responsibility for its weaker brethren was in its infancy. The governors and the respectable people living their prosperous, settled lives could only see, correctly, that the trade unions struck at the foundations of existing society. They rallied as strongly as they could to protect the structure and themselves.

Again it must be emphasized that most trade unions were in the industrial area. It was an urban movement, a product of the Industrial Revolution. Because the revolution had been born in the North of England, the first trade unions had also started in the North, and there the militancy remained. As George Loveless suggested and discussed under the sycamore tree on Tolpuddle village green, he appreciated the local difficulties he faced. What he could not comprehend was that by starting his Friendly Society he was setting an even more dangerous precedent than 'Swing'. Trade unionism might have got its foot in the door in the industrial North and spread to the Midlands and the metropolis, but in the agricultural South it had barely shown a toe. The establishment was determined that it should be restrained from doing so at all costs and this led to the pressures which built up like a geyser to blow the Tolpuddle men thousands of miles to the antipodes.

The government of the day was Whig. It had passed the Reform Bill of 1832, finally abolished the remnants of slavery in the British Empire in 1833, was introducing measures to curb the more stringent of the Game Laws that protected the wealthy and viciously penalized the poor, and to ameliorate the conditions and employment of children in the factories. The Whigs, as opposed to the Tories, claimed to be the upholders of the fundamental canons of English liberty, which to an extent they had been. While encouraging liberty whole-heartedly in theory, in practice they had frequently been as repressive as the Tories, particularly when they had indulged in a bout of reforming measures. In 1834 Lord Grey was Prime Minister but he was then seventy and he wanted to retire to the peace of his Northumbrian estates (from which it had always been difficult to prise him). Passing the Reform Bill was quite as far as Grey was prepared to go in major concessions; from choice and instinct he would not have gone so far. Having passed the Bill he felt the Whig need to demonstrate that they were as fervent believers in the rights of property, as staunch upholders of the established law, as the Tories. The result was the customary severe reaction to the forces of Radicalism, political and economic. Grey's administration actually took office in November 1829, at the height of the 'Swing' troubles, and it was the incoming Home Secretary, Lord Melbourne, who crushed the revolt. It was he who went into action far more rigorously, with even less compassion, than the previous Tory Home Secretary, Sir Robert Peel. He sent a circular to magistrates in the affected areas which gave them carte blanche to deal with 'Swing' participants in any way they thought fit and without fear of subsequent enquiry. It was he who instigated the Special Commissions.

Melbourne was the key government figure in the Tolpuddle affair. At the time of the arrests in 1834 he still held the vital office of Home Secretary, responsible for the maintenance of law and order within the country and for all civil matters, the areas seemingly threatened by the growth of trade unionism, and from 1835 onwards he held the supreme post of Prime Minister. Melbourne was a complex fascinating character. He was born William Lamb in 1779, not into one of the oldest or most aristocratic of Whig families, but to a mother whose wit and character had taken her to the heart of fashionable Whig life. (William was reputed to be Lord Egremont's son, not his titular father's.) He was educated at Eton, Cambridge and finally Glasgow University (where he went because the French Wars had made the Grand Tour impossible), and soon his own good looks, wit and charm established him as one of the most fashionable young men of the day. He led the good life, sleeping late, breakfasting hugely, strolling down to his club, riding in the afternoon, dining at those temples of Whiggism, Holland or Devonshire Houses, on to the club for gaming until 4 A.M., and so to bed.

In 1805 he married Lady Bessborough's beautiful, talented, if capricious daughter, Caroline Ponsonby. It was a love match, not a marriage of convenience. In the same year his elder brother died, and he inherited the family title, Viscount Melbourne. In 1806 he entered Parliament, and with his brains, looks and connections success seemed assured. In 1807 his son, Augustus, was born, and Melbourne's cup of happiness seemed complete. In the next twenty years, though he was never to know material lack, the contents of the cup were bitter. In 1812 his wife Caroline's famous infatuation with Lord Byron enlivened society and for sixteen long years thereafter, until her death in 1828, her capriciousness became increasingly and embarrassingly more wild, while the only son on whom the deeply wounded Melbourne lavished his hopes proved to be mentally deficient. The personal tragedies and public humiliations of these years sharpened the complexities of Melbourne's character. He had a good brain. Born into a different background, one that encouraged serious thought as opposed to flowing wit, he might have been an intellectual. A contemporary said of him in youth, 'William Lamb could do anything if he shook off his carelessness, and set about it.' The carelessness was compounded of indolence and cynicism, part inherent, part environment. The indolence could have been called the family creed – when asked to suggest the eleventh commandment, his brother George said, 'Thou shalt not bother.' Melbourne expressed his cynicism in many notes and aphorisms – 'Nobody ever did anything foolish except from some strong principle'; 'Try not to do good, and then you won't get into any scrapes'; 'When in doubt what should be done, do nothing'; 'Nobody learns anything by experience, everybody does the same thing over and over again.'

The years with Caroline strengthened Melbourne's belief that life was a ridiculous business which must on no account be taken seriously. The only thing to do with it was to enjoy it, without expectation, but the cult of hedonism can only flourish in a secure background and must, perforce, ignore the miseries of others, it being up to those others to extract the best they can from their own ridiculous lives. (Later, when *Oliver Twist* was the best seller of the day, Melbourne said revealingly, 'I do not like these things; I wish to avoid them'.) After Melbourne became Home Secretary Lord Grey commented: 'He has surprised all about him by a sudden display of activity and vigour, rapid and diligent transaction of business, for which nobody was prepared.' Maybe they were not but it was in key with Melbourne's character. Throughout his life he preferred to let sleeping dogs lie, but when public stability and as a corollary his own private security seemed threatened all the dogs could not be allowed to remain undisturbed. The cur of trade unionism was not in any case asleep, it was barking noisily. When roused Melbourne was capable of bringing his rusty but still considerable intellect and energy into action, and against the growth of trade unionism he directed their full weight. He believed that 'the resolution and acts of the trades unions ... frequently amount to a conspiracy to control their masters', that the unions were 'inconsistent, impossible and [echoing the clergyman and his pamphlet] contrary to the laws of nature'. When he took office he wrote, 'The unions of trades in the North of England and in other parts of the country for the purpose of raising wages etcetera, and the general union for the same purpose, were pointed out to me by Sir Robert Peel, in a conversation I had with him upon the state of the country, as the most formidable difficulty and danger with which we had to contend and it struck me ... in the same light.'

One of his first actions as Home Secretary was to appoint Nassau Senior, who was professor of political economy at Oxford, to investigate the activities of the trade unions and to prepare a report outlining the counter-measures that could or should be taken. This Nassau Senior did – by interviewing the masters. One of his conclusions was that the trade unionists 'conceived that they had extorted from the legislature an admission that their masters must always be rivals, and had hitherto been their oppressors, and that the combination to raise wages, and shorten the time or diminish the severity of labour, were not only innocent, but meritorious'. This was a just assessment but it was not one of which Nassau Senior approved and his recommendations to dispel this unionist notion were stringent. He did not actually advise the reintroduction of the Combination Acts, realizing this was impossible, but he recommended that all attempts to induce men to become members of a union, to persuade blacklegs to join a strike or to picket during a strike, should be severely punished by statute; that employers should be given powers to arrest trade unionists without warrant; that union funds should be confiscated. Melbourne did not implement these crippling recommendations, but the very fact that he asked for and considered the report and that such were the opinions of a professor of political economy, further demonstrate the depth of feeling against trade unionism, and the seeming urgent need to stop the urban poison spreading into the agricultural areas.

Unfortunately for the Tolpuddle men Melbourne had personal connections in Dorset. The dead Caroline's brother, William Ponsonby, with whom he remained on excellent terms, lived in the area. Consequently he was more interested in what occurred in south-east Dorset than, say, north-east Hertfordshire. Melbourne was the major government figure involved, but perhaps the man who most influenced what happened to the Tolpuddle men was the local presiding magistrate, James Frampton. The stage was set for a drama entitled 'Stamp out agricultural trade unionism before it can root'. If it had not been played in Tolpuddle it would doubtless have been played elsewhere, although its story-line would have been different. If there was little trade union activity in the agricultural areas there was some – George Loveless was not the only man in the rural South to organize a Friendly Society – but the drama was enacted in Tolpuddle and for that the personality of James Frampton was mainly responsible.

Frampton was born in 1769, at Moreton House near Tolpuddle, into a long-established family of country gentlemen, the upper-class backbone of England. Of Frampton's activities and character we have a considerable knowledge through his younger sister, Mary. She grew into the family spinster, detached, observant, listening to her relations' problems – and she kept a *Journal*. Unfortunately, Mary's *Journal* stopped abruptly in May 1833, and was not resumed until 1838, the period covering the Tolpuddle affair. It is a pity that her knowledge and observation from the forefront of the other side of the fence are missing. However, what Mary recorded up to 1833 provides a valuable picture for which we must be grateful.

All the Framptons were well-educated, and spoke and read French. It was customary for them to spend three months in London every two years, going to the theatre, keeping in contact with metropolitan life and society. Not that they were isolated or bereft of society at Moreton House. They entertained a great deal, the guests including such illustrious personages as the Duke of Gloucester. It was also customary for Framptons to be Justices of the Peace, and in due course James became a magistrate. In many ways Frampton was typical of his class and period. He believed in Church, Constitution, King and Country, that nothing finer than the English triumvirate of Church, Constitution and King could be achieved in any country. He also believed devoutly in what Edmund Burke had written many years before:

Good order is the foundation of all good things. To be enabled to acquire, the people, without being servile, must be tractable and obedient. The magistrate must have his reverence, the laws their authority. The body of the people must not find the principles of natural subordination by art rooted out of their minds. They must respect the property of which they cannot partake.

They must labour to obtain what by labour can be obtained; and when they find, as they commonly do, the success disproportioned to the endeavour, they must be taught their consolation in the final proportions of eternal justice.

Good order, the maintenance of the status quo, was essential for everybody's sake for the other road led to revolution – such as had prompted Burke's reflections – in which case everybody suffered. The upper classes might suffer most, but the poor merely exchanged one set of tyrants for another and what was the point of that? However, Frampton was more than typical. He was an activist, a man possessed of the physical and mental energy to fight for his beliefs, and he was also a romantic. He adored the concept of monarchy. As a young man he had been in France during the early days of the Revolution, and at the time his step-brother, Charles Wollaston (who also figures in the Tolpuddle drama), wrote of him, 'James is in love with the Queen'. What had happened to that Queen, Marie-Antoinette, had not diminished Frampton's passion for maintaining established society, law and order.

During the 'Swing' period in Dorset he was, as we have already briefly noted, extremely active. He harangued crowds, read the Riot Act and organized the local yeomanry in readiness to repel the revolutionary forces; while Charles Wollaston wrote of his prompt defensive arrangements, 'I found Moreton barricaded like an Irish Mansion.' (Not that the house was ever attacked.) In this surge of activity Frampton was almost alone. Indeed he felt that many of his fellow magistrates and landlords had failed both in their duty and in spirit. He was particularly displeased with one, Portman, who offered to raise the wages of his labourers, 'and by so doing', as Mary Frampton wrote, 'without the concert of the other gentlemen, greatly increased their difficulties'. Mary also noted that the brother's spirited conduct caused him to be unpopular. Among the labourers, she meant, but perhaps a few of his peers flinched, too. James's previously spirited conduct had not endeared him to the local populace. Before the 'Swing' troubles he already possessed the reputation of 'the Draco of the fields and idling labourers', and it was said that in Dorset, 'Swing' activities were only directed against unpopular landlords.

Had Frampton wanted to understand why the labourers were dissatisfied, his sister's description of Christmas dinner at Moreton during the 'Swing' period would have supplied one answer: 'The peacock in full plumage with its fiery mouth, was placed on the dinner table, with of course the boar's head. The hare appeared with the red herring astride across its back, and the wassail bowl and lamb's wool were not inferior to former years.' But reasons were not within Frampton's scope. It was the labourer's duty to revere magistrates, respect property and learn the lessons of the compensatory after-life. Anybody who did not do so was, in his fervent opinion, at best a misguided malcontent, at worst a dangerous revolutionary. Frampton's fiercely held beliefs, his dogmatic, active temperament, made him the local spearhead pulling his less 'spirited', or more reasonable and comprehending, brethren behind him. As soon as he heard of the goings-on in Tolpuddle he concentrated his formidable power and energy on stamping them out, for the renewed activity was fraught with even greater long-term dangers for the propertied classes than those presented by 'Swing'.

James Frampton was not the only person in the area who was worried about the emergence of the trade union canker in south-east Dorset. The Lord Lieutenant of the county, Lord Digby, was extremely anxious that its corrupting influence should be stopped. From the beginning of 1834 he and Frampton were in frequent correspondence, but it was Frampton who conducted the campaign. At the end of January 1834 he wrote the first of the many letters which were to pass between him and Lord Melbourne at the Home Office on the subject of the Tolpuddle men. In this letter he informed his lordship that he had been requested by several magistrates of the divisions of Dorchester and Wareham to acquaint his lordship with the fact that societies were being organized amongst the agricultural labourers of the divisions, inducing them to 'enter into combinations of a dangerous and alarming kind to which they are bound by oaths administered clandestinely'. The information only applied to a few parishes, notably Tolpuddle, and to date the magistrates had been unable to obtain specific proof against the organizers or the places of meeting. However, they were in contact with 'trusty persons in the neighbourhood' and hoped soon to have such proof. But when they had traced the proceedings and identified the ring-leaders, the magistrates were uncertain how they could proceed against the offenders and they would consequently be grateful for his lordship's advice on the subject.

Frampton and his fellow magistrates' uncertainty arose from the basic problem facing them and the government. They could no longer prosecute men merely for forming a trade union. The repeal of the Combination Acts, even in the 1825 amended version, had taken that rug from under their feet. Not that, in practice, it had ever been the best of rugs, but it had its uses. Melbourne replied immediately to Frampton's letters. He passed on his approbation of the employment of trusty persons in the circumstances outlined. Once Frampton had proof of unlawful combination, his lordship suggested he study section 25 of 57 Geo. III, c. 19, that being the 19th Act of Parliament passed in the 57th year of the reign of George III. Section 25 had 'in cases of this description frequently been resorted to with advantage'. It had, though not over-frequently, but Melbourne was addicted to it. In 1832 he had suggested its usefulness to the Duke of Wellington who was then worried about unrest in Hampshire. In 1832 Melbourne had added the rider that although the section should be called to the attention of the magistrates they must be cautioned not to proceed upon it 'except in a very clear case and upon very sufficient and unquestionable evidence'. By 1834, and two more years of trade union activity, Lord Melbourne had abandoned his caution, because there was no mention in the letter to Frampton of 'very sufficient and unquestionable evidence'.

57 Geo. III, c. 19 dated back to 1817, a panic year of suspected revolutionary plots and maximum unrest. To counter this, the government of the day had introduced an Act 'for the more effectually preventing Seditious Meetings and Assemblies', in which one of the new penalties was that members of a society or club who took an oath not required or authorized by law (i.e. any secret oath) should be deemed an unlawful combination or confederacy. Section 25 of the Act, to which Melbourne drew Frampton's attention, further stated that any society employing delegates to communicate with other societies (which all trade unions did) should also be deemed an unlawful combination. In the meantime, of course, trade unions as such had become lawful, but there was a considerable degree of vagueness about what it was legal for them to do.

Melbourne's suggestion took advantage of the lack of definition by making the subtle distinction between the legality of the unions to raise wages and the illegality of their administering oaths and employing delegates. It was subtle because it was known that all unions trying to raise wages also administered oaths and employed delegates. But it was a loophole the use of which might cripple the unions even though, or rather because, they were now legal.

However, at the end of January Frampton had no evidence about delegates travelling to and from Tolpuddle. His 'trusty persons' had failed to unearth the information about the two delegates from the Grand National Consolidated Trades Union and the initial meeting in Thomas Standfield's cottage in the autumn of 1833. Frampton and his fellow magistrates only proceeded upon sworn evidence, for they were the upholders of the law and must act by the statute book. What Frampton managed to obtain, shortly after his first letter to Melbourne, was sworn testimony from Edward Legg that a secret oath had been administered by the two Lovelesses, the two Standfields, James Brine and, on Legg's evidence, Hammett in the upper room of the Standfields' cottage in December 1833. Incidentally, the January letter exonerates Edward Legg from the suspicion of having attended the December meeting as a spy. Frampton's 'trusty persons' were generally ferreting around for information and questioning anybody suspected of having been induced to join the Society. When Legg was questioned, he cracked. The pressure brought to bear is not difficult to imagine. True, Legg was the only person who did crack, and it was solely on his evidence that the magistrates were able to act. People who betray their fellow men cannot be regarded as admirable, but why Legg did so is easily understood. He was not wicked, probably he joined the union from a desire to improve his and other labourers' lots, but he was weak, and when the implications of what he had become involved in were spelt out, he was frightened and an easy subject for intimidation. But Legg cannot have turned informant before January 30th, otherwise Frampton would have been in possession of sufficient proof by then.

We do not know the exact date on which Legg gave his vital testimony. But it was before February 22nd, because on that date the magistrates posted a Caution in the public places of Tolpuddle and the surrounding area. The wording of the Caution indicates that they had been giving their attention to the whole of the 1817 Act and the penalties they thought were contained therein. The Caution stated that it had been brought to the attention of the undersigned magistrates that 'mischieving and designing persons' had been endeavouring to induce labourers to attend meetings and 'to enter into Illegal Societies or Unions to which they bind themselves by unlawful oaths'. The undersigned magistrates therefore considered it their duty to inform all persons of the dangers they incurred by entering into such societies, namely:

Any Person who shall become a Member of such a Society, or take any oath, or assent to any Test or Declaration not authorized by law – Any Person who shall administer, or be present at, or consenting to the administering or taking any Unlawful oath, or who shall cause such oath to be administered, although not actually present at the time –

Any person who shall not reveal or discover any Illegal Oath which may have been administered, or any Illegal Act done or to be done – Any Person who shall induce, or endeavour to persuade any other Person to become a member of such Societies

WILL BECOME GUILTY OF FELONY AND LIABLE TO BE TRANSPORTED FOR SEVEN YEARS.

Next were listed the persons who could, upon indictment, also be convicted of felony and liable to seven years' transportation. These included any person compelled to take such an oath and not revealing it to the magistrates within four days, any person in correspondence with other societies and any person knowingly permitting meetings of such societies to be held in his house. The undersigned magistrates, nine in all, included Frampton, his son Henry, and his step-brother Charles Wollaston.

So the Tolpuddle men were given clear warning that they could be transported for seven years? Theoretically they were, but there were two large snags to the warning. Firstly, the magistrates must have already decided to arrest them, because February 22nd, the day the Caution was posted, was a Saturday, and the arrests occurred at dawn on Monday, February 24th. Thus any action the men could have taken would have been unlikely to have altered the course of the arrests. (And what the magistrates would have done in the event of the six grasping the implications of the Caution, admitting their guilt and casting themselves on the mercy of the bench is an interesting thought.) Secondly, the Caution spoke of 'illegal societies' and 'unlawful oaths'. Forming or belonging to a Friendly Society or trade union to raise wages was, without doubt, legal. That the administration of oaths was in certain circumstances unlawful was unknown, not only to the Tolpuddle men, but to most unionists throughout the country. Therefore the Caution had no relevance for the six men. They neither belonged to an illegal society, nor had they administered unlawful oaths.

However, George Loveless more than noted the Caution. He actually read it and put a copy in his pocket. That there must be *some* implications he was intelligent enough to realize. He probably accepted the Caution as a threat, that the going would get tougher, that if he and his friends persisted in their union activities the magistrates would be waiting for them to perform an illegal act therein stated. But he already knew that he had embarked upon a dangerous course in trying to oppose the landlords and farmers. The Caution was the opposition warning that they appreciated the threat he and his friends represented, and that the weight of the law was in their hands. Loveless does not say so, but he may have discussed the matter with the others over the week-end. They may have pondered upon the difficulties that lay ahead, on the unified strength and great care needed to overcome them. When they were arrested their minds may have flown to the wording of the Caution. But the fact that all six men accompanied the constable to Dorchester so calmly and confidently indicates the strength and assurance of their innocence. They had reason to be confident, for they had done nothing except that which was common, apparently legal, trade union practice.

On arrival in Dorchester they were taken by the constable to the house of Charles Wollaston, who was Recorder of the town. There they were questioned by Wollaston and James Frampton. George Loveless's response to the questions was that they were unaware they had violated any law, but if they had he supposed they must be amenable to that law. Edward Legg was then brought into the room and identified all six as having been present in the Standfields' cottage when an oath had been administered to him in December 1833. After the identification they were taken to Dorchester Gaol where, from the start, they were treated as felons, that is they were stripped, their clothes were searched and their heads were close shorn. (On the lesser charge of a misdemeanour people were not subjected to such humiliating treatment.) They were then locked in a room until the following Saturday morning.

The search of George Loveless's clothing produced the copy of the Caution, a key and a letter from George Romaine. The key was to a locked box in Loveless's cottage which the magistrates had opened, and which was found to contain the rules of the Tolpuddle Society of Agricultural Labourers and a subscription book. The letter from George Romaine referred to a meeting in February at which the lodge committee had been elected. The rules and subscription book were produced in evidence at the trial as proof of the unlawful nature of the combination, while the fact that Loveless had the copy of the Caution was employed generally and later. The argument was that he had obviously read it, must therefore have understood it and appreciated that what he was doing was illegal. George Romaine was a fellow Methodist and lay preacher and was the corresponding secretary of the Society, usually the most vulnerable position in any trade union as so much of the legally suspect activity devolved upon him. But Romaine was not present at the December initiation ceremony and the magistrates only proceeded upon definite information; nevertheless according to the wording of the Caution they could have arrested him, for he must have caused 'such an oath to be administered, although not actually present at the time'.

James Hammett was not present at the time either. For reasons best known to himself, but not unlikely to have been pressure from one or more of the landowning magistrates who were his masters, Edward Legg identified James Hammett as having been there. With Hammett himself never denying the accusation, his presence was accepted without demur. In his pamphlet, *The Victims of Whiggery*, written in 1837, George Loveless stated that Hammett was 'not at the lodge at the time Legg and Lock swore to our being present', although he confirmed that the others, himself included, were and his wording indicates that Hammett was a member of the lodge. It was not until 1875 that Hammett personally confirmed that he had not been present at the fatal meeting and the reason for his silence finally emerged. His young brother John had been in the Standfields' cottage and participated in the ceremony during which Edward Legg had been given the oath; a statement which emphasizes the Hammett family involvement in the Friendly Society. John's young wife was pregnant and due to give birth, and it was for true brotherly love that James stayed silent. His reasoning may have run along these lines: he had been deeply involved with the Society, so if the other five men were guilty of something so was he; therefore why implicate brother John soon to be a father? Whether he would have been quite so noble had he realized what lay ahead may be open to question. However, he had already had the experience of conditions in early nineteenth-century English prisons during his four months in the Dorchester House of Correction in 1829, so he had the foreknowledge of possible things to come. He also had a week in which to consider his decision to remain silent. It must have been discussed during those days and nights in which the men were left locked up in the room, because the other five knew that Hammett had not been present at the December initiation ceremony. They also knew of John Hammett and his pregnant wife and could therefore appreciate why his brother had decided to hold his tongue.

It was on Saturday morning, March 1st, that the six men were taken from the room, conducted to another part of Dorchester Gaol and called before, in George Loveless's words, 'a bench of magistrates'. Who composed this bench we do not know but one assumes it was the magistrates who had signed the warrant. In front of the bench Legg again gave evidence on oath about the meeting in the Standfields' cottage and identified all six as having been present, although George Loveless said that his testimony differed 'considerably from the first statement'. One can believe this, for at the trial Legg was to prove a most reluctant witness. Throughout the deliberations Hammett remained silent about the mistaken identity, and his fate was consequently sealed. The men were then committed to trial at the next Assizes and taken to cells in the gaol proper. As George Loveless recorded, the conditions were not comfortable: 'I had never seen the inside of a jail before, but now I began to feel it – disagreeable company, close confinement, bad bread, and what was worse, hard and cold lodging – a small straw bed on the flags.'

Loveless was the only one who later recorded his feelings at this period. The two uppermost were indignation and bitterness. The indignation was particularly sparked off when, soon after appearing before magistrates on March 1st, he was called into the 'conversation room'. There a solicitor promised him that if he would have nothing more to do with the unions and would tell the magistrates what he already knew about their formation and plans in the area, he would be allowed to return home immediately to his wife and children. Loveless professed not to understand what the solicitor was suggesting, whereupon the deal was spelt out. Turn King's evidence, betray your companions and you are a free man. To this Loveless replied that rather than accede to such a monstrous suggestion he would undergo any punishment. Whether a similar proposition was put to the other five men is not known as none of them later recorded the events of the trial period. George Loveless was, correctly, adjudged by the magistrates to be the leader. They may well have thought that if they could persuade him to play ball the others would follow suit. With Loveless out of the game and discredited they also presumably thought that trade unionism in the area would collapse (for otherwise the bribe would have turned into a boomerang, and the grander design of crippling unionism would have failed). In this belief they were almost certainly correct.

Loveless's general bitterness must have been shared by all the men. Here they were in the wretched, filthy, cold conditions of Dorchester Gaol, with their heads cropped, deprived of their freedom, with their families left to fend for themselves for, as they saw it, 'striving to live honest'.

A visit from the prison chaplain who informed them that they were a discontented, idle set of men, in fact much better off than their masters whom they were trying to ruin, did not lessen their bitterness. It was not their masters who were in prison, it was them. But they were spared the knowledge that would further have increased their bitterness of the legal trap that was being set for them, after their arrests, as they lay in Dorchester Gaol.

Frampton and his fellow magistrates arrested them on February 24th, without Lord Melbourne's cognizance, which they were fully empowered to do. It was not until after the session in the gaol on March 1st that Frampton informed his lordship of the arrests, and the decision to commit them to the next Assizes. Melbourne's reply requested copies of the depositions against the men and such details of the Society, its meetings and the professed objects of its oaths, as Frampton had been able to obtain. This information was required as it was the government who was to prepare the indictment. One of the reasons for the weight of the indictment may have been the alarm expressed by Frampton. He deeply regretted having to tell his lordship that Agricultural Societies were extending rapidly into other parishes previously uninfected and that the present picture and future outlook were highly unfavourable.

In his first letter of January 30th, Melbourne had merely referred Frampton to the 1817 Act, specifically the 25th section. On that date he had not considered it necessary for Frampton to refer to the Acts on the statute book relative to the administration of secret oaths. However, Frampton had framed the Caution, and the arrests, on the possible penalties attached to such administration. On this line Melbourne had to proceed. By March 6th he was happy to be able to inform Frampton that the statutes on which the magistrates had issued their Caution were unaffected by the repeal of the Combination Laws. But to what degree they were unaffected Melbourne himself was not, apparently, certain, because on March 10th he wrote a most important letter, not to Frampton, but for the urgent attention of his law officers, the Attorney- and Solicitor-Generals. In the letter he outlined the various societies in various parts of the kingdom connected together by correspondence, with the professed object of increasing wages, at whose meetings 'secret oaths not to divulge or make known the proceedings' were administered. He asked his law officers to consider the repeal of the Combination Acts in conjunction with the 1817 Act and other statutes relating to illegal oaths, and to inform him (a) whether in their opinion members of such societies could be punished by law, independently of their administering illegal oaths and (b) whether such societies administering their secret oaths were illegal, and if so how they could be proceeded against. The postscript to the letter states that 'Viscount Melbourne is desirous of obtaining the law officers' opinion as soon as possible.' The law officers' reply to Melbourne's urgent enquiries is unfortunately missing. But as it was the government who prepared the indictment, the law officers must have pointed out to Lord Melbourne the following facts. The 1817 Act made the members of societies taking oaths not required by law guilty of belonging to unlawful combination within the meaning of an earlier Act, 39 Geo. III, c. 79. This had been passed in 1799 'for the more Effectual Suppression of Societies Established for Seditious and Treasonable Purposes' (in other words trade unions); and it was a section of this 1799 Act that had originally made members taking secret oaths guilty of unlawful combination. The 1799 Act established a few exceptions, notably the Freemasons, who were allowed to continue to administer their secret oaths. But the Freemasons were virtually the only persons who were, a fact which the law officers did not presumably point out as it was eventually to help salvage the Tolpuddle men. However, the 1799

Act itself referred back to yet another Act. Those taking unnecessary oaths became guilty of unlawful confederacy within the meaning of 37 Geo. III, c. 123. This had been passed in 1797 and was a most specific Act relating to the Spithead and Nore naval mutinies of that year. But Acts of Parliament were then in two parts, a preamble which stated the intention of Parliament in passing it, followed by the enacting part which promulgated the new laws and penalties for infringement. The preamble to the 1797 Act made it clear that Parliament was concerned with 'divers wicked and evil disposed persons' who had 'of late attempted to seduce Persons serving in His Majesty's forces by Sea and Land . . . and to incite them to Acts of Mutiny and Sedition', and that Parliament's intention was to curtail future threats of mutiny in His Majesty's forces. However, one of the clauses of the enacting part made it a felony to administer an oath binding a person not to reveal an unlawful confederacy (which a society within the armed forces certainly was). Unfortunately, the enacting part did not state that it was only referring to the administration of oaths, and societies, within the armed forces. Thus the passing of the 1799 and 1817 Acts had brought a wider administration of oaths than had originally been intended within the meaning of the 1797 Act. Despite the repeal of the Combination Acts, anybody who administered an oath not required or authorized by law was guilty of an unlawful confederacy. Moreover, if the oath thus administered bound the participants not to reveal the activities of their society, the offence became a felony under the 1797 Mutiny Act. The law officers must have made clear to Lord Melbourne that if he wished to impose the felonious sentence, it was essential that the 1799 and 1797 Acts be used in conjunction. For under the 1799 Act the offence of belonging to an unlawful confederacy was a misdemeanour for which the maximum sentence was three months' imprisonment or a £20 fine. It was only by referring to the 1797

Act that the felonious charge could be ensured, whereby the sentence could be seven years' transportation. Lord Melbourne, with his general fears of trade unionism and the specific Dorset alarms of Frampton in mind, wished to impose the maximum sentence (or at least present the judge with an indictment whereby he could impose it). The Tolpuddle case, thanks to Frampton's drive and energy, presented an excellent opportunity not merely to cripple the unions but to kill them. For how many would stay in or join the unions if they were liable to seven years' transportation for so doing? Thus the 1797 Mutiny Act became the spike on which the Tolpuddle men were impaled. Having used the words 'trap' and 'spike' it must be stressed that their actions were not, by government or magistrates, considered Machiavellian or taken with specific malice. Assuredly, Lord Melbourne had no inkling of the furore that was to be unleashed upon his head following the sentences. Had James Frampton been told as he busied himself during the months of February and March 1834 that he would be remembered by future generations as the man who issued the warrant for the arrest of 'The Tolpuddle Martyrs' his astonishment would have been beyond belief. Both men were merely performing an efficient job of crippling trade unionism, a task which, in their joint opinion, would be warmly applauded by respectable citizens throughout England.

6: 'An Act for the More Effectually Preventing the Administering of Unlawful Oaths'

The Spring Assizes to which the men were committed opened in Dorchester on Friday, March 14th, 1834. This means the government had to work quickly in preparing the indictment against them. In view of the short time factor – Melbourne's letter to his law officers on March 10th, the indictment in Dorchester by March 14th – one author has queried whether Melbourne's letter was requesting general rather than specific information on the Tolpuddle case. The author was the Honourable Mr Justice Evatt and he raised the point in his interesting book on the legal aspects of the Tolpuddle case, *Injustice within the Law*.[1] But if Lord Melbourne had the relevant statutes and penalties to hand and already knew that the Tolpuddle men were to be indicted on the 1797 Mutiny Act, the need to ask urgently whether societies administering secret oaths were illegal and if not on what count they could be indicted is not apparent.

On March 7th, a local landowner, Portman, who had displeased James Frampton by offering to raise his labourers' wages during the 'Swing' period, wrote to Frampton, asking, 'Do you mean to proceed at the next Assizes? It seems to me desirable to expedite the Blow and to allow it come from the Judges, if possible at once.' It had already been decided to commit the men to the Assizes, but the information was obviously not generally known even to close friends and interested parties. Portman's letter does not dissipate the aura of haste, albeit purposeful, surrounding the Tolpuddle case. Lord Melbourne did not know of

[1] Mr Evatt later became Deputy Prime Minister and then Chief Justice of Australia.

the arrests and committal until March 3rd, and it was the government, not the magistrates, who framed an indictment based on the 1797 Mutiny Act. It therefore seems likely, if not proven, that the indictment was prepared between March 12th and March 14th.[2]

The Assizes opened in the afternoon of the 14th when the judges and their retinues arrived in Dorchester from Salisbury. However, only the traditional ceremonies occurred on the 14th: the official opening in the County Hall, the reading of the commission for the Assizes, and the procession to the parish church of St Peter for divine service. Legal business did not start until the next day. Early in the morning of Saturday, March 15th, the six Tolpuddle men were taken from Dorchester Gaol to the cells beneath the Crown Court of the County Hall. The cells were individual boxes, a few feet wide and a few feet deep, without windows or light, the walls running with damp and extremely claustrophobic. They lay either side of a narrow corridor leading from the gaoler's room, and each had a Judas hole. When the Tolpuddle men were locked in 'some wet and green brush-wood was serving for firing', as George Loveless recorded (presumably in the gaoler's room). The smoke from the fire together with the dampness, as Loveless further recorded, 'amounted nearly to suffocation'. From the foul atmosphere he in particular was to suffer.

The business to be performed on March 15th was the finding of a True Bill against the six men (and other prisoners). Shortly after nine o'clock in the morning the judge, Mr Baron Williams, entered the Crown Court. The usual reading of 'His Majesty's most gracious proclamation against vice and immorality' took place, and the names of

[2] It is known who prepared the indictment for the government: Serjeant Wilde, M.P. He stated this in the House of Commons debate on the Dorchester Unionists, June 25th, 1835. Unfortunately, he did not clarify the circumstances of the preparation.

the grand jury were called and they were then duly sworn. It was the task of the grand jury to determine whether an indictment against a prisoner, or prisoners, was valid. if the grand jury decided it was, then the cause went to trial before a petty jury which, as today in Britain, consisted of twelve good men and true whose verdict was accepted. The grand jury whose names were called on March 15th, 1834, in the panelled walls of the Dorchester Crown Court included among its members James Frampton, his son Henry, his step-brother Charles Wollaston and other magistrates who had signed the warrant for the Tolpuddle men's arrests, while its foreman was William Ponsonby, Lord Melbourne's brother-in-law. If this seems a heavy loading of the dice – the same people who had arrested the men and committed them to the Assizes deciding whether the case should go to trial, with a relation of the Home Secretary thrown in for good measure – it was. However, there was nothing abnormal about it. Grand juries consisted of magistrates.

Apart from the biased nature of the legal system of the time, the Tolpuddle men had another factor weighted against them. This was the character of the judge, Mr Baron Williams. These Dorchester Assizes were the first over which Williams presided. He had only been appointed a Baron of the Exchequer[3] on February 28th, 1834. He was probably, therefore, to some extent suffering from first-night nerves and the accompanying determination to prove himself as a judge. This factor, together with his personality and previous disappointments, made him a particularly unfortunate and formidable opponent for the Tolpuddle men. Williams was born in Cheshire in 1777 and educated at Manchester Grammar School and Cambridge. He was

[3] 'Baron of the Exchequer' was the title given to judges of the Court of Exchequer. This Common Law Court was abolished and became part of the Queen's Bench Division later in the nineteenth century. The title then became extinct.

called to the bar in 1804, but was not appointed a KC until 1827, and his elevation to Baron of the Exchequer had only just been made. The main reason for the slowness of his promotion was not the lack of ability, but lay within Williams' temperament. He was a prickly, passionate man who allowed bitter personal feelings to enter his professional life. He had, in fact, in the 1820s succeeded in introducing much needed reform into Chancery proceedings, but in so doing he had crossed swords with Lord Chancellor Eldon and thus retarded his advancement. The light in which he was regarded by his fellow jurists was clarified by Lord Chancellor Brougham. When asked to perform what he regarded as a particularly villainous task Brougham exclaimed, 'No, it won't do, it's only a fortnight since I made Johnny Williams a Judge!' It was this prickly man, with years of disappointment behind him and one of whose passions was devoted loyalty to the Whig party – he had himself been a Whig M.P. – who sat in judgment on the Tolpuddle men.

From the start of the grand jury proceedings, Williams made his bias apparent and his feelings known. He delivered a lengthy speech in which he called the grand jury's attention to the case in the calendar where six persons were charged with combining together and administering secret 'or as they were more properly called, unlawful oaths'. He presumed the jury were aware of an Act of Parliament, 37 Geo. III, c. 123. This was the first public mention of the 1797 Mutiny Act, and it was extremely unlikely that all the jury were then aware of its provisions. The Act, Mr Baron Williams continued, seemed to allude to seditious societies. It did, he said. However, it had been decided that a combination need not be for a seditious purpose for it to come within the meaning of the Act. Combinations for other unlawful purposes were therein embraced. Therefore, if the grand jury had evidence that persons had administered oaths binding them to secrecy, there was no doubt the offence would be within the meaning of 37 Geo. III, c. 123, even though there was no evidence that the combination was for a seditious purpose. This theme was to be enlarged upon at the trial. Suffice to say for the moment that in his address to the grand jury Mr Baron Williams went to the nub of the legal proceedings, the 1797 Mutiny Act, and left no doubt as to its validity. This he was entitled to do. Part of a judge's task was to assist the jury, whether grand or petty, on points of law.

Having clarified the legal aspects Williams was not content to let the matter rest. He felt he must comment on 'the nature and quality of the offence'. This he was not entitled to do. Such comments should be left for the summing-up, after the nature and quality of the offence has been adduced at the trial. Williams held forth at length upon the current proliferation of secret oaths which was bringing into disrepute the administration of oaths altogether, and thereby affecting the sanctity, the essential purity of the judicial oath upon which English law depended. It would be an evil day for England when men came to prefer private tribunals to the open courts of the realm. He then dealt with the miseries of such cases as the one they were called upon to examine. The first misery, in his strong opinion, was that men subjected themselves to the irresponsible conduct of others. Worse, and he personally knew of many instances, men were compelled by the force of the oath they had taken to pay large subscriptions and contributions from their scanty means. Most heinous of all, having taken the oath the grossest oppression was practised upon them. They were forced to obey the commands of those irresponsible and dangerous persons running the societies. If they refused to obey it was often 'at danger to life and limb', while 'the common right obligation of every man of labouring as he pleased for whom he pleased' was taken away. The fact that trade unions were being formed because men could not labour for whom they pleased at a wage that kept them, let alone pleased, did not enter Williams' mind or argument.

He was not the only person locally making known his views about the evils of trade unionism. From February 27th, the *Dorset County Chronicle* had been intermittently holding forth on the subject. On that date they printed the full version of the magistrates' Caution, too late for its warnings to be of use to the Tolpuddle men as they had already been in Dorchester Gaol for three days. On the same date, the paper also printed a version of the oath as administered by Friendly Societies: 'I do before Almighty God and this loyal lodge most solemnly swear that I will not work for any master that is not in the Union . . . and if ever I reveal any of the rules may what is before me plunge my soul into eternity.' What was 'before me' was presumably a six-feet-high painting of Death the skeleton. They also printed a selection of the laws of the Society, the ones most likely to put the fear of God into the masters, namely, no working with illegal men, inducing other men to join, keeping all the secrets of the union, using money only for the union, not writing or causing to be written 'either on stone, marble, brass, paper, or sand, any thing connected with this order'. On March 6th there was a homily upon the twin dangers of revolution and trade unionism. The *Dorset County Chronicle* had hoped their county might have been spared these illegal combinations which were part of a lawless association threatening the whole country, and were a matter of the deepest concern 'to all men of property, of whatever party'. Further on March 13th, there was an editorial dealing with the linking effects of the spread of popular education and the growth of criminal activity (such as trade unionism). There was 'a mania for diffusing amongst the lower orders an education altogether unsuited to their station in society'. Education should be limited to teaching the lower orders their duty towards God. Anything beyond that and it turned from a blessing to a curse.[4] The case of the Tolpuddle men was not directly mentioned in either of these editorials, nor, confirming the haste of the indictment, were the six men listed in the criminal calendar for the Dorchester Spring Assizes which the paper also printed on March 13th.

Having doubtless read the *Dorset County Chronicle* (whose views they shared), and listened to Mr Baron Williams' address (which also echoed their sentiments), the members of the grand jury withdrew into a private room. There, witnesses for the prosecution gave their evidence and the prisoners themselves were examined. The only person apart from the grand jury who could enter into these proceedings was the solicitor for the prosecution, if invited. Nobody on the prosecution side ever revealed what occurred during the deliberations on the morning of March 15th, and George Loveless's only comment was 'the grand jury appeared to ransack heaven and earth to get some clue against us, but in vain'. By this statement he meant in his view 'in vain'. Having deliberated, the grand jury then re-entered the court, where the Clerk of the Assizes asked them whether they had found a True Bill or not. Needless to say they had.

On Monday morning, March 17th, the actual trial opened. For this the petty jury was in attendance. George Loveless's opinion of them was that they were 'land-renters', as opposed to the land-owning grand jury, and that self-interest would induce them to return a verdict of 'Guilty'. There was truth in his allegation. The petty jury had, as Loveless also alleged, been specially selected. Officers had been sent round the area prior to the trial to

[4] The editorial attributed the current rise in the infanticide rate to the fact that women were being taught to read. The logic of this is not apparent. Did the editor mean to imply that basically women hated babies? So give them an education and the infant population would be decimated?

enquire into the characters of those nominated for jury duty. One man, a Mr Bridle who lived at Bere, was rejected because he was a Methodist. (Later Mr Bridle was to show active sympathy for the Tolpuddle wives and children.) Having gone to considerable trouble in preparing an indictment based on the 1797 Mutiny Act, it seems reasonable that care should be taken by the local representatives of the Crown to select a jury most likely to reach the desired verdict. In fact, it would have been more difficult to find a jury likely to say 'Not Guilty'. Juries did throw out cases, even in 1834 (and before), but not in areas such as south-east Dorset where entrenched authority and the old ways were paramount. It was the radical, faintly anonymous, artisan city juries who defied the Crown, not the conservative, intimately known, rural shopkeepers and small farmers.

With the court convened, the six men were led from their foul cells, through the gaoler's room, along a narrow corridor and up the wooden steps that wound directly into the prisoners' box in the Crown Court. The place was packed for, as the *Sherborne, Dorchester and Taunton Journal* reported, 'this case excited deep interest'. Whether any of the prisoners' wives and families were among the crowds we do not know. They would have had to walk the seven miles to Dorchester, and they may have preferred not to see their menfolk indicted as common felons. Nor do we know how, at this stage of the proceedings, the families were faring, without even the meagre wages of their menfolk on which to live. If the wives had already applied for parish relief, they had received a vindictive answer, as we shall shortly see. With or without their presence, the trial proceeded.

The charge against the men was that they 'feloniously and unlawfully did administer and cause to be administered unto one Edward Legg a certain Oath and engagement purporting and then and there intended to bind the said

82

Edward Legg not to inform or give evidence against any associate confederate or other person of and belonging to a certain unlawful combination and confederacy before that time formed and entered into by the said George Loveless, James Loveless, James Brine, James Hammett, Thomas Stanfield and John Stanfield and divers other ill disposed persons and which said oath and engagement was then and there taken by the said Edward Legg against the peace of our said Lord the King his Crown and dignity against the form of the Statute in that case made and provided ...'[5] and so on for eleven more counts. In fact the indictment started with a mis-statement, in that 'George Loveless late of the Parish of Tolpiddle otherwise known as Tolpuddle in the County of Dorset, labourer, and the others, on the *24th day of February* [my italics], in the 4th year of the reign of our sovereign Lord William IV had caused the said oath to be administered.' February 24th was the day they were arrested, not the day the oath was administered, but nobody made any reference to this error. Neither did the indictment mention the Acts on which it was framed. However, Mr Baron Williams had already drawn attention to the nub of the prosecution's case, the 1797 Mutiny Act, and nobody was left in any doubt during the trial.

Mr Gambier opened the case for the prosecution. We have already examined the three Acts on which the prosecution case was built, the 1797 Mutiny Act, and the 1799 and 1817 Acts, and the reasoning behind their triple use. We will now see how Mr Gambier unwound the threads of the intricate legal web in the Crown Court of Dorchester County Hall.

The prisoners, Mr Gambier informed the court, were

[5] Standfield was spelt without a 'd' in all official documents and newspaper reports. The family itself spelt it with the 'd'. So unless a direct quotation is involved, the name has been given as Standfield, with a 'd'.

charged with having administered an unlawful oath to Edward Legg in December 1833, the dual purpose of that oath being to bind Legg not to reveal any of his associates, nor to say that an unlawful oath had been taken. Mr Gambier admitted that the indictment was framed on 37 Geo. III, c. 123. He knew the court would be aware that the preamble related to seditious societies and mutiny within the armed forces. However, the enacting part was 'of a more general nature', and the court would also be aware that Lord Ellenborough had ruled in the case of *The King* v. *Markes* that the enacting part was not limited by the preamble, but that it extended to all societies whose objects were unlawful and, as specifically in *The King* v. *Markes*, to trade unions. But was the Society to which the prisoners belonged unlawful? To establish this, Mr Gambier directed the court's attention to 39 Geo. III, c. 79 (the 1799 Act) whose second section made the members of societies, with certain exceptions, taking oaths not required or authorized by law into unlawful combinations. He further directed the court's attention to 57 Geo. III, c. 19 (the 1817 Act). He felt sure that when he presented his evidence to the court they would be in no doubt that the prisoners had administered an oath not required or authorized by law to Edward Legg, and therefore according to the 1799 and 1817 Acts, they were guilty of unlawful combination. At this juncture Mr Gambier admitted that the provisions of the 1799 and 1817 Acts made those who committed this offence guilty only of a misdemeanour (for which the penalty was a £20 fine or three months' imprisonment), but he quickly returned to the foundation of the indictment. If the prosecution could prove to the court's satisfaction that the prisoners had been members of an unlawful combination (and by reference to the 1799 and 1817 Acts it obviously could), then the prisoners were guilty under the 1797 Act because they had administered to Edward Legg an oath binding him not to reveal an unlawful combination. And societies for seditious purposes, bent on overthrowing the government, to which the 1797 Act seemed to allude, did not enter the matter. Under the 1797 Act anybody administering such an oath became guilty of a felony, and the sentence could be seven years' transportation. Mr Gambier did not say this, but he clearly established the felonious charge, and the sentence was implicit.

It was a beautifully spun web – it was fool-proof and it was legal. For as the *Law Magazine* later said, 'It is not with administering an oath not required or authorized by law, that the Dorsetshire Labourers stood charged, as still seems to be imagined by the leaders of the Unions . . . but with administering an oath not to reveal a combination which administers such oaths.' You may need to read this subtle distinction a few times, but once absorbed, it explains how the indictment was strictly within the letter of the law. Whether it was within the spirit is another matter, as are the reasons which motivated the indictment.

The prosecution called Edward Legg and John Lock to give evidence about the meeting in Thomas Standfield's cottage in December 1833. George Loveless commented scathingly on the two men's testimony: 'The greater part of the evidence against us, on our trial, was put into the mouths of the witnesses by the judge.' The *Law Magazine*, which was not a supporter of the Tolpuddle men, upheld Loveless's accusations thus: 'The witnesses had in their depositions given a much more detailed and circumstantial account of the transactions in which they had partaken than they chose to adhere to in the Box. The evidence, which was drawn from them with the utmost reluctance and by a severe questioning, did not at all equal in amount (though it did not contradict) that which they had voluntarily given.' The *Law Magazine* considered this was because 'they were under the influence of terror or some sinister motive'. By 'sinister motive' it presumably meant intimidation from the trade unions. The assessment of terror seems the more likely. Legg and Lock were frightened out of their wits at having to stand up in court and help convict their ex-companions. They certainly do not seem to have enjoyed their roles. As John Lock was one of James Frampton's gardeners it is more surprising that he found the courage to join the Friendly Society in the first place than that he was prevailed upon to give evidence. But again, as with Edward Legg, he could not have attended the December meeting as a spy, otherwise Frampton would have had the necessary evidence in his possession before January 30th.

John Lock gave evidence that he saw James Brine in the street some time before Christmas and that in the company of Edward Legg, James Hammett and three others he went to Thomas Standfield's cottage. Legg himself stated that Brine and James Hammett called upon him before Christmas and asked him to go to Standfield's cottage, and that he did so in the company of the three other men named by Lock. At the cottage George and James Loveless and John and Thomas Standfield were waiting. The naming of Hammett does not assist in confirming that he was a member of the Society, because we know it was a case of mistaken identity and that it was John, not James Hammett, who participated in the initiation ceremony. In connection with the initiations and the vital administration of the oath, very little was dragged from the reluctant Lock and Legg by Mr Baron Williams' repeated questioning – 'Now think, I will give you another minute to consider'. They told about going to the upstairs room of the cottage, of blindfolding their eyes, of words being spoken, of the Lovelesses in their surplice-like smocks and of the picture of Death the skeleton in the corner. They offered such vague statements as, 'Some one read again, but I don't know what it was', and 'I saw a book which looked like a Bible', and 'Something was read concerning something of

striking for wages during the time we were kneeling down.'
The nearest to an overt statement was that made by
Edward Legg, under direct cross-examination by Mr Baron
Williams: 'We were to keep it secret, and not to reveal
anything that was done or said there ... But I don't
understand much of what they were saying; we kissed the
book directly after we had repeated the words.' What 'the
words' were, was not elicited from Legg. The *Dorset County
Chronicle* might have printed the oath on February 27th,
but in court neither Lock nor Legg ever admitted that it
had been administered. Under cross-examination by the
defence counsels both men testified to the good character
of the accused. John Lock said, 'I have known John
Standfield, Hammett and Brine three or four years. They
are labouring men, and have always borne good characters.' According to *The Times* report, Edward Legg said, 'I
know Hammett and Thomas Standfield; they are respectable hard-working men.' According to the *Dorset County
Chronicle* he said, 'I know all the prisoners; they are all
hard-working men, and I never heard a word against any
of them.' Further cross-examined by Mr Baron Williams
he added, 'I did not know Hammett before the summer
previous to last.' However, 'the summer previous to last'
was a sufficient length of time for him to be able to
recognize James Hammett from John. So why he ever
identified James as being present at the initiation ceremony,
when it was John, remains a total mystery.

The next witnesses for the prosecution were a Mr and
Mrs Whetham, and their apprentice, from Dorchester. Mr
Whetham kept a paint shop in Dorchester, and Mrs
Whetham stated that in October 1833 James Loveless had
visited the shop and presented her with two designs, one of
Death and one of a skeleton, which he wanted Mr
Whetham to paint, six feet high on a dark background,
with 'Remember thine end' printed over the head of Death.
Loveless, according to Mrs Whetham, told her they were

wanted for a secret society. If he did the statement seems to enhance Loveless's innocence and naïvety, and it could hardly be called a secret society if Loveless went around advertising its existence. Mrs Whetham handed the designs to her husband but he would have nothing to do with them. The apprentice then confirmed that later in the month James Loveless called to collect the paintings, but that Mr Whetham had refused to execute them. Unfortunately, the designs had been destroyed so they could not be produced in evidence. This testimony neither proved that the Society was illegal nor that an oath had been taken. What it did corroborate was Legg and Lock's evidence about the painting of Death in the corner of Standfield's cottage (obviously obtained elsewhere, and whoever painted it was not discovered by the prosecution). The Whethams' testimony also helped to imprint upon the jury's mind the mysterious, sinister nature of the Society.

The final witnesses for the prosecution were a turnkey and the governor of Dorchester Gaol, a 'tithingman of Tolpuddle', James Frampton's bailiff and Frampton himself. These five appeared briefly, their roles being to supply the link that allowed the letter from George Romaine about the election of the lodge committee and the papers found in George Loveless's locked box to be admitted in evidence. The turnkey had taken the letter and the key from Loveless's person and given them to the governor of the gaol. He had felt it his duty to deliver them to Charles Wollaston. Wollaston, who did not appear, had presumably felt it his duty to hand them over to Frampton because it was Frampton's bailiff and the tithingman who had proceeded to Loveless's cottage, obtained and opened the box and given the contents to Frampton. In court Frampton merely identified the copy of the rules and regulations, plus an account book containing a list of subscriptions, as those found in Loveless's box. They were then produced in evidence.

The account book proved to the satisfaction of the court that all six men were members of the Society; not that this would have been a difficult feat. The book is no longer extant, nor can the membership list be traced that Walter, later Sir Walter, Citrine claimed to have seen when he wrote the story of the Tolpuddle men in the T.U.C.'s lavish centenary book. So it cannot now be absolutely proven that the James Hammett who stood trial was ever a member of the Friendly Society. Certainly the court, and every newspaper, accepted the membership of all six men, Hammett included. As this was thus accepted, the reading of Romaine's letter proved that they were deeply involved in the Society's activities. The admission in evidence of the rules and regulations proved the Society's concrete existence and underlined its secret nature, though it did not demonstrate that of itself the Society was an unlawful confederacy. However, if it was proven that the six men had administered an oath not required or authorized by law to Legg, the rules stated that he must not reveal the activities of the Society. The elaborate detail and intent of the rules were such as to frighten any respectable citizen or man of property, including those who made up the petty jury. It was with this final imprint of fear, of the labourers organizing themselves against their masters, that the prosecution rested its case.

It was not, evidentially, a strong case. Vital testimony was given in a reluctant and blurred manner. Few witnesses were called. However, only one piece of evidence was really needed – that an oath had been administered to Edward Legg. Once that was admitted everything proceeded in a neat circle and snapped shut. Perhaps the greatest irony of the trial of the Dorchester Unionists was that while the prosecution failed to prove in court that the oath had been administered, without doubt it had been.

The men were not allowed to give sworn evidence in their own defence. This right did not come into effect until 1898 (and many present-day jurists believe it to be a two-edged weapon, defendants mainly being less intelligent, certainly less-versed in the arts of cross-examination, than barristers, and frequently convicting themselves out of their own mouths or by a poor performance in the witness-box). However, in 1834, a defendant could, if he wished to and was capable of so doing, conduct his own defence, cross-examine witnesses and make speeches on his own behalf. But the Tolpuddle men neither wished nor knew how to defend themselves legally. Even had they been allowed into the witness-box the most they could have hoped to have achieved would have been to create an impression of good character. Explanations as to why they had founded the Society, their belief in its legality, their ignorance of the law would not have assisted at law. Had they been asked under cross-examination whether the oath had been administered, one of them might have admitted this non-proven fact.

They were, of course, defended. How their defence counsels were selected, how long the counsels were given to prepare their briefs, what access to the prisoners was granted to them, remains unknown. George Loveless was the only person closely connected with the trial who later gave an account of it. Loveless was too engrossed in the injustices of the indictment and the opposition's behaviour to make much comment upon the nature of the defence, or the barristers involved. No official transcript of the trial was ever produced, so for the defence case, as for the prosecution, we have to rely upon newspaper reports. Fortunately the trial was widely covered and the reports are remarkably similar. From them we learn that the defence was undertaken by two barristers, Mr Butt representing John Standfield, James Brine and James Hammett; Mr Derbishire representing George and James Loveless and Thomas Standfield. As reported, the defence of Mr Butt emerges as inadequate, that of Mr Derbishire as excellent. It could have been that Mr Butt and Mr Derbishire consulted before the trial and decided that one would pursue a certain line of argument while the other followed with different arguments, because either all six men would be found guilty or all acquitted. The likelihood of an exception being made was remote. It could have been that the newspapers cut Mr Butt's arguments while reporting Mr Derbishire's more fully, on the premise of not doubly boring the reader, or it could have been that Mr Derbishire was the more experienced barrister and put forward the more attacking lines of defence. Assuming that reasonable access was given to the two counsels to interview their clients and hear their side of the story, obviously nobody mentioned to Mr Butt that James Hammett was not present on the fatal day because the subject was never raised. Hammett stuck to his decision to remain silent.

Mr Butt was the first to address the court on behalf of John Standfield, James Brine and James Hammett. He submitted that insufficient evidence had been presented to justify his lordship, Mr Baron Williams, sending the case to jury. He read the lengthy preamble to the 1797 Mutiny Act in full, and reminded his lordship that it had been framed for the protection of soldiers and sailors against evil-disposed persons, at a time of great danger, and was no doubt a very proper measure – in 1797. He contended that a very strong case was needed to bring the three men he represented within the provisions of the Act, and no such case had been adduced. He then dealt with *The King* v. *Markes*, which Mr Gambier had cited in the prosecution's address. He reminded his lordship that in that particular case the application before the court had been for the prisoners to be allowed bail. He could not accept that it provided a precedent for this case, nor that Lord Ellenborough's ruling that the preamble covered all societies whose objects were unlawful could be regarded as 'a formal decision'. He trusted that his lordship would be of the same opinion. Finally, he submitted that there was no evidence that the Friendly Society to which it was alleged the prisoners belonged was for mutinous, seditious or indeed illegal purpose; and that the prosecution had failed to prove the administration of an illegal oath, therefore 'the case ought not to be left to the decision of the jury'. Apart from the full reading of the preamble to the Mutiny Act, Mr Butt's submissions were made starkly. There was no elaboration, no reasons why he thought the prosecution had failed to prove its case, no counter-arguments or mitigating circumstances were presented.

After Mr Butt came Mr Derbishire. He opened his address with the similar submission that there was insufficient evidence to put the case before the jury, but he proceeded to give the reasons why he was of this opinion. He crisply delineated the two factors that needed proving before the indictment, based on the 1797 Mutiny Act, could be sustained: (a) that the prisoners had entered into an illegal combination and (b) that they had administered an oath to Edward Legg binding him not to reveal the activities of an illegal combination. He dealt with (b) first. What had the prosecution proved but that 'two stupid persons ... had chosen voluntarily to blind themselves, some words were uttered by someone they did not know, about something they did not understand ... but in which they recollected the words "eternity" and "soul" for what purpose introduced they could not imagine'. An indictment could not be sustained upon such evidence, or lack of evidence, about the administration of the oath. For the 1797 Act required – and even more, justice required – that the administration should be explicitly proven. If, however, his lordship should be satisfied that there was sufficient evidence in connection with the oath to justify the case going to the jury, he would deal with point (*a*). Precisely what evidence had the prosecution presented to suggest that the prisoners had formed a society that came within the meaning of the 1797 Mutiny Act? Not only the preamble to the Act but the enacting part of the first section declared that it was for the suppression of mutiny and sedition and of societies deliberately formed to disturb the public peace. Had the prosecution presented any evidence whatsoever to connect the prisoners with any such society? The rules and regulations of the Tolpuddle Friendly Society, as admitted in evidence, showed that it was 'the exact reverse of an illegal combination', that it was not for seditious or mutinous confederacy, that it had not violated any known law. The purpose of the Society was to provide a fund, 'a kind of Agricultural Savings Bank' to help the prisoners in their hours of need. Mr Derbishire then reminded the court that the prisoners were poor labouring men with wives and children dependent upon them, liable to be thrown out of work or fall sick, and he failed to see how an association 'to provide against seasons of scarcity and obviate starvation' could possibly be called an illegal combination. On the contrary he thought the prisoners had acted 'in a spirit of prudential foresight in forming an association for such purpose in times when so many changes in the law were in contemplation'. The changes to which Mr Derbishire referred were the agitation for the repeal of the Corn Laws and the new Poor Law. He said the prisoners could not fail to be aware of topics that were being discussed in every parish and newspaper in the country. Nor could they be ignorant of the likely effects of these changes, if enacted, namely, that the removal of the protective duty offered by the present Corn Laws would ruin agriculture, with the heaviest loss falling on the lowest paid and that the new

Poor Law would forbid parish relief to those labourers whose wages were inadequate. The question the court should ask itself was what 'animus' had prompted the prisoners to form their association. Surely men in a position such as the prisoners, their livelihood and means of subsistence threatened by the proposed changes in the Corn and Poor Laws, were entitled to protect themselves by forming associations? Surely 'the poor man had as much right to protect the property he had in his labour, as the rich had to protect his accumulation of wealth'? It would be a hard measure of justice, and one that could never have been intended by the Legislature that had framed the 1797 Mutiny Act, to treat as felons and condemn to transportation men whose 'only crime was conspiring to protect each other from the evils of possible starvation'. Mr Derbishire then proceeded to remind his lordship, gently, that the Combination Laws had been repealed, that there was no longer any restriction upon men forming societies to raise wages, and that the prisoners were entitled to this fact in their favour. As men were legally entitled to enter into combinations to raise wages, he could not see that the administering of an oath to members of a legal society could possibly be a violation of the 1797 Mutiny Act. He then returned to his point that no explicit evidence had been adduced as to the oath's administration: 'Upon that all was as vague and mysterious as the nondescript figure Mr Whetham was called upon to paint.' Finally, he dealt with the case of *The King* v. *Markes*, and again he was more detailed in his counter-attack than Mr Butt had been. In this earlier case there had been strong evidence not only that the association was for an illegal purpose, but that the accused had forced people to take an oath. This element of coercion 'constituted a broad line of distinction between the two cases'. Moreover, *The King* v. *Markes* pre-dated the repeal of the Combination Acts, occurring at a time when the formation of trade societies was illegal. Therefore the use of the 1797 Mutiny Act at that time could be considered 'not to be at variance with the general policy of the Laws'. As this was no longer true, Lord Ellenborough's ruling which had been cited by the prosecution could no longer apply. Confidently, Mr Derbishire submitted that there was no case to put before the jury.

It is difficult to see what more or better pleas or arguments Mr Derbishire could have offered. The late Sir Stafford Cripps (in the T.U.C.'s book *The Martyrs of Tolpuddle*) criticized him, for failing to use the repeal of the Combination Acts sufficiently, but it seems that Mr Derbishire was in a grave dilemma. Of course the repeal had altered the position of the trade unions. In theory the repeal had negated the previous statutes aimed against them, and in theory the case should not have been brought into court. In practice it was, because the statutes against them had not all been repealed. Mr Derbishire knew this. He realized he could only press at the intent of the 1797 Act, and the nature of the Tolpuddle Friendly Society. More importantly, he realized the light in which trade unions were currently regarded, nowhere more blackly than in such an area as south-east Dorset and to such people as those who sat on the jury. He also knew – who could fail not to? – the judge's opinion of trade unions. Thus, if he hit too hard at the legality of unions to raise wages (and all that entailed) he was more likely to terrify the jury than to convince it of the prisoners' rights. That is surely why he talked about 'agricultural savings banks' and times of sickness and the prisoners' foresight in providing not only for themselves but for their families. This sounded wise and sensible and the fact that to do this they had to organize themselves against their masters was neatly side-tracked. Mr Derbishire did bring the repeal of the Combination Acts into his speech twice. He did say he considered that the repeal should be in the prisoners' favour, while his arguments in connection with the prisoners' prudence and foresight in forming their society verged towards the radical. That 'the poor man had as much right to protect the property he had in his labour, as the rich had to protect his accumulation of wealth' was not a widely or popularly held view of 1834.

After Mr Derbishire had concluded his arguments for the defence, Mr Gambier for the prosecution submitted to his lordship that his learned friends had indulged in 'a latitude quite unprecedented'. At this juncture the prisoners were asked if they wished to say anything. George Loveless was prepared for such a moment and his brief, written statement on behalf of all six men was passed to the judge. He had written, 'My Lord, if we have violated any law, it was not done intentionally; we have injured no man's reputation, character, person or property; we were uniting together to preserve ourselves, our wives and our children, from utter degradation and starvation. We challenge any man, or number of men, to prove that we have acted, or intended to act, different from the above statement.' Mr Baron Williams asked him if he wished to have his words read in court. Loveless said he did, but recorded, 'It was then mumbled over to a part of the jury, in such an inaudible manner, that although I knew what was there, I could not comprehend it.' However, one or two newspapers managed to report the drift of his words, if not the whole statement. Also at this juncture – according to George Loveless – one of the defence counsels said that if the prisoners were found guilty a great number of persons, himself included, would be dissatisfied. If the remark was made, the sentiment expressed proved only too true, and the speaker was surely Mr Derbishire.

There was never really any doubt that Mr Baron Williams would submit the case to the jury. The last flickering doubts as to what the verdict might be were scattered to the four corners of the court by his summing-up. Later, in

The Victims of Whiggery, Loveless accused Williams of saying that if trade union societies were allowed to continue 'they would ruin masters, cause a stagnation in trade and destroy property'. The *Dorset County Chronicle*'s wording was different – it had Williams saying such societies were calculated to shake the foundations of society and bring the country into extremely perilous circumstances. The sentiment was the same. Loveless also recorded Williams as telling the petty jury that if they should find the prisoners 'Not Guilty' he was certain they would forfeit the opinion of the grand jury. Officially, the grand jury disappeared from the case after the finding of the True Bill. However, it was customary for them to remain in court during the trial to see how matters proceeded. The grand jury box in Dorchester County Hall was situated above the well of the court. Thus throughout the trial and when they recorded their verdict the petty jury were surveyed from above by the magistrates who comprised the grand jury and whose opinion they were instructed not to forfeit.

Most newspapers contented themselves with a less forthright summary than that recorded by George Loveless and the *Dorset County Chronicle*, but nonetheless damning. Most of the reports had Williams saying that the jury must be satisfied of two things, and then proceeding to deal at length with one only, the vital fact that an oath had been administered to Edward Legg that came within the meaning of the 1797 Mutiny Act. To satisfy themselves that it did, the jury must be convinced that it was not a formal oath, i.e. one drawn up on affidavit or administered in court, that it was an oath intending to bind the mind and conscience, and that it had been administered by persons not authorized to do so (and its precise nature, what it bound the participants to, 'was not a material subject for their enquiry'). If the jury did not feel the administration proven, well then the whole case collapsed. Mr Baron Williams next refreshed the jury's memories of the Lovelesses in their surplice-like smocks, the drawings of the skeleton and Death 'intended to strike awe on the mind of the person to whom the oath was administered', and of Mr and Mrs Whetham's evidence which enabled him to mention Death and skeletons again. He concluded with a selection from the rules of the Friendly Society and by reading the prisoners' names from the subscription book. If, after this, the jury felt the administration proven, then they would inform him whether they were of the opinion that the prisoners belonged to a society whose members were pledged to secrecy and who administered binding oaths.

The jury withdrew and within five or twenty minutes, according to which newspaper you read, not surprisingly returned a verdict of Guilty. Mr Baron Williams did not pass sentence immediately and the six men were led back to the foul cells beneath the court. Whether any of them understood how they had been indicted is doubtful. Perhaps George Loveless grasped the complicated legal arguments, although he could not possibly have heard of 37 Geo. III, c. 123 or 39 Geo. III, c. 79, but that they had been found guilty of administering unlawful oaths they all realized only too well. For over thirty-six hours they were left in their cells, prey to the nightmare despair of being trapped in an inexorable machine from which it was impossible to escape, struggle as they might, feel innocent as they might.

It was on Wednesday, March 19th, that the six men were conducted to the bar of the court to have sentence passed upon them. Mr Baron Williams told them that the delay was due to the objections raised by their learned counsel. Why Williams delayed sentence for over thirty-six hours and what sort of objections the defence counsels raised are fascinating questions which, unfortunately, can only be answered by conjecture. A judge delays sentence to hear reasons for mitigation, to obtain expert advice from another judge if the case has been a complicated, specialized one outside his field or, if he is not the strongest-minded of men, to seek support of a decision. Williams was not a weak character, the Whig government he so loyally supported had gone to immense pains to frame a cast-iron indictment based on the 1797 Mutiny Act and he had demonstrated in his address to the grand jury how strongly he disapproved of trade unions. So why should he consider? Did the defence counsels press so hard on the fact that the 1797 Mutiny Act had been used against six agricultural labourers that Williams had momentary doubts? Not so much about the employment of the Act – the indictment in any case had been prepared by the government and he assuredly considered it justified to stop the spread of trade unionism – but about his imposition of the maximum sentence? As the characters of the six men had emerged in court as uniformly good, did Williams wonder whether a lighter sentence might not only be more humane but achieve the desired result of stamping out agricultural unionism? Ironically, even a very light sentence would have drastically curtailed the formation of other Friendly Societies. The mere facts that the Tolpuddle men had been arrested, sent for trial and sentenced at all would have been sufficient to dampen the already limp spirit of the majority of agricultural labourers. But one reverts back to the other facts that the 1797 Mutiny Act, with its felonious penalty, had been the basis of the indictment, that it would not have been employed unless the government had wished to present the judge with the opportunity of passing the maximum sentence and that Williams was both a loyal Whig and a fierce opponent of trade unionism.

In the event, having considered the validity of the defence counsels' objections (whatever they might have been) Mr Baron Williams decided there was none. He told the six men that he had noted their plea that they had not intended to harm anybody by their actions and sententiously observed, 'What your intentions were can only be known to yourselves.' Leading on from this he said there were cases whose effect on public security was such that an example had to be made, whatever the intentions of the participants. Into this category their offence came because they had withdrawn themselves from the recognition of the law and had kept their conduct private and secret from the rest of the world. He then made the revealing statement that was to be pounced upon not only by Radicals but by all shades of political opinion: 'The object of all legal punishment is not altogether with the view of operating on the offenders themselves, it is also for the sake of offering an example and a warning.' Finally, having deliberated well and seriously upon the evidence, he felt he had no discretion in the matter but was bound to pronounce the sentence which the Act of Parliament had imposed. In fact Williams did have discretion in the matter, he could have imposed a sentence of seven days' transportation. However, in dealing with a felony light sentences were not passed, and when dealing with the 1797 Mutiny Act judges were instructed to impose the maximum of seven years. This Mr Baron Williams duly did on Wednesday, March 19th, 1834, in the Crown Court of the Dorchester County Hall when he adjudged, 'that you and each of you be transported to such places beyond the seas as His Majesty's Council in their discretion shall see fit for the term of seven years.'

Loveless managed to borrow some paper on which he scribbled a poem, which presumably had been gestating in his head. As he was led from the court-room, a convicted felon, he threw the poem into the crowd:

God is our guide, from field, from wave,
From plough, from anvil, and from loom;
We come, our country's rights to save,
And speak a tyrant faction's doom:

We raise the watch-word, liberty,
We will, we will, we will be free.

God is our guide! No swords we draw.
We kindle not war's battle fires:
By reason, union, justice, law,
We claim the birth-right of our sires:
We raise the watch-word, liberty,
We will, we will, we will be free!!!

It has been claimed that the poem was not original, by Walter Citrine in the T.U.C.'s 1934 book, and that evidence of its use at earlier Radical meetings existed. But James Hammett's grand-daughter said, 'Of course George wrote it. After all, he was brought up on Charles Wesley's hymns.' In 1834 the authorship was certainly attributed to Loveless, and as the 'Song of Freedom' the verses rang round England.

Once the sentence was passed, the six men were manacled together and escorted back to Dorchester Gaol. As they were conducted through the crowds outside the court, George Loveless tossed the piece of paper on which he had written 'God is our guide' amongst the watching people. The paper was retrieved by the guards and delivered to Mr Baron Williams (who eventually returned it to Loveless). The gesture had a defiant panache. George Loveless intended to allow nothing and nobody to quench his spirit.

Two days after being returned to the gaol he was taken ill, which he attributed to the foul atmosphere he had endured in the cells beneath the Crown Court. He must have been very ill, a severe fever or bronchitis, as he was removed to the prison hospital. It was initially because of his illness that he became separated from his companions. For on March 27th his brother James, the two Standfields, Brine and Hammett were led from Dorchester Gaol, hands and legs individually fettered and linked together by a long chain. In the yard a coach waited, to the outside of which they were further chained. Then the coach set off for Portsmouth, with its human monkeys clinging on – its destination the hulks.

The hulks were old battleships of the line, sold to the government once their days of action had ended. Their rotting carcasses lay off the shores of such southern towns as Woolwich, Chatham, Portsmouth, Deptford, Sheerness, Devonport and Plymouth. The use of the hulks as floating prisons dated back to 1776 when the American War of Independence and the loss of the American colonies put an end to the practice of shipping to the United States those sentenced to transportation. In 1779 an Act of Parliament confirmed that 'daring and atrocious offenders' should be incarcerated in the hulks and employed during the day in cleansing the River Thames and other ports; confinement not to exceed five years for those sentenced to seven years' transportation, seven for those to fourteen years. In 1799, after New South Wales had been officially established as a fresh repository for convicts, offenders were, in the main, sent only temporarily to the hulks prior to transportation across His Majesty's high seas. After 1799 an Inspector of the Hulks was appointed – previously the prisoners had been left to the mercies of private contractors – and conditions improved. What they must have been like before this date is almost unimaginable, if the description of literate prisoners who arrived after 1799 is accepted.

One such literate prisoner, an engaging ebullient 'con man' named James Hardy Vaux, who managed to get himself transported not once but thrice, by which time even his ebullience was flattened, wrote of the hulk at Woolwich:

> Of all the shocking scenes I had ever beheld, this was the most distressing. There were confined in this floating dungeon nearly six hundred men, most of them double-ironed; and the reader may conceive of the horrible effects arising from the continual rattle of chains, the filth and vermin naturally produced by such a crew of miserable inhabitants, the oaths and execrations constantly heard among them . . . Nothing short of a descent into the infernal regions can be at all worthy of comparison with it . . . All former friendships or connections are here dissolved, and a man will rob his best benefactor or even messmate, of an article worth one halfpenny. The guards were commonly of the lowest class of human beings; wretches devoid of all feelings; ignorant in the extreme, brutal by nature, and rendered more tyrannical and cruel by consciousness of the power they possess. No others but such as I described would hold the

situation ... They invariably carry ponderous sticks with which, without the smallest provocation, they will fell an unfortunate convict to the ground, and frequently repeat their blows long after the poor sufferer is insensible ... The water in which the beef was boiled is thickened with barley, and forms a mess called 'smiggins' ... The cheese is commonly bad ... The beef generally consists of old bulls, or cows which have died of age or famine.

Prisoners were permanently chained, before and after 1799. There were usually three decks containing, as Vaux wrote, between five and six hundred prisoners each. The lowest deck was the worst, as the bilge water slopped through constantly. Newcomers were normally committed to the lowest deck and it was a question of fighting or bribing your way upwards to the less damp conditions and the less foul air. Scrofula, consumption and scurvy were endemic, while periodic epidemics of cholera, dysentery and smallpox swept through the rotten ships and reduced the passenger list. The odds on a long-stay prisoner surviving his term of sentence was one in three. Punishments, inflicted by the guards Vaux described, were frequent and arbitrary. They included flogging within an inch of life and then having salt rubbed into the lacerated back which, as many recorded, was worse than the flogging; near starvation; enormous weights attached to the permanent chains; and solitary confinement in the 'Black Hole' below bilge-water level. Prisoners were taken out during the day to work, though not necessarily for cleansing the river, or port. Over the years any hard, dirty, unwanted task was allotted to the inmates of the hulks. They often, although not always, worked in chain gangs. From sunset to sunrise they were battened down in the holds. The food, as James Hardy Vaux said, was literally lousy. However, after 1799, there was usually a chapel on board, although what in the physical circumstances it was hoped to achieve by spiritual ministration is difficult to imagine. There was also a library in which the literate or lucky convict could find a calm if temporary oasis. By 1834 a prisoner's stay on board a hulk was usually short-term, being the weeks or months between sentence and actual transportation, which depended on the space available on the convict ships and their sailing schedules. However, even in 1834, the records show that men had been on board the hulks at Portsmouth since 1823 – eleven hideous years.

It was not only 'the daring and atrocious offenders' specified in the Act of Parliament who were incarcerated on the hulks. The inmates over the years included boys of fourteen who had been sentenced to fourteen years' transportation for having stolen 'some cheese, two ferrets and a tinder box', and young men similarly sentenced for having stolen a silver spoon, victims of the belief that 'nothing but the terror of human suffering can avail to prevent crime'. They also included educated political prisoners, participants in the Irish rebellion of 1798, Luddite rioters, Scottish trade unionists, hundreds of decent, ordinary young men who had become entangled in the 'Swing' revolt and, of course, six men from Tolpuddle.

Transportation itself was first established under a Vagrancy Act of Elizabeth I. Magistrates were empowered to remove intractable criminals from the confines of decent society and send them overseas. One of the ideas behind the system, apart from ridding society of its villains, was redemption. With a fresh start in a new land the offenders might discover the paths of righteousness. By the eighteenth century transportation was a regular practice and the field of offenders had widened considerably. The dumping ground was the American colonies where there was a great demand for servants and cheap labour in general, but the War of Independence, as we have just noted, put an end to American transportation and the hulk system was introduced. Within a few years the hulks were overflowing.

Because Canada had remained loyal during the American War, it was not thought proper to burden Canada with England's unwanted criminals. In 1770, New South Wales had been annexed for Britain by Captain Cook, and needed colonizing. It was the Younger Pitt who adopted the suggestion that the crush in the hulks could be relieved – and the new colony opened – by transportation to Australia. Botany Bay in New South Wales was selected as the site for the convict settlement and the first transport sailed in 1787. In fact Botany Bay was found to be unsuitable and the settlement, named Sydney in honour of the Home Secretary, was built farther along the coast. In 1779 an Act of Parliament had established transportation to colonies other than the now-lost American ones. These included Barbados, where a small penal settlement was made, but the major traffic was between England and the new colony of New South Wales and its dependency, Van Diemen's Land.

At the start of the great export of human cargo to New South Wales, merchant ships carried the convicts. The owners were paid from £20 to £30 a head, so it was to their financial advantage to pack the ships as tightly as possible. In 1790 a ship called the *Neptune* sailed with 502 convicts on board, of whom 158 died en route, and the survivors had to be carried ashore, half dead, on arrival. In 1802 the government took over. Special convict ships were built or converted, and a naval surgeon was appointed superintendent. He received a bonus for each convict landed alive and the death rate consequently decreased. In those early years there was little to choose between the middle passage endured by the Negro slaves en route from Africa to America and that suffered by the white convicts en route from England to Australia. If the hulks were for male offenders only, transportation was not, and thousands of women and children were also shipped out. By 1834, transportation to Australia was in full swing, with the grisly routine of sentence, followed by confinement on the hulks for the men and imprisonment for the women and children, the move to the convict ships and the final sailing.

On arrival in Portsmouth on the evening of March 27th, the two Standfields, Brine and Hammett were taken to the hulk *York*, while James Loveless was taken to the *Leviathan*. In fact, the *York*'s records state that all five men went there but the Dorchester Gaol records say that James Loveless went to the *Leviathan*. Officialdom regarded both Lovelesses as ring-leaders and certainly George was to remain separated, so probably James was removed, either as a bad influence or to punish him for being a ring-leader. On board the hulks the men were stripped and their fetters were removed. They were given convict clothes – coarse grey jackets, waistcoats and trousers, flat hats and heavy nailed boots – then fresh and heavier irons were riveted to their legs. But their stay on board the hulks was mercifully brief. Two days later, on March 29th, they were taken to the convict ship *Surrey* at Spithead. On March 31st, the *Surrey* sailed for Plymouth, where it arrived on April 2nd and lay at anchor for nine days, taking on supplies and further convicts.

If conditions on the hulks remained grim, they were not much better on the convict ships. By 1834 a small bed, pillow and blanket were allotted to each convict and, as George Loveless later wrote, they would have contributed greatly to the convicts' comfort 'had there been room sufficient to have lain upon them, but we could not. A berth about 5 feet 6 inches square was all that was allowed for six men to occupy day and night.' One of the worst features of the convict ships and of those endless weeks sailing along the south coast, lying at anchor, then sailing across the high seas, was the fact that there was nothing to do. Prisoners did get off the hulks to work, but you could not get off the ships. You were confined, with your legs in chains, for twenty out of twenty-four hours – only two hours in the morning and two in the afternoon allowed for exercise – to those 5 feet 6 inches with five other men, hemmed in by hundreds of men similarly trapped. At worst they were the scum of England, at best they were full of despair, terrified and sea-sick, and the panic that usually set in when the ship sailed, or first hit heavy seas, was fearful as few if any convicts had ever been to sea or had any conception of a ship's movement. George Loveless reported laconically of conditions on board his ship that, 'I now began to think I had seen or heard but very little', while John Standfield wrote of the horror of 'being confined down with a number of the most degraded and wretched criminals, each man having to contend with his fellow or be trodden underfoot'.

Rations too were little better than on the hulks. They were commonly known as 'six upon four' – six convicts sharing the amount issued for four sailors. John Standfield said, 'The rations . . . were of the worst quality, and very deficient in quantity owing to the peculations indulged in by those officers whose duty it was to attend to that department . . . and the badness and the saltness of the provisions, induced disease and suffering that it is impossible to describe.' The discipline that had to be maintained among those sullen, frightened, angry, hungry, wicked and above all bored cargoes can be imagined. The naval surgeon appointed superintendent was invested with summary powers of punishment which meant he could do what he wanted with the convicts. How much he did, and how effective the discipline consequently was, can be gauged from the fact that during the eighty years of transportation to Australasia there was not one successful mutiny on board a convict ship. There were attempts, and one ship did successfully disappear (to Montevideo in 1797) but that was because the crew mutinied, not the cargo.

On April 11th, 1834, the convict ship *Surrey*, with John and Thomas Standfield, James Loveless, James Hammett and James Brine on board, weighed anchor and sailed from Plymouth Sound on the start of its journey across the world to New South Wales. Visitors were not allowed on the convict ships, but letters were. John Standfield managed to write to his mother from Plymouth and received her answer two days before the *Surrey* sailed. As the undulating, green, hedged fields of Devonshire receded – hedged as a result of the Enclosure Acts which were partially responsible for their presence on board a convict ship – John Standfield wrote of 'the agonizing reflection that we had done nothing deserving of this punishment, and the consciousness that our families, thus suddenly deprived of their protectors, and a stigma affixed to their names, would probably be thrown unpitied and friendless upon the world'.

In the meantime George Loveless, ill in Dorchester Gaol, had been left behind. On April 2nd, the day the *Surrey* and his companions arrived in Plymouth, he was visited by Charles Wollaston. His visitor enquired after his health and said how sorry he was to see a man of Loveless's intelligence and good character in such a situation. But he was afraid it was Loveless's own fault because he had listened to the words of the evil men who were going around the country deceiving people (i.e. trade unionists) and had failed to heed the warnings of the magistrates. At this reference to the Caution Loveless launched into the attack. How could he have heeded the warning when it was issued nine weeks after the event for which he had been arrested, and about which it warned, had occurred and when within three days of the issue he was in gaol? Wollaston then said, 'Ah, it is of no use talking to you.' To which Loveless replied, 'No, Sir, unless you talk more reasonable.' One assumes Wollaston visited Loveless with kind intent, grieved that such a man should have been so 'deceived'. He was the only magistrate who took the trouble, but he should not have expected Loveless to have been in a responsive or contrite mood.

On the same day, Loveless heard that his brother and friends had already left the gaol for the hulks and immediately asked to be sent to join them, but it was not until April 5th that he was declared fit to travel. He, too, was chained to the outside of the coach before it set off for Portsmouth. However, as it approached Salisbury, the accompanying officer offered to remove Loveless's leg irons. He explained that the streets of the town were so narrow they would have to walk part of the way and the rattling of the chains would cause people to stare. Loveless asked if the chains would be restored once they had passed through Salisbury. The officer said that regretfully they must be, so Loveless declined the offer. His reason was that he had done nothing to be ashamed of and if people wanted to stare at the chains the authorities had inflicted upon him, they could. The refusal demonstrates his confident, righteous integrity – and his courage, because it could not have been pleasant to walk through a busy cathedral city in convict garb and chains. It also probably showed his bitter resentment, for refusing a well-meant gesture is the sort of action one takes when one feels deeply wronged. The offer itself indicates the effect George Loveless had on others. It was he who was given the opportunity of freedom if he betrayed his companions before the trial, who Wollaston visited, who received this offer in Salisbury. Loveless must have been a very strong, compelling character.

On arrival in Portsmouth, where he was taken to the *York* and stripped and re-chained as his friends before him, even Loveless's courage faltered. He was 'struck with astonishment' at the sights that greeted his eyes, and as the fresh fetters were riveted to his legs he half fainted. But he was conducted to the best and quietest ward of the *York*, in consequence of the good character reference the governor of Dorchester Gaol had forwarded. It was as well the governor performed this kindness, because Loveless was to stay on board the *York* for six weeks, and on top of his recent illness six weeks in the lowest deck, with its bilge water and general foulness of men and conditions, could have undermined even George Loveless, both mentally and physically.

Loveless could have been sent to join his brother and friends, as he had begged, because he was fit to travel on April 5th, and the *Surrey* did not sail until April 11th. However, the likelihood of his being especially escorted direct from Dorchester Gaol to Plymouth was remote as the official routine – gaol to the hulks, hulks to the convict ships – had to be followed. Whether as the ring-leader, he would have been separated despite his illness remains unknown. In the event he was kept on board the *York*, working during the days on the gun-wharf, battened down at night, until May 17th. On that day he was taken to the convict ship *William Metcalfe* at Spithead. Its destination was not New South Wales, but Van Diemen's Land. Loveless does not seem to have known of the destination. He spoke of sailing for Botany Bay – but then everybody tended to use Botany Bay in connection with convicts, wherever they were going. Even had Loveless been told that he was en route for Van Diemen's Land the information would not have conveyed much. His self-education did not extend to geography. And the general geographical ignorance, apart from the awful ignorance of what transportation entailed, is pathetically illustrated in a young convict's letter to his mother: 'Oh, please tell poor Mrs Hart it is out of my power to enquire for Henry Hart, as Sydney is 2000 miles from me.'

The *William Metcalfe* passed Land's End on May 26th, the black rocks of Cornwall being the last sight of England. As his brother and friends five weeks before him, George Loveless sailed without knowing whether he would ever see, not only England, but his wife and children again.

Particularly his wife to whom he had written on the eve of departure, 'I thank you, my dear wife, for that kind attention you have ever paid me, and you may safely rely upon it that as long as I live it will be my constant endeavour to return that kindness in every possible way, and hope to send to you as soon as we reach our place of destiny, and that I shall never forget the promises made at the altar; and though we may part a while I shall consider myself under the same obligation as though living in your immediate presence.' Further he wrote, 'Be satisfied, my dear Betsy, on my account. Depend on it, it will work together for good and we shall yet rejoice together. I hope you will pay particular attention to the morals and spiritual interest of the children. Don't send me any money to distress yourself. I shall do well for He who is the Lord of the winds and waves will be my support in life and death.'

While the six men were being sent to the hulks and then to the convict ships, a great deal was happening in England in respect of their case. The uproar started immediately after the sentences. First into the field was the *Dorset County Chronicle* which, by virtue of proximity and publication day, was able to print the sentences on March 20th. The *Chronicle* stoutly upheld the official view. The extent to which combinations of an unlawful nature were spreading had rendered it imperative that an example of severity should be set which would operate as 'a wholesome example' to other misguided or discontented men who would now realize 'That the laws of England are not to be defied with impunity; that there is still a power to maintain public security'. An attempt had been made to prove that the punishment for unlawful combinations did not extend to transportation. This attempt had failed. The magistrate's Caution and the judge's wise deliberations had shown that those who committed this crime were 'doomed to a long and wearisome exile from their native land, severed from their families, friends and connections, and wearing out their days in a state of slavery of the most oppressive and laborious kind.' No longer could men plead ignorance of their misdeeds and their just punishment, and viewing the punishment awarded 'as useful in its operation as a warning, rather than as a measure of revenge upon the unfortunate convicts', the *Chronicle* was glad the laws upon the subject were so severe, and that those who administered them had been willing to enforce them.

The *Chronicle* returned to the subject on April 3rd when it informed its readers that the misguided men had been removed to the *York* hulk. On the same day it told *The Times*, the *Globe* and the *Standard* that they would not be supporting the Dorchester Unionists if they knew the true facts (for by this date most newspapers had rallied, if for various reasons, to the defence of the Tolpuddle men). The true facts were that proper warning of the penalties had been carried in the columns of the *Dorset County Chronicle* 'for several weeks beforehand'. It depended on the interpretation of 'beforehand'. The first warning appeared in the *Chronicle* on February 27th, three days after the arrests, but before the trial. Moreover, continued the *Chronicle*, one of the men had in his possession a copy of the Caution when arrested, and had therefore clearly understood the implications. The men were educated: the Lovelesses, whom it named James and John,[1] were itinerant preachers while James Loveless had written a set of verses after his sentence – and the *Chronicle* printed 'God is our Guide' to demonstrate their horrid, unrepentant but educated nature. The argument that had been put forward – that trade unionists in the towns had gone unpunished – was ridiculous. The fact that illegal combinations in the towns were so rampant was all the more reason for agricultural societies being checked and labourers prevented from becoming urban tools. It finished by embellishing the theme that the convictions should be viewed as an act of mercy, in deterring others. After April 3rd the *Chronicle* mainly kept silent. Of the proliferating activity in London it reported not a word. It reverted to news of royalty, singular outrages and dreadful happenings in Dorset, and its favourite themes of everybody knowing their proper place (that of women being in the home), the Protestant religion and the maintenance of law and order.

[1] The *Chronicle* can be excused the confusion of names. There was generally a great deal of misspelling and misinformation about the six men. Loveless was frequently spelled Lovelace, Brice and Bruce for Brine, Hammett was much mangled, emerging as Harris and Hamilton; Thomas Standfield was credited with eight children; while Hammett's age was given as fifty and six children were attributed to him, the eager researcher having confused him with his father.

The attacks of those opposed to the sentence started on March 21st, allowing a day for the news to travel to and be printed in London. They were multifarious but can roughly be divided into two categories: committed Radicals and trade unionists forming one; anti-Radicals and anti-unionists who queried this particular sentence and the methods by which it had been obtained forming the other. Lord Melbourne, Frampton, the magistrates and the government in general may rightly have felt that the majority of respectable citizens wanted the unions put down but they overlooked several facts and forgot the human element. They chose to indict six men, a manageable number for the general public. It is difficult to identify with hundreds or thousands of victims (as in the case of the 'Swing' labourers) because the numbers swamp the imagination, but six the average mind can encompass. The six they chose to indict were good, honest men. Nothing evil or vicious could be proved against them (and the government soon abandoned the attempt, as we shall see). The indictment and sentence might be legal but it had only too evidently needed a sharp scraping of the statutory barrel to obtain them. How could six labourers from Tolpuddle have been expected to have known of the 1797 Mutiny Act? Although the government could not actually be accused of taking a sledgehammer to crack a nut – for the trade unions represented more than a nut – they could be indicted from the David and Goliath angle. They appear to have failed totally to anticipate this emotional, human and very English reaction – the long-cherished, if not always operative, tradition of fair play and justice, as opposed to unfair play and legality. They also do not seem to have appreciated that the trade unions would recognize that the Tolpuddle case, if allowed to go unchecked, represented their death sentence; that trade unionists would consequently contest the verdict and raise the greatest possible outcry with all the strength and desperation of those fighting for their lives. Or perhaps the government simply underestimated the spirit and conviction and will to fight of the trade unions.

Newspapers such as *The Times*, the *Morning Herald*, the *Globe*, the *Morning Post*, the *Sunday Herald*, the *Morning Chronicle*, were all quick to point out how much they disapproved of trade unions. The *Morning Post* asserted that 'the trade unions are, we have no doubt, the most dangerous institutions that were ever permitted to take root, under the shelter of the law, in any country', while the *Sunday Herald* (in fact a Radical paper but anti-unionist) viewed them 'as a wreaking of the revenge of the working classes upon the capitalists, who themselves are only the fellow sufferers in the political oppressions of an unjust government'. But these newspapers also spoke of the unjustifiable severity of this particular sentence upon six poor, misguided, ignorant labourers. The *Morning Herald* voiced a common view of the methods employed when it stated that the unions should not be attacked by 'a side-wind', not by a verdict that showed 'the treachery rather than the energy of the law, by throwing the noose of an Act of Parliament over the heads of sleeping men'. The unions should be grappled with manfully and upon proper occasion. The *Morning Chronicle* expressed another common view, namely that the men were being punished for having joined a union rather than for an illegal act they had personally performed, when it wrote, 'A man is never punished in England for that which he is found guilty.' The main thing to be said for the pro- or anti-government but anti-union newspapers was that they all discussed the case of the Dorchester Unionists at length. (The name Tolpuddle was not used at the time, it was always Dorchester, although the description 'martyrs' first appeared as early as April 5th, 1834.)

The Radical and trade union newspapers obviously represented those with most to gain and lose. There were a fair number of them, mainly Radical rather than specifically trade unionist in colour, though due to the lack of funds and to the swingeing stamp duty, their birth and death rates were alarmingly high. (In 1836, during his second Ministry, Lord Melbourne in fact lowered the duty from four – old – pence to one penny per issue.) Among them were the *Republican*, the *Pioneer*, the *Poor Man's Guardian*, the *True Sun*, and the *Political Register* in which William Cobbett had been thundering away for years. But in 1834 Cobbett, one of the greatest of English journalists, was a sick man – he died a year later – and his defence of the Dorchester Unionists lacked much of his old fire and passion. The standard of production among the Radical newspapers was generally lower than that of the wealthier Whig and Tory ones, but the content was often as high, notably in the *Poor Man's Guardian* and later the *Northern Star*. In the newspaper world it was the *True Sun* that took up the cudgels on behalf of the Tolpuddle men. It was not averse to rhetoric or purple passages, but nor was any contemporary newspaper; it over-simplified the issues no more than any of its rivals, whom it attacked with as great a verve and vigour as they attacked the *True Sun*. There was intense rivalry, and little quarter given, between the opposing papers. The *True Sun* did not put down the cudgels until justice, as it understood the word, had been finally effected for the Tolpuddle men. Fortunately, it lasted long enough, until 1837, to see its efforts rewarded.

In the first editorial of March 20th, 1834, the paper grasped the fact that 'a large number of persons ... including the whole of the members of the numerous and daily increasing Trades Unions' were liable to the same penalties on the same grounds as the Tolpuddle men. It had not then appreciated that they included the members of Orange Lodges (Grand Master, His Royal Highness the Duke of Cumberland), Oddfellows and sundry other societies. The next day, when it had the sentences in its possession, it launched into a fuller attack. It spoke of 'The unwarrantable stretching of an Act of Parliament', and presciently said, 'Our judges and legislators may rely upon it, this is a case which will never be forgotten.' Practically, it announced that a public meeting would be held at the National Institution, 14 Charlotte Street, Rathbone Place, on Monday next at twelve noon, to petition the legislature against 'the cruel and oppressive sentence'. It urged everyone who valued his liberty to attend. It hoped the public voice at large would make itself loudly heard to prevent the sentence being put into effect as there was yet time to save the men from the horrors of transportation. On Monday, March 24th, the public in London responded in numbers anywhere between five and ten thousand (contemporary estimates cannot be relied upon, as they vary wildly according to source) at the 'Grand Meeting in Favour of the Agricultural Unionists Convicted at Dorchester'. In the chair was Dr Arthur Wade, D.D., Vicar of St Nicholas church in Warwick, 'chaplain to the metropolitan trade unions,' leading Radical and enthusiastic supporter of the Tolpuddle men (a letter to *The Times* was later to enquire whether Wade was *still* a vicar in Warwick, as he patently spent no time amongst his parishioners). The principal speaker and organizer of the meeting was Robert Owen, founder of the 'model town' of New Lanark and the Grand National Consolidated Trades Union, idealist, believer in the power of reason, disbeliever in class conflict. In a general speech on trade unionism Owen asserted that the working classes of Great Britain and Ireland were in a worse condition than any slaves in any country in any period of the world's history, that 'it was right and just that all people of the earth, without reference to class, party, sect, country or colour, should determine to carry out this principle of eternal justice, that they are the owners of their own labour'. These were not sentiments calculated to enthral the government or the respectable citizens of

England, but Owen believed them with all his heart and his audience stoutly approved. Owen moved the resolution that the sentence on the Tolpuddle men was 'not to be defended, and was cruel and severe, and the proceedings of both judge and jury seem to have been totally misconceived'. There followed the type of argument on a matter of detail – whether the word 'misconstrued' would not be more accurate than 'misconceived' – with which socialism has always tended to bedevil itself. In the end 'misconceived' won, and the resolution was carried unanimously. A petition was prepared for presentation to the King and the final resolution was that they would not cease in their exertions until a remission of sentence had been obtained.

Thus, from the start, the Tolpuddle men attracted the vital, articulate, urban, and specifically metropolitan conscience. The Radical and trade unionist organizers may have acted from self-preservation, but they believed passionately in what they were trying to preserve – the right of the working classes to have a decent share in the capital they helped produce. They also sincerely believed that an Act of Parliament had been unwarrantably stretched, and the sentences had been unduly harsh. The *True Sun* reported the meeting of the 24th in full, and took the opportunity to appeal to members in those hot-beds of trade unionism – Manchester, Birmingham, Ashton-under-Lyne, Bolton and Sheffield – to make known their feelings on the subject.

On March 26th the first petitions were presented which was fairly quick work. In addition to the Owenite petition, presented by William Cobbett who implored the merciful consideration of the King, there was one from Oxford to Parliament. (Such petitions were usually presented to the King who had the power to pardon, but they could be presented to Parliament where they would be certain of discussion.) The Oxford petition was signed by 1,563 persons from 'a city which did not now, nor ever did, contain a single political or trades union'. It pleaded for a remission of sentence on the grounds of its severity, the victims' good character and ignorance of the law and the fact that Druids and Oddfellows took similar oaths. In the short exchange that followed, one M.P. wanted to bring in a Bill to amend the 1797 Act, another maintained that the law was unclear, and the important question was asked whether the government was considering a mitigation of the sentences? To this the government spokesman replied that he thought it was the intention of Ministers to recommend mitigation to the King. The petition was then ordered 'to lie on the table' and on March 26th Parliament went into the Easter recess.

The agitation outside Parliament continued. On March 29th there was another protest meeting at the National Institution in Charlotte Street, and on March 30th a deputation took a petition to Lord Melbourne, while a crowd of up to twelve thousand waited to hear the results. After the interview, the deputation announced that Lord Melbourne had assured them that the sentence would not be carried into effect until the petition was in the King's hand. This appeared to be a step forward and to substantiate the parliamentary statement that the government was considering recommending mitigation to the King. On March 31st there were large meetings in Birmingham and Nottingham and on April 3rd there was a further gathering in the National Institution in London at which lengthy speeches were made and 'Rule Britannia' and Loveless's verses of 'God is our Guide' were rousingly sung.

A few days later the Secretary of State's office refuted the assurance that Lord Melbourne was alleged to have given. In any case the petition had been laid before His Majesty but he had not been 'pleased to signify any commands thereupon', consequently, 'all the persons who were convicted at Dorchester for administering unlawful oaths were now on their passage to Botany Bay'. As a result of this statement the *Morning Post* waded into the attack. This paper, as we have already noted, strongly disapproved of trade unions and accepted the sentence. However, on April 7th it wrote that Lord Melbourne's assurance of March 30th had been understood 'not by Trades Unions only, but by all mankind to convey an intimation that the sentence would be mitigated at least'. If, a few days after the assurance, it was announced that the men were already en route, Lord Melbourne must have known of their imminent departure when he accepted the petition. Therefore his presenting it to the King, at a moment when the men were about to sail, or indeed had already sailed, was a mockery and insult to which the *Morning Post* strongly objected.

In fact the men were not yet actually en route. George Loveless remained in Dorchester Gaol, while the other five were on board the convict ship *Surrey*, but it lay at anchor in Plymouth Sound until April 11th, so they could have been taken off if the authorities had so desired. However, the likelihood of this being done was almost non-existent, as the wheels were in motion and the *Surrey* had sailed from its starting point at Spithead. Although the government was strictly untruthful regarding George Loveless (and it did know of his illness), technically it was accurate about the others. Whether the Radical and other newspapers appreciated the technicality at the beginning of April is doubtful. By April 16th Lord Howick stated in Parliament that the *Surrey* had gone round from Portsmouth to Plymouth and he had every reason to believe it had sailed from the latter place – which by then was true, except that George Loveless was not on board. Certainly nobody campaigning for the remission of sentence was aware that Loveless remained in England until nearly the end of May. The lack of clarity on the government's part was undoubtedly deliberate. Their swift action – for only two days on a hulk was most unusual, anything up to nine months was still possible – stemmed from the belief and hope that once they announced the *fait accompli*, as no way of retrieving the men from the high seas was possible, the agitation would die down.

The reverse was true. The deliberate opaqueness of the government's statements, the unseemly haste with which the sentences had been effected only added fuel to the newspaper barrage. The *Republican* decorated the windows of its office with black stickers saying, 'Mr Guelph, alias the King, sanctions the exile of the Dorchester Unionists.' The *True Sun*'s efforts were unremitting. Every evening they had a leader, an article, or an editorial on the subject of trade unions and Radicalism in general – 'The hour of trial for English reformers is at hand' – and the Dorchester Unionists in particular. From time to time they held their own 'opinion poll', printing dozens of other newspapers' views, metropolitan and provincial, for and against, over-whelmingly proving that the majority view in this instance was on their side. They drew everybody's attention to a case in which sixteen men were due to be tried at Exeter on 'a charge similar to that on which Loveless and the other Unionists were tried at Dorchester'. The loud noises they, and others, made on behalf of these sixteen men ended in triumph. The prisoners were allowed bail, the case was deferred until July 21st and when it came to trial the case was dismissed. The *True Sun* also pressed at the fact that half of England could be transported for the same offence as the Tolpuddle men. This was a popular theme. The *Spectator*, for example, asked: 'Were the Dukes of Cumberland and Sussex aware that they were liable to a transfer for seven years from Kew and Kensington to the pickpocket quarter of the world?' The protest meetings continued from Manchester to Southwark, and passed resolutions not to cease until the freedom of the Dorchester Unionists had been obtained.

With the reassembly of Parliament, on April 14th, the

petitions begging for remission of sentence started to pour in. Also with the reassembly the biggest gun of the day, Daniel O'Connell, came into action. O'Connell was born in Kerry in 1775 and educated in France (because the Relief Bill which allowed Catholics a Catholic education had not in his youth been passed). In 1794 he came to London to study law, was called to the bar in 1798 and within a few years was the leading Irish barrister. He was ever a flamboyant, commanding character, six feet tall and broad as an oak, possessed of great pride and intelligence, with a fluency of speech, a strong natural sense of theatre and an attacking boldness. But above everything he was an Irishman. He loved Ireland, all Ireland, Protestant and Catholic, with a devouring passion. Everything he did was for Ireland. Over the years he twisted and turned, veered and tacked, but his objective remained clear – the repeal of the Act of Union, an Irish Parliament in Dublin, although firmly fixed within the framework of the British Empire. The *Leeds Mercury* said of him, 'If there be one man who more than another stands out in bold relief from the mass of characterless men of modern times, that man is O'Connell. He reminds us of the heroes of antiquity . . . O'Connell and Ireland. They are body and soul.'

He was elected an M.P. in 1828 but, as a Catholic, refused to take the oath of supremacy to the King. Lord John Russell supported the claim that O'Connell need not be subject to the usual oaths, but it was rejected by the House. A new election was ordered, but after the passage of the Catholic Emancipation Bill in 1829 O'Connell was returned unopposed, and thus became the first Catholic to take his seat in the House of Commons without tendering the oath of supremacy to the King. He was not basically a Radical. O'Connell was as firm a believer in law and order as the nearest Whig or Tory. What he wanted for Ireland, a decent measure of independence, he hoped to obtain through the law and without disorder. Nor was he a particular friend of the trade unions whose activities he had previously regarded with more than a little alarm. However, his passionate nature embraced injustice, whether Irish based or not, and the Tolpuddle men had, in his view, been victims of gross injustice. The politician in him knew that 'the people' were strongly of the same opinion, and O'Connell needed a ground-swell of public opinion to assist him in his battles for the repeal of the Act of Union. Perhaps, by and by the Tolpuddle swell, strongly supported by him, could be steered towards Ireland. Thus the weight of the most colourful character of the day was brought into play on the side of the Dorchester Unionists.

Other M.P.s who stoutly supported the cause included Joseph Hume, the old Radical and co-campaigner with Francis Place for the repeal of the Combination Acts; and Feargus O'Connor, a barrister and powerful orator like his compatriot Daniel O'Connell, but unlike O'Connell a passionate if unstable Radical, later to be one of the Chartist leaders.

On the day Parliament reassembled, a petition was presented from Cheltenham. In the ensuing exchange, O'Connell raised two points. First he posed the question of why the government had raked up 'this slumbering statute', and then gave the answer, 'to strike terror into the trades unions'. Secondly, he drew attention to the liability of members of Orange Lodges, at whose head were many illustrious persons, to be similarly indicted. Two days later further petitions were presented from Yeovil, Liverpool and Kingston-upon-Hull, the latter being the largest. It was presented by Mr Hutt, Hull's M.P., and was signed by seven thousand members of the Grand National Consolidated Trades Union there. Mr Hutt said he was not personally in favour of trade unions as he thought they were 'most mischievous in their operations'. However, he himself was a member of a society that administered secret oaths, and he considered it clear that the six men had been punished for being members of a trade union, not for administering oaths. It was in this discussion, of April 16th, that Lord Howick (who was one of Prime Minister Grey's many sons) stated that to the best of his knowledge the men had sailed from Plymouth. Two days later another petition was presented from Leeds, the result of a meeting attended by over twenty thousand people. The figure was probably an exaggeration, but all the petitions were the result of large protest meetings up and down the country. A further parliamentary exchange followed in which Joseph Hume spoke of the higher classes forming their unions and administering their oaths with impunity, and in which Howick replied at some length for the government. The trade unions were not contenting themselves with raising wages, but were attempting to usurp the rights of industry, and it was the imposition of the oath that rendered unions illegal. He admitted that the Dorchester Unionists may not have known of the precise Act of Parliament under which they had sinned. However, they had known they were doing wrong, witness the secrecy in holding their meetings at night. Two of them had been Methodist preachers and could not therefore have been as ignorant of the law as people were making them out to be while another had previously been sentenced to hard labour, therefore neither could they be as virtuous as people were imputing. Feargus O'Connor took up the point that it was difficult for labourers working all day to meet at any other time than at night. There was more discussion about their suffering for the imagined crimes of trade unions in general, and about those members of other societies who took illegal oaths and were not prosecuted, and the petition was again laid on the table.

After this there was a ten-day respite from petitions to Parliament, but it was far from quiet outside the House.

10: 'Labour Put Its Hat upon Its Head and Walked towards the Throne'

The mid-April agitation for the remission of the Dorchester Unionists' sentence, including the greatest demonstration of all, partly stemmed from reaction to the activities of the authorities.

Lord Melbourne was applying the brakes. To him the Dorchester Unionists were never a cause. They were the spanners who happened to have been on hand to jam the trade union works. The spanners had, unfortunately, become a major issue, though exactly why they had, apart from political opportunism, Melbourne never comprehended. Compassionate identification, the cult of the underdog, the earnestness of campaigners, were beyond his reach. Thus, while considering the ends justified the means and were justifiable, he could see no point in exacerbating the situation. Let it lie, like the petitions on the table of the House of Commons, and die a natural death. However, for James Frampton, the Tolpuddle men remained a passionate cause, part of the wide framework of trade unionism which must be pursued to the death and not allowed to die of its own accord. Immediately after the sentence he wrote to Melbourne suggesting that the farmers turn off all labour known to belong to a union. In reply he received two letters, one through the normal channels from the Under-Secretary at the Home Office, but the other marked 'private and confidential' from Melbourne himself. Both advised against any such action, Melbourne's personal letter at considerable length. Unions themselves were now regrettably legal, provided they did not resort to violence or administer illegal oaths. The government could not, therefore, advise farmers to discharge men for doing what was not only legal but, if the farmers were not paying decent wages, might be just and reasonable. Would not farmers acting in such a manner 'take upon themselves great responsibility, incur much odium and subject themselves to observations which it would be very difficult to reply to?' Moreover, if the government's experience of master manufacturers in the towns was anything to judge by, the likelihood of the farmers themselves being united was remote. After this warning, Melbourne agreed that standing by with arms folded in the face of the union activity was unthinkable, but he could only recommend firmness, resolution and vigilance and, of course, prompt action should any violation of the law occur. In his reply Frampton begged to assure his lordship that he would do everything in his power to adhere to the advice and instructions contained in his lordship's private letter, the receipt of which had been a great honour.

In another letter, written at the end of March, Frampton outlined the importance of the trial and sentence, as viewed in Dorset and, he inferred, elsewhere. Its course had been followed 'with the greatest anxiety by all Classes in this County'. The farmers had known that their future control over their labourers depended on the result, for the latter had been merely waiting for the result to see whether they could join the unions with impunity. The conviction and prompt execution of the sentence had given 'the greatest satisfaction to all the Higher Classes' and would, Frampton had no doubt, have a very great effect among the labourers. To implement the effects Frampton had, by the end of March, taken further action that lay within his power, though not on Lord Melbourne's advice. While the men were still in Dorchester Gaol he had refused permission for Betsy Loveless to visit George, for Diana Standfield to see either of her brothers or her son (though she was allowed to see her husband, Thomas), and for Catherine Brine to see her son James. These refusals were reported in the *True Sun*, with great indignation, as an indication of the vindictiveness and callousness of the 'Higher Classes'. More important, because of its practical effects, Frampton had also refused to grant parish relief to the dependants of the six men, and had urged his less spirited fellow magistrates to do likewise. Diana Standfield, with five children to support, was told, 'You shall suffer want. You shall have no mercy, because you ought to have known better than to have allowed such meetings to have been holden in your house.' Frampton gave as one of his reasons for refusal the fact that if the families could have afforded to pay one shilling to join the union and a penny a week thereafter, they did not need parish relief. He callously overlooked the more recent fact that the women who were being refused relief no longer had anybody to provide one shilling or one penny. Another general reason given, by him and other magistrates, was that the men and their families would soon appreciate that the leaders of the trade unions had deceived them. Having been refused parish relief, they would be forced to turn to the unions who neither intended nor were able to support them. Frampton's reasoning was, by his standards, logical. Why show compassion at this stage? The families must suffer, too. But when Melbourne heard of his next scheme, to refuse relief to all or any unionists thrown out of work for belonging to a union, he did not approve. It appeared to him doubtful that such refusal could be justified legally, and by implication he disapproved of the withholding of parish relief from the Tolpuddle wives and mothers. Urged on by Frampton, the magistrates' cry to Diana Standfield, Elizabeth Loveless, Sarah Loveless, Harriet Hammett and Catherine Brine was, as the *True Sun* reported, 'Go to your Union Club, and see if they will assist you now.'

The answer of the unions was to provide all possible support. The first mass meeting at the Institute in London on March 24th had announced the inauguration of a fund to assist the wives and children. On March 31st, the *True*

Sun reported the refusal of the magistrates to grant relief, underlining the urgent necessity for assistance. By April 12th the *Pioneer* was pleased to announce the receipt of individual subscriptions from all over the country, and from the unions of silk weavers, gardeners, shipwrights, joiners, cordwainers, journeymen, tailors, caulkers, coach painters, trimmers and brushmakers. The subscriptions were quickly put to good use. On April 8th Frampton informed Lord Melbourne that 'a very well-dressed person, tho' not a gentleman' had arrived on the London mail coach at Milbourne, a village half-way between Blandford and Dorchester. This person had immediately enquired about the six Unionists and their families. A few days later Frampton was able to inform his lordship that he was 'about 5 feet 4 inches high, dressed in a black coat and trouser, dark waistcoat and dark cravat', that the features of his face were 'short and compressed together' and that he had a sore on his upper lip. Moreover, he had been to Bere where he had called on a Mr Bridle, a Methodist who kept the draper's and grocer's shop. (Mr Bridle was the jury member rejected by the Crown at the trial.) The stranger had then reappeared at Milbourne accompanied by Betsy Loveless and her eldest son. Their intention had been to catch the mail coach to London, but it had been full on arrival in Milbourne so Mrs Loveless and the child had returned to Tolpuddle. A week later Frampton had further information about the activities of the mysterious visitor whom he was now able to identify as a Mr Newman, a cabinet-maker of Grays Inn Lane, London. Mr Newman had visited the area 'to convey money to the wives and families of the convicts'. Frampton understood that he had given money directly to Mrs Standfield and the two Mrs Lovelesses, leaving a further supply in the care of Bridle. He further understood that Bridle was shortly to go to London where 'the regular rate of pay to be allowed to these women and children' would be finally settled. Prior to Newman's visit the Tolpuddle vicar, Doctor Warren, had been contacted by another member of the relief committee in London with a request to distribute money to the wives and families of the convicts. But Doctor Warren, although he had been willing to distribute the charity, had heard no more on the subject. Perhaps the organizers of the relief money had decided to by-pass Warren and make their own arrangements, hence Newman's visit. Lord Melbourne displayed little interest, either in Frampton's or the relief committee's activities. By August 1834, an official 'London Dorchester Committee', with Robert Hartwell as its secretary, was established. It was to be the focal point of the continued agitation, and of moral and financial support for the wives and children.

At the end of March, Frampton was also busy supplying information to the government about the six men. This Melbourne had requested sensing, only too correctly, that the reassembly of Parliament would occasion 'much observation . . . upon the six men lately convicted of administering unlawful oaths at Dorchester'. Frampton's character references were inevitably not flattering. Thomas Standfield was described as 'the owner of the house in Tolpuddle where the meetings of the Union were held and also a Methodist Meeting House there, where he preaches occasionally'. Nobody else ever mentioned Standfield's owning a Meeting House, but it is likely that Methodist gatherings were held in his cottage and Frampton's 'trusty persons' who supplied him with this information were confused. Thomas Standfield was also referred to as 'a very discontented man, and if any disturbance is going on he is sure to be in it'. John Standfield was similarly marked out as being a Methodist and 'very saucy and ready for any disturbance'. The description of James Brine started in a more flattering manner. 'At the time of the Riots in 1830 . . . he behaved well and tried to keep out of them.' But then went on to say that since that time he had become 'very idle and kept company with James Hammett ... He has been wandering about the whole winter under a pretence of seeking work but there is every reason to believe he has been employed during all that time by the Lovelesses and Standfields, with James Hammett in enticing persons to join the Union.' Hammett himself was described as 'always a very idle man and ready for mischief', with the additional information that he had been previously sentenced to four months' hard labour for stealing iron. Frampton's statement that it was Hammett who had been the downfall of young James Brine, and that the two of them had spent the winter enticing people to join the Union, emphasizes his strong belief that Hammett was a key member of the Society. James Loveless was noted as being a Methodist preacher, and 'very active in the riots of the winter of 1830'. The longest report was devoted to George Loveless. He had also, according to Frampton, been very active in the 'Swing' riots, was registered as a Methodist preacher and it was he 'who set the Union on foot in this neighbourhood'. There were further details about the list of those who had belonged to the Union being in his handwriting, and the papers relating to the Flax and Hemp Trade Union and the letter from George Romaine being found on his person.

It was on the information supplied by Frampton that the government based its statement to the House of Commons of April 18th. Fortunately, Melbourne took the information with a pinch of salt and there was no reference to the Lovelesses and the 1830 riots. Indeed, in his next letter to Frampton he asked for further information 'of the grounds on which it is stated that James and George Loveless were active in the riots of 1830'. The grounds as outlined by Frampton demonstrate the frightening gullibility of the sincere but closed mind. For they consisted of a statement made by a local farmer, referring to an incident that had occurred four years previously, during which, in murky early morning light, he thought he had recognized George Loveless's voice among a mob. While all that could be said of James Loveless's participation was that he had 'appeared much dissatisfied, and tried to persuade the men to go and join the mob which had assembled at Piddletown'. On receipt of this vague information, Melbourne immediately wrote back to ascertain whether Hammett's previous conviction came into the same unsubstantiated category. In this instance Frampton was able to produce confirmation, which he did by enclosing a copy of the 1829 certificate from Dorchester Gaol. However, Melbourne wisely remained unconvinced about the men's bad characters, and thereafter the government eschewed attacks from this quarter. The field was left for the campaigners to elaborate upon the goodness, honesty and industry of the six men.

Among the groups who campaigned for the men's release, official Methodism was not to be found. From their brothers in religion, the five men received no support. (Young James Brine was not a Methodist, though later in life he became a convert to the creed.) Orthodox Methodism then resided in the personage of Jabez Bunting, a born dictator if ever there was one. Four times Methodist President, sometimes simultaneously head of the Theological Institution and the Missionary Committee, if Bunting decided something was not to be, it was not. (On one notable occasion he adjourned the Methodist Conference in full session because he needed to go to London.) Bunting held to the view that good Methodists were as opposed to democracy as they were to sin, and the notion of any of his adherents using their brains to organize themselves democratically to bargain with their masters did not appeal to him. Methodist historians, however, point to the growing opposition to Bunting and his emphasis on the tenets of John Wesley the authoritarian politician, rather than John Wesley the reforming evangelist, which led to breakaway sections. Although there was no official Connexional support for the five men in their hour of trial, in the light of Methodist Chartist activity only a few years later, the historians believe individual Methodists were among the campaigners.

The next large protest meeting, organized by the Radicals, was held on April 18th at the Crown and Anchor Inn in London. It was notable not only because of the large attendance, 'the room was crowded to suffocation', but because of its speakers, among them Feargus O'Connor and the mighty Daniel O'Connell. The preliminaries were of an emotional nature, with a lady who had travelled from Dorchester putting 2s. 6d. on the table to defray the expenses of the meeting, a butcher's boy giving a shilling, and Daniel O'Connell contributing his mite 'in the name of God and Mercy'. In his speech, Feargus O'Connor asserted that as a lawyer he was convinced that the six men were not only morally but legally innocent, while as a member of a trade union he would support the movement to the death, so long as its object remained just. But it was the considered verdict of O'Connell, leading barrister as well as major figure, that everybody wanted to hear. O'Connell said he could only judge from the newspaper reports but he thought the sentence was probably legal (he was to change his mind twice about the legality). He had asked the government for a copy of the indictment which they had initially promised to give him but had since refused. From this he adjudged the case might be weak. However, the families could apply for a copy and the government could not refuse them. If there was a fault in the indictment then a writ of error could be brought. There was a fault, in the date the oath was said to have been administered, but it was not a major one, and certainly not the sort of error on which one could demand a re-trial (although, initially, the defending counsels might have obtained a brief postponement). For whatever reasons the families did not apply for a copy of the indictment, so this legal point was not raised again. O'Connell said that Mr Baron Williams could have sentenced the men to seven days' transportation rather than imposing the maximum sentence. He then turned to the subject of trade unions generally. They must proceed by legal means and never put themselves in the wrong, as they had done by taking oaths. If they proceeded legally and were not misdirected, he now thought 'the English trades unions would set an example to the world', but they patently needed legal advice and he offered his services as counsel. He also thought they needed representation in the House of Commons, though 'an ugly house it was'. O'Connell was correct. The unions needed both, and temporarily they were to be given both. O'Connell acted as their counsel, until Ireland regained his whole attention, and their case was well supported in the House. But it was to be a long time before they could afford to pay legal advisers, as opposed to receiving temporary free aid, and before they had their own representatives in Parliament.

What the Tolpuddle case did *at the time* was help establish the unions. William Lovett, founder of the Working Men's Association in 1836 and later Chartist leader, wrote of the Grand National Consolidated Trades Union, 'Soon after its formation, a great stimulus was found in the transportation of six poor Dorchester labourers belonging to a friendly society of agricultural labourers, having for their object the improvement of their miserable wages; their alleged offence being the taking of an oath on their admission as members.' While Francis Place believed that the Tolpuddle affair saved the unions from extinction, if 'saved' is the right verb. For Place, the architect of the repeal of the Combination Laws, thought that the impetus for trade unions had arisen from the government's opposition, that once the illegality was removed the need would disappear and the unions would cease to exist. In this belief Place was curiously and historically wrong, but he expressed it strongly in a letter written in April 1834:

> The Unions were fairly at an end. I told Mr Young more than three months ago that they would die out if left alone. This was really the case when the worse than stupid condemnation of the Dorchester Labourers so rapidly carried into effect gave the stimulus the people needed to set them to their work again full vigour. Ça ira – Ministers have furnished the stimulus. We were very much in the condition you predicted we should be in. We are now on our legs again. Ça ira ... Had sentence been passed upon the Dorchester Labourers and then been remitted. Had a proclamation been issued declaring the law and the determination henceforth to enforce it been made, an end would have been, at once, put to all Trade Unions.

Place's assessment was not correct. The need for unions went deeper than the setback the sentence and immediate remission would have caused, and they would have re-emerged. But as it was, the trade unions were on their legs, and kicking for all their worth. They delivered the strongest possible indication of their reborn vigour on April 21st. On that April Monday of 1834 a mass demonstration and procession was organized by the Metropolitan Trades Unions. According to Place, the original intention was to call for 'a long holiday' throughout the country, but owing to the exertions and influence of 'a very sedate discreet man, a leader in the Central Union Committee', assuredly influenced by that sedate, discreet gentleman called Francis Place, the decision to have the one-day demonstration in London was reached. Again according to Place, who regarded himself as the éminence grise of all reforming activity, it was he who instructed the organizers in the laws relating to the carrying up of petitions.

The plan for April 21st was that the demonstration would meet on Copenhagen Fields, near King's Cross, 'the old rendezvous of disturbance' according to *The Times*. In orderly procession they would then march to, and past, the Home Office in Whitehall, over Westminster Bridge to an open space near the Bethlem Hospital where they would halt. In the meantime the deputation from the Central Committee, of not more than ten (as instructed by Place), would present a monster petition for remission of sentence on the Dorchester Unionists to Lord Melbourne. The results of the interview at the Home Office would be communicated to the waiting crowds at the Bethlem Hospital who would then disperse peacefully. Apart from two alterations this plan was carried out. It was achieved by the meticulous organization of the unions, and by lack of panic on the part of the government, stemming from the character of the man whose duty it was to maintain law and order, Lord Melbourne.

Francis Place was not involved in the organization, he merely gave advice. But Robert Owen was, actually hiring Copenhagen Fields for April 21st so that the assembly should be on private, union-owned property and free from police intervention. Prior to the 21st, Owen and the Central Committee separately visited Lord Melbourne to give him the full details of the intentions of the procession and the route to be taken. While expressing his disapproval of the plan, Melbourne received them with 'his accustomed courtesy' and informed them that he would be at the Home Office from 11 A.M. to 5 P.M. on the day. Both Owen and the Central Committee also saw the Metropolitan Police to acquaint them with the details and impress upon them the peaceable intentions. The police reply was that they had instructions only to protect the procession and, if necessary, property. However, Lord Melbourne took some extra precautions, bringing in detachments of Lancers, the Queen's Bays and the Royals from Croydon, and eight battalions of infantry and 'twenty-nine pieces of ordnance' from Woolwich. But wisely and sensibly he did no more than order them to be held in readiness at nearby barracks in case of emergency.

The events of April 21st started early. At 7 A.M. a light waggon festooned with blue and red calico was carried on to Copenhagen Fields by twelve bearers. On top of the waggon was an iron frame carrying the petition for remission of sentence. The petition itself was on a wooden roller, was two feet broad and three feet in length, and bore between two hundred thousand and three hundred thousand signatures. By 8 A.M. the approaches to the Fields were packed with members of the various lodges marching from their earlier assembly points. There were tailors 'distinguished by the jauntiness of their appearance', smiths and metal-workers 'a little dingy', coal-heavers 'in their frocks and fantails', and the silk weavers whose appearance 'told a tale of squalid misery which every man must regret to know exists'. But this was no day for squalid misery. The human traffic jams converging on Copenhagen Fields sorted themselves out, and the leaders of each lodge placed their banners temporarily in front of Copenhagen House. According to *The Times* there were thirty-three banners, according to the *True Sun* 'nineteen facing London and twenty to twenty-five facing Hampstead'. They made a brave spectacle, fluttering in the wind, shining in the sun – and it was a fine spring day. By 9 A.M. the vast area of the Fields was filled with a mass of people thick and tight as grass on a well-maintained lawn. *The Times* said the scene was 'most imposing; the utmost decorum prevailed, and the *coup d'oeil* was most striking, inasmuch as it bore so strong a semblance of military array, discipline and good order'. Decorum and discipline were the order of the day. At 9.30 A.M. a rocket was fired as the signal for the procession to start. In front were the horsemen, including Joseph Hume; next came the Central Committee of the

Metropolitan Trades Unions; then the twelve bearers carrying the festooned waggon with the monster petition, with the members of the delegation who were to present it to Lord Melbourne walking immediately behind. Among these were Doctor Wade in full canonicals, with his hood as doctor of divinity, and Robert Owen. William Lovett was also among the throng.

The procession followed the prearranged route from King's Cross, through to Russell Square, across into Tottenham Court Road, along Oxford Street, down Regent Street, into Waterloo Place, along Pall Mall to Charing Cross, into Whitehall and then to the Home Office. All the streets were lined with thousands of spectators and business in London, the City apart, came to a standstill. At Tottenham Court Road, Robert Owen left the procession and went as quickly as possible to the Home Office by himself. For Melbourne had earlier sent two messages to the Central Committee at Copenhagen Fields, saying he had decided he would not receive the petition. But at the Home Office Owen was refused an audience with anybody, high or low, the reason being given that he was not a member of the official deputation.[1] While Owen was being refused an audience, the rest of the procession was continuing on its way to Whitehall. Its head, with the officially constituted deputation, reached the Home Office at twelve noon. They were allowed to enter, but Melbourne refused to meet them or accept 'a petition presented under such circumstances, and in such a manner', although he would accept and lay before the King any petition delivered in 'a proper manner'. The deputation then asked if the petition was refused and were given the same answer. It must be presented in a

---

[1] Owen tended to play a lone hand. Although he founded the Grand National Consolidated Trades Union in 1833, he only became a member himself after the Tolpuddle sentences, in order to make it easier for him to fight for remission.

proper manner. They accordingly left the Home Office, with the petition still in their possession.

This was the first alteration to the grand design. However, the refusal did not in any way affect the procedure or behaviour of the main body of the procession. It continued to march down Whitehall and over Westminster Bridge, the banners fluttering as the wind whipped up the Thames. At the Bethlem Hospital, the plan had to be altered for the second time. The space in front of the hospital was found to be too small to hold the incoming thousands, so with excellent discipline and up-to-the-minute organization the procession was kept on the move. It wound its way past the Elephant and Castle, past Newington Church to Kennington Common, where it waited patiently until the deputation arrived with the news that Lord Melbourne had refused to accept the petition. Then it dispersed, and by five o'clock Kennington Common was empty. Neither frenzy nor uproar greeted the news of Melbourne's refusal. What mattered on the day of April 21st was the fact that thousands of men and women could be roused by the sentence to sign the monster petition in the first place; the fact that they could be organized into 'one of the most remarkable processions that perhaps ever walked through the streets of London'; the fact that they were trade unionists, or currently in sympathy with the unions; that this was the day when 'Labour put its hat upon its head and walked towards the throne'; and that it walked in a sober, decorous, disciplined manner.

How many thousands were involved in this most remarkable procession? Estimates varied from twenty thousand to two hundred thousand. *The Times*, partly in the interests of accuracy, partly to denigrate the wilder claims of the trade unions, devoted over six hundred words to a mathematical analysis. It had reporters stationed at Charing Cross, watching the procession as it wheeled into Whitehall; it accepted that the members of the procession walked on average at five abreast; it noted that the time the whole length took to pass Charing Cross was two hours, twenty-five minutes; therefore *The Times* calculated that thirty-five thousand people were involved. It also printed a letter from an eye-witness, who had likewise been stationed at Charing Cross and had done his own calculations. He concluded that the procession 'could not possibly exceed 32,000, and it might be somewhat less than 30,000'. His estimate was corroborated by 'several old officers who had been at the balconies of the Junior United Services Club'. *The Times*' own figure of thirty-five thousand was accepted by the *True Sun* which also thought the estimates of two hundred thousand were over-optimistic (although if you included the numbers *watching*, as well as those *participating*, more than two hundred thousand people could well have been involved). But thirty-five thousand was no mean figure, and a procession which lasted two and a half hours, whose tail was still in Copenhagen Fields when its head had already reached the Home Office in Whitehall, was no mean procession.

The demonstration was generally acknowledged to have been a success, if in some quarters grudgingly. *The Times* said, 'It was but justice to the whole body assembled on this occasion, to add, that nothing could have been more orderly than their demeanour throughout the long line of the procession.' The *Morning Herald*, *Morning Post* and *Globe*, like *The Times* no friends of the unions, admitted the same. The *Morning Post* expressed surprise at the orderly behaviour but thought the demonstration was the thin end of the wedge, which indeed it was, although the wedge had a long way to go before it prised open the opposition. The *Globe* considered that the job of presenting the petition could have been performed as efficiently by half a dozen men. The job was, in fact, done by the deputation and it was surely naïve of the *Globe* to imagine that half a dozen men entering the Home Office would have attracted one-hundredth of the attention drawn by the mass procession. The Radical papers naturally regarded the day as a glorious triumph. Who after such a display, asked the *True Sun*, could say the working classes were unfit to vote?

A triumph April 21st may have been, and in the long run the effects were beneficial to the Tolpuddle men and the trade unions, but the immediate, short-term effects were not so obvious. The monster petition was later accepted, but on April 28th the Central Committee received 'another of those evasive and unmeaning answers . . . The King has not yet been pleased to issue any commands thereupon.'

On the same day, April 28th, the matter of the Dorchester Unionists was discussed in both House of Commons and House of Lords, although only obliquely in the latter. In the House of Commons, Joseph Hume presented petitions for remission of sentence from Newcastle upon Tyne, Belfast, and two from Scotland. In the exchange that followed Hume asked what rights the repeal of the Combination Laws had granted to the trade unions? He also said that the sentence had given rise to the general opinion that men were punished for one thing which was not illegal, under the name of another of which the illegality was doubtful. Another speaker said that the government's motives were the suppression of trade unionism, but the grand meeting of April 21st had disposed of the likelihood of this happening. Supporting the sentences, two members gave as their reasons (*a*) that if trade unionism was allowed to continue, the framework of society would collapse, and the whole thing end in Republicanism; and (*b*) that the raising of wages was not the sole object of the unionists, but that they aimed to intimidate their masters and the government (this, of course, had been part of the government's own argument). The main speaker was Daniel O'Connell. He repeated much of what he had said at the

141

Crown and Anchor meeting on April 18th, his being refused a copy of the indictment, his consequent doubts about the legality and strength of the government's case, his becoming counsel to the unions. In addition he read at emotional length a letter received from a gentleman named Mr Ewett who had been present at the trial in Dorchester. The opinion of Mr Ewett was that 'the evidence was given in a very loose and indistinct manner', that the taking of the oath was never proven, that the appearance and demeanour of the prisoners 'entirely supported their defence, which was, that they did not know that they were doing anything against the laws, that they united to support themselves and their wives and families', and finally, 'supposing the conviction to be legal, the extreme punishment awarded in this case, was a most indiscreet and cruel application of the law'. That a gentleman, not a trade unionist, should have been sufficiently roused by what he had witnessed to communicate his emotions, at length, was why O'Connell read the letter. Inevitably, O'Connell managed to bring Ireland into his speech. Providing they kept within the bounds of the law, he now thought the unions could possess a degree of moral force that boded nothing but good, particularly in respect of the cheap labour being imported from Ireland which was putting extra money into the masters' pockets.

The debate in the House of Lords was supposed to be about the better observance of the Sabbath. Within a short time the Duke of Newcastle had progressed to the disgraceful proceedings of certain bodies of persons, calling themselves trade unions, who were in the habit of congregating in London in great numbers under various pretences. Lord Londonderry concurred. The crisis was alarming with thousands of people assembling in the neighbourhood of the parks, specifically Copenhagen Fields although he did not say so, 'for what object he could not conceive'. Lord Melbourne speaking, according to *The*

Times, 'in a very low tone of voice'[2] agreed that the situation was an unhappy one but, again applying the brakes, pointed out that there was no means of stopping such proceedings unless the laws were violated. When Lord Chancellor Brougham rose the brakes were released, and the governmental carriage hurtled along, mowing down both Tolpuddle men and trade unions. He said he entertained not a shadow of doubt that the men were lawfully and justly convicted. It was the most audacious assessment, the most foul and unpardonable calumny against the judges of the country and the laws of the land, to assert that the six men had been sentenced and punished because they were members of a trade union. They had been tried and convicted, and were now suffering punishment for one of the worst offences that could be conceived. The administering of secret oaths was an offence most dangerous in itself, fraught with worse dangers still, leading to the violation of the rights of property, even to assassination itself. Brougham then directed his passion against the unions themselves, and he was one of the ablest orators of the day. Of all the worst things, of all the most pernicious devices that could be imagined to injure the interests of the working classes, not forgetting the interests of the country at large, nothing was half so bad as the existence of the trade unions. He implored unionists and would-be members to listen to the wholesome advice of those who had no interest in deceiving them. The leaders of the unions were idle, good-for-nothing agitators, a set of pernicious counsellors who for their own private advantage were intent on leading the working classes astray. It was because he was a sincere

---

[2] Melbourne himself had once written, 'In the House of Commons, whether it be from apprehension, or heat, or long waiting, or the tediousness of what I hear, a torpor of all my faculties almost always comes upon me, and I feel as if I had neither ideas nor opinions, even upon the subjects which interest me most deeply.' The same torpor presumably overcame him in the Lords, too.

friend of the working classes that he was an enemy of the unions.

It was, in a way, an odd speech for Brougham. It should have been delivered by the bluest of Tories, not by an erstwhile reformer, not by the man who had effected so many beneficial legal changes and who cared for the education of the working classes. But Brougham was the least consistent of men, his brilliance and boundless energy lacked balance, he shot off in tangential passions, and his worst enemy was not the unions, but himself. The *True Sun*, naturally, thought his speech was monstrous while *The Times*, equally naturally, gave it a special column, separate from the general report of the Debate. The *True Sun* also considered it 'a little odd' that in neither House had anyone commented on the actual petition, signed by three hundred thousand people, for the release of the Dorchester Unionists.

For the time being pressure, in and out of Parliament, slackened, partly because everything possible had been done, partly because it is not possible to maintain human pressure indefinitely. Throughout the weeks of high tension and activity George Loveless remained in England, working during the day on the gun-wharf at Portsmouth, battened down from sunset to sunrise on the hulk *York*.

11: 'In Short the Convict Is, Properly Speaking, a Slave?'

William Cobbett said that the immediate agitation for the release of the six men was 'to the eternal honour of England, and indeed of Scotland and Ireland too'. (He made no mention of Wales.) The agitation had no practical value for the men. George Loveless was on the hulk at Portsmouth, while his brother and friends were en route for New South Wales. The five men had already discovered what being a convict meant, briefly on the hulk, less briefly on board the *Surrey*, for it was after four months at sea that the *Surrey* sailed past the Heads and entered Sydney Harbour, on August 17th, 1834. They were then to discover what being a convict in Australia entailed.

At the first protest meeting, Robert Owen had said that the working classes of Great Britain and Ireland were in a worse condition than any slaves at any period in the world's history. Cobbett had often asserted that the agricultural labourers of England endured less freedom and greater hardship than the Negro slaves of America, and Cobbett had lived in the United States. But neither he nor Owen had visited Australia and seen the convicts there. New South Wales, it must be remembered, was established as a penal colony. Not only did the convicts build the towns, clear the forests and push the roads through the bush and mountain, but they also manned the early schools and lower ranks of government. From the start it was inevitable, given the circumstances and the period, that the discipline needed to contain this mixture of evil men, of indifferent men sucked down by the fight for survival, of the spirited and rebellious, should be ferocious. Almost from the start penal settlements within the penal colony were established, places to which the 'refractory' convict could be removed. The most notorious of these was Norfolk Island, a small volcanic island about a thousand miles off the Australian mainland. Of Norfolk Island it was variously said that it was the hell on earth from which no man returned alive; 'Let a man be what he will when he comes here, he is as soon as bad as the rest; a man's heart is taken from him, and then is given to him the heart of a beast'; 'I would not hesitate to prefer death, under any form that could be presented to me, rather than such a state of endurance as that of the convict at Norfolk Island'; and that those condemned to death there gave thanks to God, and those reprieved cried to Him for mercy.

As the statement 'Let a man be what he will when he comes here' implies, it was not only the refractory convicts who were sent to penal settlements. What happened to the transported convict was a total lottery, and his life was one of continual and demoralizing uncertainty. On arrival the convict became the property of the Governor but increasingly as the years went by, and after 1818 when free emigration to New South Wales was established, the Governor assigned – a euphemism for sold – the convicts to free settlers. Again it was an absolute lottery whether the convict went to a good or bad master. One young assigned convict said, 'All a man has got to mind is to keep a still tongue in his head, and do his master's duty, and then he is well looked upon.' It was not as simple as that. If the master was a monster who regularly beat or starved the convict, he might in the end be driven to absconding. If he was caught the punishment could be a penal settlement such as Norfolk Island. If the convict retained any spirit and tried to object, again the punishment could be the same. Even if he said nothing the end result might be Norfolk Island because men were sent to penal settlements for 'insolence of expression'. The same young convict admitted that if you did *not* do your duty satisfactorily – or happened to have an uppity expression – 'you may as well be hung at once, for they would get you 100 lashes, and then get you sent to a place called Port Arthur'. (This was a penal settlement on Van Diemen's Land.) Flogging was a commonplace of convict life, not only in the penal settlements but in direct government employ or on assignment.

In 1834 direct government employ included the road parties which were still opening up the country. It was generally admitted that to be sent on arrival to a road party was the worst thing that could happen. On assignment there was a chance of having a good master; on the road parties there was little hope. Men worked fourteen hours and more a day, in temperatures up to 115°F, at the mercy of overseers, herded at night into 'Belly Bots' which were boxes holding twenty to twenty-eight men, with no room to lie down. The overseers were bullies, because the job demanded it, and sometimes sadists, and for any infringement or for 'idleness', which could mean absolute exhaustion, the punishment was being tied to the 'triangle' and the infliction of fifty or a hundred lashes on the bare back. One convict who killed an overseer said, 'I was tired of the whole damned business. Life was just hell. All I wish is that I was to swing for killing a hundred blasted overseers, instead of just one, you lot of miserable tyrants.' Worse than the road parties were the road gangs where the men were permanently chained, and the floggings severer and more arbitrary. But the road gangs were a form of punishment.

The power of sending a man to the road gangs, along with many other powers, lay with the magistrates. Officially any convict had the right to appeal to a magistrate in a case of severe ill-treatment. In practice it was impossible for a convict in direct government employ to appeal because no one was going to say that the government was wrong. In practice, too, it was very difficult for an assigned convict to appeal. The magistrates were the pivot of the day-to-day system that kept the convict in his place. The likelihood of their upholding the despised and feared convict against his master was remote. Occasionally it happened, but as a witness before the 1837 Select Committee on Transportation said, 'Legal redress is rarely sought for, and still more rarely obtained by the injured convict.' Even should the magistrate agree that the convict had been severely maltreated, he had no powers to punish the master. The most he could do was ask for the convict's reassignment, or suggest that the master was unfit to be one. The magisterial powers were directed *against* the convict, and they were wide. On a complaint being laid by a master, the magistrate could order up to a hundred lashes and/or send the convict to road gangs or a penal settlement. In one week of 1834 the Weekly Statement of Offences and Punishments issued by a magistrate included:

Having taken and concealed a bundle of kangaroo skins, the property of their master – hard labour 12 months. Recommended at penal settlement.

Feloniously receiving and partaking a quantity of potatoes – 12 months hard labour. Chain gang recommended.

Making frivolous and vexatious charge against his master – 3 months hard labour on a road gang.

Being seen with a quantity of potatoes, strongly suspected to have been stolen – 12 months hard labour on a chain gang.

Out after hours – 6 months hard labour on a chain gang.

A most determined runaway – 75 lashes, two years penal settlement.

Giving away, and accepting, mutton, the property of his master – 12 months hard labour on a chain gang.

In 1834 the number of summary convict convictions in New South Wales was twenty-two thousand, the number of floggings inflicted just under three thousand. The total convict population was then twenty-eight thousand, male and female, so the odds on your being able 'to keep a still tongue in your head' and be 'well looked upon' were not high. It will be noted from the list of Weekly Punishments that three of the offences were connected with food. They frequently were as hunger was another of the lotteries. Rations varied, they were higher in Van Diemen's Land than in New South Wales, but on average a convict received ¾ lb. fresh meat or 8 oz. salt pork, 1½ lb. bread, 10 oz. flour, 1½ lb. potatoes and ½ oz. salt per week, while tea, sugar and milk were 'indulgences' which could be withdrawn for ill-behaviour. On the chain gangs and in the penal settlements there were horrifying accounts of men killing each other for a bone and picking the grains from the excrement of oxen.

There was a reverse side to the grim coin of transportation and convict life, although it was an unequally balanced coin and few saw the brightness. If the convict was assigned to a good master (or mistress which particularly applied to women convicts) life could be better than in England. If by luck, cunning, or sheer dogged endurance he managed to keep clear of summary punishments there was a piece of cheese in the mousetrap in that his sentence could be cut and tickets-of-leave could be awarded for good conduct. Once he had a ticket-of-leave, he was free to seek his own employment although he still remained a convict. Conditional pardons were granted which gave the convict his freedom although he had to remain in the colony. Absolute pardons were also, though more rarely, granted in which case the convict could return to England if he so desired and had the necessary money.

The early Governors of New South Wales mainly saw their task as keeping the unruly labour force in order while opening up the country. In 1809, General Lachlan Macquarie, a Highlander, was appointed Governor. He believed in what had been one of the main ideas behind transportation which others had forgotten, namely that it was meant to redeem the convict, to give him a fresh start in a new world. Macquarie made life more tolerable by establishing a muster roll so that convicts officially existed, by building a hospital and by reorganizing the law courts so that justice was a little less summary than it had been. In particular he encouraged the emancipists, as freed convicts and their children were called, and even appointed one emancipist as a judge. By his actions he aroused the hostility of the free settlers, who started to emigrate after 1818. (There were free settlers before this date, but they consisted of the higher ranks of government employees and those few who for various reasons were given parcels of crown land.) Macquarie was followed by Sir Thomas Brisbane who reigned, briefly and ineffectually, until 1825 when Ralph Darling arrived. Darling was a rigid, arbitrary man with an overweening sense of his own importance – for example, in 1815 he wrote to the Duke of Wellington asking for command of the British forces in Belgium; the reply he received from the Iron Duke was succinctly negative. Darling managed to make himself unpopular on nearly all sides, with the Press on which he tried to impose total censorship, and with free settlers who accused him of favouritism in the disposal of crown lands, but convicts and emancipists were the greatest sufferers from his régime. He adhered to the popular view that convicts were the scum of the earth, otherwise they would never have become convicts in the first place, and were to be treated as such. In the battle between emancipists and free settlers, he was firmly on the side of the latter. For had not emancipists been convicts? How could it be said that they were entitled to the same rights as decent, respectable free settlers? Darling was finally removed in 1831, and later, in 1836, a committee was appointed in London to enquire into his behaviour as Governor. He was exonerated from the charges levelled against him, but was not again given office. However, William IV expressed his approbation of Darling's conduct by knighting him.

The man who succeeded Darling in 1831 and was Governor when the five Tolpuddle men landed in Sydney was Sir Richard Bourke. He was born in Dublin in 1777, and was a relation of the celebrated Edmund Burke. He qualified for the bar but instead became a soldier, serving under Wellington in Portugal. In 1825 he was appointed Lieutenant-Governor of the Cape of Good Hope, and in 1831 was promoted to the full Governorship of New South Wales. Bourke was a liberal man and helped steer the colony through extremely difficult years. For by the time he took office the situation was explosive, and a clash between emancipists and free settlers seemed possible. By 1834 free settlers outnumbered the convicts. In Sydney the ratio was forty-five thousand freemen to twenty-five thousand convicts, but these freemen included emancipists and New South Wales was still basically a penal colony. In the Macquarie years the emancipists had been encouraged, in the Darling era they had been repressed. Bourke tried to steer a middle course between free settlers and convicts, while fully realizing that the future of the colony, indeed of the whole country (for explorers had pushed the boundaries well beyond New South Wales), lay in everybody being free. The current state of flux was greatly concerned with the future. Was the country to remain a series of penal settlements? Were the convict ships to continue to transport the troublesome and degraded from the mother country? How could a decent class of free immigrant be encouraged when armed banditti consisting of the most desperate convicts roamed within twenty miles of Sydney? When the vicious circle of convict crime and punishment had produced the highest criminal statistics in the world?[1] When drunkenness and juvenile prostitution were rampant? (Remember how many adolescents were transported, and how many female convicts were, or soon became, pregnant.) In 1834 it was already strongly felt by many people, for many and varied reasons, that the whole question of transportation and colonization by convict labour was in urgent need of examination and review. Also in 1834 the convict system was still very much in existence, the merry-go-round of fear, misery, deprivation of rights, being flogged and working in chain gangs, subject to the whim and caprice of master and magistrate, with the spectre of Norfolk Island dangling in front, and the hope of redemption lagging behind. It was on to this merry-go-round that John and Thomas Standfield, James Brine, James Hammett and James Loveless stepped on September 4th, 1834, not knowing when or if they would be able to jump off.

The men were kept on board the *Surrey* for nearly three weeks before disembarkation. The time varied from ship to ship, according to the degree of organization on land, for, with the vagaries of sail and storm, nobody knew the exact arrival time of any ship. The convicts were examined while on board by a doctor, to ensure they had not suffered too greatly en route and were fit for work, and by an official from the Colonial Secretary's Office who noted their details, with particular attention to physical description. In the absence of photography, such information as to whether a convict had scars or moles or extra distinguishing marks

[1] Criminal offences in the United States then stood at 1 per 3,500 inhabitants; in England it was 1 in every 740; whereas in New South Wales it was 1 in 22.

was the only means of identifying him, should he later abscond. The details of the five Tolpuddle men were recorded thus:

[No.] 1576/62 Brine Jas; Aged 21; Education – R. W. [indicating that the convict could Read and Write]; Religion – Protestant; Unmarried; Native place – Dorsetshire; Trade – farm servant; Offence – unlawful oaths; Tried – Dorset Assizes, 14th March, 1833; Sentence – 7 years; Previous convictions – none; Height – 5ft. 5 in.; Complexion – ruddy; Hair – brown; Eyes – hazel/grey; Physical details – scar right eyebrow. Scar under left nostril. Scar back of left thumb. Scars on face and one back of middle finger of left hand.

1575/61 Hammett Jas; Aged 22; Education – R.W.; Religion – Protestant; Married, one child; Native place – Devonshire; Trade – farm servant; Offence – unlawful oaths; Tried – Devon Assizes, 14th March, 1834; Sentence – 7 years; Previous convictions – 4 months; Height – 5 ft. 6¾ ins.; Complexion – ruddy; Hair – brown; Eyes – grey; Physical description – Forehead narrow. Scar centre same. H.H. inside lower right arm. J.H. 1829 inside left wrist.

1572/58 Loveless James; Aged 25; Education – R.W.; Religion – Protestant; Married, two children; Native place – Co. Dorset; Trade – farm servant; Offence – unlawful oaths; Tried – Dorset Assizes, 14th March, 1834; Sentence – 7 years; Previous convictions – none; Height – 5 ft. 5¾ ins.; Complexion – dark sallow; Hair – brown; Eyes – brown; Physical description – eyebrows meeting. Small mole lower part of right side of neck. Scar on forefinger and thumb of right hand. Scar back of left hand. Scar back of forefinger of left hand. Two moles inside lower left arm.

1773/69 Stanfield Thos. Aged 45; Education – R.W.; Religion – Protestant; Married, five children, one on board; Native place – Dorsetshire; Trade – farm labourer; Offence – unlawful oaths; Tried – Dorset Assizes, 14th March, 1834; Sentence – 7 years; Previous convictions – none; Height – 5 ft 6¾ ins.; Complexion – dark sallow; Hair – black and grey; Eyes – brown; Physical description – Lost canine teeth in upper jaw. Lower front teeth irregular.

1774/60 Stanfield John. Aged 21; Education – R.W.; Religion – Protestant; Unmarried; Native place – Dorsetshire; Trade – farm servant; Offence – unlawful oaths; Tried – Dorset Assizes, 14th March, 1834; Sentence – 7 years; Previous convictions – none; Height – 5 ft. 7¼ ins.; Complexion – ruddy; Hair – dark brown; Eyes – grey; Physical description – lower front teeth irregular. Nose thin and inclining a little to the left side. Several moles on right cheek and neck; scar back of right hand near the knuckle of forefinger. Small scar back of the forefinger and thumb of left hand.

Fate, if not himself, was determined to make James Hammett the odd man out. Whereas the information on the other men was in the main correct, Hammett was not, of course, a native of Devonshire, nor tried at Devon Assizes. The 'J.H. 1829' inside the left wrist may have related to his period in the House of Correction in Dorchester, while the 'H.H. inside lower right arm' was, one assumes, a tattoo. Hammett's wife's name was Harriet and, presumably, he had her initials tattooed on his arm. The other error was in the date of James Brine's trial – it was 1834 not 1833. The main variation for the similar details recorded in Dorchester Gaol was in the heights of the men. Thomas Standfield had acquired an extra half-inch during the four months' passage from England, but the others had shrunk. James Brine had lost three-quarters of an inch, James Hammett half an inch, John Standfield one inch, while James Loveless had decreased from 5 feet 7½ inches to 5 feet 5¾ inches. Hammett's eyes had also changed colour; in Dorset they were blue, in New South Wales, grey.

To these details were added the convict's destination – government employ or the name of the master if assigned. These were then filed in Sydney, while a shorter version of the convict's arrival and assignation was sent back to London. For the five Tolpuddle men the details returned to London were:

654 Brine Jas. Arrived Surrey, 17th August 1834. Sentence 7 years. Assigned Jas. Mitchell, General Hospital.

2759 Hammett James. Arrived Surrey etcetera. Assigned E. J. Eyre. Woodlands.

3459 Loveless James. Arrived Surrey etcetera. Assigned D. McMillan J.P. St Vincent.

5302 Stanfield Thos, etcetera. Assigned Timothy Nowlan. Hunter River.

5303 Stanfield John etcetera. Assigned Richard Jones, M.C. Sydney.

On September 4th the convicts were taken off the *Surrey*, chained four abreast, and marched through the streets of Sydney. The first town to be built on the Australian continent was already a good size. It covered over two thousand acres, had many wide and spacious streets and buildings of brick and freestone, while the mansions of the wealthy overlooked the town and the magnificent harbour from the lush Surrey Hills. The five Tolpuddle men saw little of the town. They were marched with the other convicts to Hyde Park Barracks, where they waited until their masters or overseers were ready either to collect them or for them to be despatched. Of the five, young James Brine was the first to leave. What fear or panic he felt we do not know. Each, except Hammett, was later to record his experiences but the recording was mainly limited to a statement of what happened, not to what was undergone emotionally. Up to this moment they had been together in their sufferings. They had been able to talk, to have the comfort of shared misery. Now each had to face the lottery of convict life on his own. Brine was assigned to James Mitchell, a surgeon in the General Hospital in Sydney, but he did not stay long at the hospital being quickly sent to a farm run by Scott at Glindon up the Hunter River. Brine himself speaks of 'his master' as one Robert Scott whom he says was a magistrate. He definitely went to a farm run by Scott at Glindon, but he was never officially reassigned. Throughout his years in New South Wales James Mitchell remained his assignee, so either Robert Scott was a tenant of Mitchell's running the farm at Glindon for him, or if he were the owner (which, as a magistrate, seems likely), some private deal was made between him and Mitchell regarding assigned convicts.

That James Brine 'we was sent to a farm at Glindon', is the literal truth. Convicts were despatched, rather like parcels, to their destinations. They were put on their way but were by no means guarded for the whole distance which could be hundreds of miles, and there was no guarantee of safe arrival. However, most of them did arrive because there was little else for them to do. The alternatives were absconding and trying to lose yourself in the back streets of Sydney, or joining the banditti in the bush, if you could find them, stomach them and if they would have you. Newly arrived convicts were unlikely to consider these alternatives. It was the old hands who absconded or took to the bush.

James Brine, in any case, was a law-abiding young man, and off he went, by steamboat to Newcastle and part of the way up the Hunter River. He was dropped off thirty miles from Glindon, given a small bed and blanket, a suit of 'new slops' and a shilling, and told to make his own way there. Whilst he was asleep one night under a gum tree, everything was stolen from him by bush-rangers – his new slops, bedding, blanket, shoes and money. Whether he was sleeping so soundly that the bush-rangers whipped the bedding from underneath him or whether he had a fight with them, he did not clarify but he arrived at Glindon with nothing except the clothing he had been sleeping in. He was taken to Mr Scott, explained what had happened, and asked for replacements. Mr Scott did not believe a word of his story, and according to Brine, he said to him, 'You are one of the Dorsetshire machine-breakers, but you are caught at last. If you utter another word of complaint, I will put you in the lock-up; and if you ask me for another article for six months to come, and if you do not do your work like another man ... I will send you up to Mr Moody [a magistrate] where no mercy will be shown you.'

For six months Brine went without shoes, change of clothing or bedding. He wrapped iron hoops around his feet, but he had to sleep on the bare ground without covering at night. Part of the work he was ordered to do was in the pool, washing sheep. For seventeen days he worked up to his chest in water. Without a change of clothing, or bedding to keep him warm at night, he consequently caught 'a severe chill'. He then asked Mr Scott for a blanket but the reply was, 'No. I will give you nothing until you are due for it. What would your masters in England have had to cover them if you had not been sent here? I understand it was your intention to have murdered, burnt, and destroyed everything before you, and you are sent over here to be severely punished, and no mercy shall be shown you.' Mr Scott also said, 'You damned convict, don't you know that not even the hair on your head is your own?' Brine must soon have absorbed this fact, and the best that can be said for Mr Scott, if Brine's record of his character is accurate, is that he did not send him before the magistrate in the fifteen months that the young man remained as one of his assigned convicts. That, bearing in mind the offences for which convicts were sentenced, was something.

James Loveless and Thomas Standfield, who had remained in Hyde Park Barracks, were given their marching orders on September 5th. Thomas bade an emotional farewell to his son John, and left for the farm of his master, Timothy Nowlan, which was also up the Hunter River, near Maitland, then 'a rising township'. Thomas did not suffer hardship en route, but he had the misfortune to be assigned to work as a shepherd which was one of the more arduous of tasks. He was not a young man and he had six hundred sheep to guard in what he described as 'an immense forest of trees and brushwood, with here and there a clear spot of ground' on to which the sheep had to be driven. At night he slept in a watch box, 6 feet by 18 inches wide, 'where the wind blew in at one end, and out at the other, with nothing to ward off the pelting of the pitiless storm', and to obtain his rations he had to walk four miles. If fortune was unkind in the job to which he was assigned, it was favourable in that young John was also sent to a farm up the Hunter River, only a few miles from his father. John left Hyde Park Barracks on September 8th for the house of his master, Richard Jones, in Sydney. However, Mr Jones owned a farm at Balwarra, three miles from Maitland, and it was there John was assigned to work. Before leaving Hyde Park Barracks he had discovered the whereabouts of his father – a discovery which underlines the general initiative of the Tolpuddle men. Obtaining information from government departments, particularly information you are not supposed to have, has never been an easy task. It required a high degree of persistence, persuasiveness and self-control for a convict to obtain any in 1834. When John learned that he was going to Balwarra and that it was near his father, he must have been delighted. His journey, too, was uneventful and Mr Jones appears to have been a good master with a well-run farm, and there is no word in John Standfield's narrative of ill-treatment at Balwarra.

However, once he had arrived and settled down in his job, John had to obtain permission to visit his father. Earlier concessions regarding time-off had been withdrawn by 1834 and convicts were not allowed to do anything without the permission of an overseer or master, nor did they have any official free time. Again John demonstrated his powers of reasoned, persistent persuasion, and leave to visit his father was granted. He found Thomas out in the bush, tending hundreds of sheep, and in great distress. Three weeks later he obtained permission for a further visit and his father was then 'a dreadful spectacle, covered with sores from head to foot, and weak and helpless as a child'. John tried to get his father moved to an easier job, but in this he was not successful. Over the next nine months he saw Thomas as often as possible, once or twice a month, and the visits must have helped to sustain the older man. In the spring of 1835, Thomas was transferred to another farm owned by his master, Timothy Nowlan, on the Williams River, which made further visits from his son impossible. What work Thomas did at the new station is not recorded, but we may assume it was easier and that Thomas's age and ill-health were brought to the attention of Timothy Nowlan because he was later to write of Nowlan's kindness to him.

In the meantime, James Loveless had left Hyde Park Barracks on September 5th. His destination was the farm of Mr McMillan, J.P., at Strathallan in the county of St Vincent. Loveless stated that it was three hundred miles from Sydney. Although St Vincent was the county bordering on what is now the State of Victoria and a long way from the New South Wales capital, the farm was in fact less than three hundred miles away. As James was provided with a blanket and bedding, a ration of flour and raw beef, and had to walk the distance by himself, he can be forgiven for adding the extra miles. The journey took him fourteen days, sleeping under gum trees at night, but he arrived safely. He, too, appears to have found a reasonable master in that he did not record any ill-treatment.

Finally, there was the silent Hammett who never printed a word of his experiences. However, many many years later he did briefly speak of his arrival in New South Wales. He said he was taken to the barracks in Sydney and described the scene that first greeted his eyes: 'A man was brought in, a barrel rolled into the middle, the man stripped, lashed across the barrel, and given twenty-five lashes on the bare back, twenty-five on the backside and twenty-five on the calves of the legs.' After this salutary introduction to convict life he said, 'We were sold out as slaves at £1 a head.' Having been sold, he was taken to his master's agent in Sydney and given the address of his destination. He asked where it was and reported the following laconic conversation:

'Oh, not far, 400 miles.'
'Who's going with me?'
'No one.'
'How am I to find the right road?'
'You'll find the road right enough . . . Go to Brickfield Hill, and enquire for Liverpool. You're sure to find your way.'

In fact Hammett's destination was less than four hundred miles away, being Woodland on the Molomglo Plains, near Queanbeyan, close to the present site of the federal capital, Canberra. As he too walked the whole way by himself, sleeping at night under the trees, stripping off their bark for shelter, he, like James Loveless, can be forgiven for exaggerating the distance. His feet, as he said, were tender before he started, having been cramped on the convict ship and given only two hours' exercise a day for nearly four months, so it probably seemed like four thousand miles. Hammett further said that he was given rations for twenty-two days but they ran out long before his arrival. Even if starving, he did, as the agent had airily indicated, somehow find the right road and somehow arrived at Woodlands. Whether he was well or ill treated and to what task he was assigned, he did not record. However, he went to work for Edward John Eyre, the most illustrious master among the five men, and a considerable amount is known about him. He was born in 1815, and was only nineteen, three years younger than Hammett, when the Tolpuddle man was assigned to his farm. Fate had been kinder to Eyre than to Hammett. He was born into an old-established English family and went to Australia when he was seventeen, partly for health reasons (he was a delicate child) and partly from character, for he had an adventurous nature. He acquired the land and farm at Woodlands, though he cannot have spent much time there. He was soon off exploring the interior of New South Wales, and later, in 1840, mounted an expedition to open communications between South and Western Australia. Eyre was concerned about the fate of the aborigines, and in 1841 he was appointed their protector in the Moorundie region of South Australia. So it is possible that he also cared about the welfare of the English convicts, though this does not necessarily follow, and that Hammett found a reasonable billet.

Throughout most of 1835, the five men remained at their various posts and tasks in New South Wales, without rights, thousands of miles from home, separated from their families. The most the future seemed to offer was that if they kept out of trouble they might in four years' time be granted ticket-of-leave. Their first fifteen months in the penal colony, viewed in the wider context of what could and did happen to other prisoners, upheld the contention of the young convict that if you kept a still tongue in your head and did your master's duty you would be all right. It was not a contention which was likely to have cheered the Tolpuddle men.

12: 'The Great Gaol to the Empire'

In the meantime George Loveless had arrived in Van Diemen's Land. The convict ship *William Metcalfe* sailed into Storm Bay and dropped anchor off Hobart Town on September 4th, 1834, the same day his five companions set foot on Australian soil. The sail up the Derwent River to Hobart was, Loveless admitted, beautiful, past ranges of hills, verdant with box and lightwood, cherry and wattle, pine, cedar and peppermint. But his only feeling was that he had come to the wrong end of the world.

Van Diemen's Land was first discovered by the Dutch explorer Tasman in 1642. Its native inhabitants were left undisturbed until 1803 when it was annexed for Britain, and soon became a penal sub-colony to New South Wales. Conditions for the convicts were much the same as on the mainland. There were penal settlements within the island, at Macquarie Harbour (abandoned in 1832) and at Port Arthur (flourishing in 1834). Free emigration to Van Diemen's Land was established in 1817, the year before its establishment in New South Wales and by 1834 some of the same sort of problems between emancipists and free settlers were fermenting. However, there were differences in Van Diemen's Land which stemmed from the personality of the Governor.[1]

Colonel George Arthur was appointed Lieutenant-Governor in 1824. He was born in Plymouth in 1784, entered the army in 1804 and served during the Napoleonic Wars in Italy, Egypt and on Walcheren. In 1814 he was appointed Governor of British Honduras and displayed a

---

[1] Van Diemen's Land had, in fact, a Lieutenant-Governor, while New South Wales had a full Governor, but their roles were separate and autonomous. Arthur was always referred to as Governor Arthur.

ruthless hand in the suppression of the slaves' revolt in 1822. Arthur was an extremely capable, efficient man, possessed of great energy with equal measures of vanity and self-esteem. He wore fancy costumes of a semi-military design, and whenever possible rode on horseback so that his striking appearance could be duly noted while he surveyed the minions beneath him. He was deeply religious, and could quote the Bible to suit his text. He believed with an absolute certainty that he was right, and would brook no argument. He was also described as 'the most enduring quill-driver of his own or any other age' – a verdict upheld by the quantity and length of his despatches to the Colonial Office in England. During his years in office he, and his various relations and sycophants – for his temperament did not welcome the spirited – amassed large fortunes for services rendered in the assignment of convicts, from the sale of crown lands and from the hastening of official or legal processes. Arthur was not a full-blown monster, but he was a dictator who ran, and enjoyed running, his fiefdom to his own advantage and with rigid discipline.

The discipline was more rigid in Van Diemen's Land than in New South Wales. In 1834 there were fifteen thousand summary convictions and fifty thousand lashes were inflicted on a convict population of just over fifteen thousand. The main reason for the harshness of discipline and punishment was Arthur's wholehearted belief in transportation. He regarded Van Diemen's Land as a vast prison to the Empire where the convicts, if they behaved themselves, had it in their power to redeem the character they had lost. It was within his power, more it was his duty, to see that they suffered in the cause of redemption, for did not the Bible speak of an eye for an eye, a tooth for a tooth, the cleansing of guilt through suffering? However, in the process of ensuring that no convict escaped his due redemptive punishment, in tightening the security in the Empire's gaol, Arthur enacted stringent laws that also affected the free settlers and deprived them of many rights. The free settlers did not warm to being treated as, at worst, second-degree felons, at best as naughty schoolboys who had to report their every action to their masters. Nor did Arthur's tight coterie at Government House, and his system of paternal bribery, enchant the more liberal or spirited of inhabitants. There was, consequently, less friction between emancipists and free settlers on Van Diemen's Land than in New South Wales, and a mounting common front against Arthur's dictatorship.

It was into this beautiful, verdant prison that George Loveless stepped on September 12th, 1834. Prior to landing the usual medical examinations and details of prisoners were held and taken on board ship. Loveless's were recorded as follows:

Trade – Ploughman; Height – 5 ft. 4¼ in.; Age – 37; Complexion – brown; Head – Small; Hair – Brown; Whiskers – Dark Red; Visage – small; Forehead – low; Eyes – Dark hazel; Nose – Small; Mouth – Med. Wide; Chin – Small Dimpled; Remarks – Small scar on upper lip, Scar on L. arm; Native Place – Nr. Dorset.

Apart from the normal examination Loveless was subjected to several interrogations of a more searching and less customary nature. Perhaps the home government had sent extra information that he was a trade unionist and trouble maker, or the authorities in Hobart may have read the London newspapers of March and April, which would have arrived by September, and were taking their own precautions. Loveless himself recorded three interrogations – one on board ship, two ashore – of which two were conducted by the assistant police magistrate, Thomas Mason, and one by the Governor himself. Governor Arthur was in the habit of addressing the fresh boat-loads of convicts as they landed on his territory,[2] so he may have had a special word with this trade unionist ring-leader. Certainly a statement was taken from Loveless on September 15th by Thomas Mason. Governor Arthur forwarded a copy to London in December, 1834, with the comment that it was from 'a convict named George Loveless, relative to the proceedings of one of the Trades Unions in London. If this man's statement is to be credited, it is evident that he and his companions have ignorantly become the victims of more artful men.'

Loveless's statement, as officially recorded, was straightforward – he explained about contacting his relative, Robert, in London, the visits of the delegates from the Grand National Consolidated Trades Union, the reading of the rules of the Society, the decision to form what seemed a legal union. He said the initiations were held, and that subsequently Legg made a confession in which 'He told of nine who were in the cottage, three of them . . . were the magistrate's own neighbours and they were not tried.' His statement had a simplicity and dignity, and there was no attempt to blame or blacken or incriminate others. However, Loveless obviously felt he had been deceived about the legality of the unions. This viewpoint was accepted by Governor Arthur.

Loveless's own reports of the conversations with Mason and Governor Arthur are detailed, suspiciously so. Few people, if any, have total recall, and without pencil, paper and shorthand one cannot later give a verbatim report of a conversation. This is not to impugn Loveless's veracity. He was a truthful man, but writing after an event there is a tendency to mingle what one would have liked to have said with what was actually said. The following are extracts

[2] He noted that the 'Swing' labourers transported to Van Diemen's Land in 1831, 'seemed to feel more deeply than any other convicts I ever saw the punishment to which they were subjected'.

from Loveless's reported dialogue, and assuredly some of the words were spoken, on board the convict ship, on the Hobart quayside and in the Hobart police-office in September 1834. Those that were not, expressed what Loveless wanted to say.

MASON: What is all this about these Unions? You think of doing great things, I suppose. Now tell me what you meant.

LOVELESS: We meant nothing more, Sir, than uniting together to keep up the price of labour, and to support each other in time of need.

MASON: Now, I know this is false. There is some secret sign of conspiracy at the bottom, is there not?

LOVELESS: No, Sir, quite the reverse of that, for every man that is a member of the Union is under an obligation not to violate the laws.

MASON: Yes, surely, I know you mean they are bound not to break any of their laws.

LOVELESS: I mean they are under an obligation not to violate the laws of their country.

Mason then asked questions about a secret sign whereby all unionists knew when and where to meet. Loveless replied that he knew nothing of any such sign.

MASON: Now, you pretend from a scrupulous conscience that you cannot reveal the secret to me. Let me tell you that you ought to tell all that you know about them. And if you have taken an oath not to reveal, *you are sinning against God and man, until you break that oath*, and if you still refuse to tell me you shall be severely punished.

The conversation ended with Mason threatening to report Loveless to the Governor. It was, according to Loveless, Mason who pointed him out to Arthur on the quayside, as a trade unionist who was 'very backward to say anything about the union'. Arthur then came over to speak to Loveless.

ARTHUR: What a fool you must have been for having anything to do with such things. What object had you in view for doing so?

LOVELESS: The motives by which we were influenced were to prevent our wives and families from being utterly degraded and starved.

ARTHUR: Poh, poh! No such thing. What? Cannot labouring men live by their labour.

LOVELESS: Not always now, Sir.

ARTHUR: I mean good labouring men. Surely they can live comfortable?

Loveless explained that they could not.

ARTHUR: But you know that you did very wrong, do you not?

LOVELESS: I had no idea whatever I was violating any law.

ARTHUR: But you must know that you broke the laws, or how came you here?

LOVELESS: By some means or other I was sent here. But I cannot see how a man can break a law before he knows that such is in existence.

The final interview with Mason, according to Loveless on September 13th, though the official record places it two days later, was in the presence of a clerk and this was when his statement was taken. At the interview Loveless recorded Mason as saying 'Well, I have to tell you that you was ordered for severer punishment. *You were to work in irons on the roads.* But in consequence of the conversation you had with the Governor yesterday, his mind is disposed in your favour. He won't allow you to go where you were

ILLUSTRATIONS

THE RETURNED 'CONVICTS'

JAMES BRINE
Aged 25

THOMAS STANFIELD
Aged 51

JOHN STANFIELD
aged 25

GEORGE LOVELESS
Aged 41

JAMES LOVELESS
Aged 29

A contemporary drawing entitled *The Returned 'Convicts'* which appeared in *Cleave's Penny Gazette*, May 12, 1838

Lord John Russell painted by F. Grant in 1854

Lord Melbourne painted by Landseer in 1838.

An etching of the York hulk
in Portsmouth harbour
by E. W. Cooke, 1828

Contemporary instruments of punishment on board the *Success.* This was never in fact a convict ship, although it was exhibited as such in England and the United States

The mass demonstration at Copenhagen Fields, April 21, 1834

Colonel George Arthur, Lt.-Governor of Van Diemen's Land

Wall decorations of the old Dorchester exhibition at Wimborne
The inscription reads: 'Evangelists and their followers seem to
have always been the object of persecution by their fellow men.
These peaceful disciples of John Wesley associated themselves

'ith a movement for bettering their conditions of labour,
nd in consequence were sentenced to transportation.
eorge Loveless is seen under the Martyrs' Tree exhorting
is companions to keep the peace.'

"TOLPUDDLE MARTYRS"

ERECTED IN HONOUR
- OF THE -
FAITHFUL and BRAVE MEN
OF THIS VILLAGE,
WHO IN 1834 SO NOBLY
SUFFERED TRANSPORTATION
IN THE CAUSE OF
LIBERTY, JUSTICE
AND RIGHTEOUSNESS,
AND AS A STIMULUS
TO OUR OWN
AND FUTURE GENERATIONS.

GEORGE LOVELESS.
JAMES LOVELESS.
JAMES HAMMETT.
THOMAS STANDFIELD.
JOHN STANDFIELD.
JAMES BRINE.

"WE HAVE INJURED NO MAN'S
REPUTATION CHARACTER PERSON
OR PROPERTY. WE WERE UNITING
TOGETHER TO PRESERVE OUR-
SELVES, OUR WIVES AND OUR
CHILDREN FROM UTTER DEGRADA-
TION AND STARVATION."
(GEORGE LOVELESS DEFENCE.)

UNVEILED BY
ARTHUR HENDERSON M.P.
27. MAY 1912.

Thomas Standfield's cottage, Tolpuddle

New House Farm, Greensted, Essex, into which the Lovelesses and James Brine moved on their return from Australia

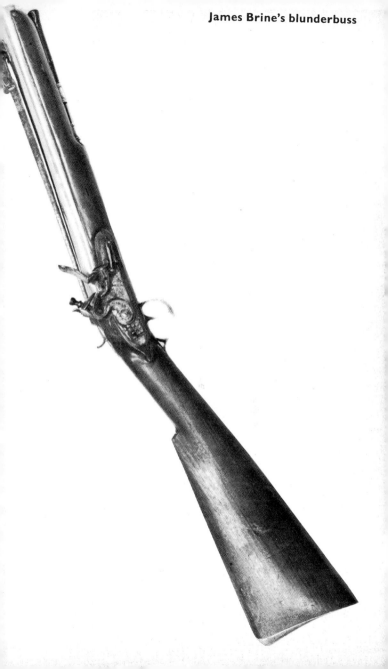

OUR PARENTS GRAVES

GEORGE LOVELESS
DIED
May 6, 1874.
Aged 77 Years

ELIZABETH
Beloved Wife of
GEORGE LOVELESS.
DIED
Mar. 9, 1868.
Aged 71 Years

The grave of George and Betsy Loveless
in Siloam cemetery, London, Ontario

assigned to. He intends to take you to work on his farm.'
The Home Government could, and did, send orders for
certain convicts to be worked on road parties, and even in
some instances to go straight to penal settlements (this was
usually in the case of vicious and hardened criminals). The
official returns to London for the *William Metcalfe* show
that it had 240 male convicts on board of whom 121 were
assigned, 28 were immediately placed in chain gangs, 6
were ill and sent to the Colonial Hospital while 27 were
boys unfit for assignment and the remainder were employed
'in the various Departments of the government'. The
Appropriation List, kept in Van Diemen's Land, records
that George Loveless aged thirty [*sic*] was sent to the
Domain Farm, which was a government establishment for
the production of 'Vice-Regal and institutional vegetables
and meat'. As the orders that Loveless should be worked
in irons are not extant and the Appropriation list states
only that he went to the Domain Farm, there is no
documentary evidence to prove the truth of his own account
of what Thomas Mason told him. But George Loveless
was an honest man and the horrors of transportation were
bureaucratically documented on thousands of pieces of
paper, without his needing to invent an extra gruesome
detail. Two years later in 1836, when Governor Arthur
was under heavy fire, the *Tasmanian* partially defended his
character and conduct by stating that in the case of the
Dorchester Unionists, when orders were sent from England
for Loveless 'to be worked in irons on the roads', Governor
Arthur refused to effect them. If the Home Government
did send such orders they were not only as cruel and severe
as the initial sentences, they were callous and vindictive
too. The orders would have come from Lord Melbourne,
as the Home Secretary. Either they demonstrate the less
pleasant, compassionless side of Melbourne's not
unpleasant character, or they show how deep ran the fear

of trade unionism in rural areas. Yet again the Tolpuddle men were to be savagely treated *pour encourager les autres*.

George Loveless recorded that for just over a week he was worked on a chained road gang, sleeping at night on the stone floor of a barracks without bed or blanket. Laconically, he reported, 'I now began to feel the effects of transportation.' On September 22nd he said he was removed to the government farm where conditions were better – the men were not chained, the overseers were less bullying, the work was less back- and spirit-breaking. However, the conditions were nevertheless grim. Loveless slept in a hut, with five beds for eight men, and it was not until 'some of the older hands unfortunately got into trouble, that I was entitled to a bed'. Then he could 'lie in a bed and view the stars in fine weather, in foul weather feel the wind and rain'. He started to suffer from rheumatic pains 'first brought on by cold irons round the legs, and which in all probability will be my companions until I reach the tomb'. He was appointed shepherd and stock-keeper. His daily round started at sunrise when he took the sheep to grass and he then returned to the farm to milk the cows. The rest of the day was spent in watching the sheep to see the dogs did not worry them, preventing the cattle from straying into the bush, more milking sessions, looking after the ewes in lambing time, and attending the calves at various times. Rations were not high, though Loveless said they received four pounds of wheat and four pounds of maize, with some beef or mutton of inferior quality as their weekly allowance, which was higher than average. But the diet was not calculated to keep up a man's strength, and hunger was a constant companion. Loveless also said that if you complained about the food you 'got married to the three sisters', i.e. tied to the flogging triangle, so you did not complain.

This hard, wretched round continued for over a year. In November 1835 Loveless was put on a charge of 'neglect of duty' and brought before the magistrate. His marriage to the three sisters for fifty lashes seemed imminent, but Loveless managed to bring off the coup that was so rarely accomplished. He spoke in his own defence and obtained legal redress – the charge was dismissed. The overseer's accusation was that nine of the wild cattle, which were in Loveless's care as much as the domesticated animals, had been taken to the public pound and Loveless had not missed them until the following morning. Loveless's defence was generally that he had far too much to do, specifically that he had been weaning the lambs, the sheep were consequently restless, so he decided to stay with them. As he could not be in two places at once, that was how and why nine wild cattle had strayed and been taken to the pound. The magistrate then asked the overseer how long Loveless had been doing the job, and if there had been any previous cause for complaint. The overseer said there had not. The magistrate replied, 'Do you not think that the man has more duty than he can perform here? I really think it is a great pity you should have brought the man here. I shall return you to your duty, go to your duty, my man.' With only a reprimand entered on his sheet, without fifty lashes across his back, Loveless went. He was fortunate in his magistrate. People were flogged for much less. Again the force of his character is shown. To escape the charge he must have presented his evidence in a clear, cogent and reasoned manner which impressed the magistrate.

Loveless went back to work, tending the lambs, milking the cows, combing the bush for strays, and it is doubtful that he received help in his labours. Throughout those weary months in Van Diemen's Land he observed. His keen eye had been recording its impressions of the island from the moment the *William Metcalfe* sailed up the Derwent River, and later he was to transfer his impressions to print. The appearance of Hobart from the sea was 'not inviting', as the best of it was lost to view in the flat land between the harbour and Mount Wellington. However, the best was impressive, the streets were wide, many were 'macadamized', while the shops and houses were not inferior to those of London. (Country-bred Loveless may not have seen London, indeed any town, before he left Dorset but he had seen London before he went into print.) Mount Wellington, covered in snow for eight months of the year, dominated the town. At its summit was a lagoon which supplied Hobart and the surrounding area with fresh water, while at its foot was the factory for female convicts. The rest of the country, or that part of it which Loveless saw, was wild and romantic, range upon range of wooded hills, and soaring mountains covered with lofty trees, with here and there a few acres of land cultivated by the settlers. In the lowlands the soil was fertile, peaches grew in the orchards 'like apples at home' and there were 'beds of grapes', thick hedges of geranium and sweetbriar. Wild animals abounded, forester and brush kangaroos, wild cats and bandicoots, ringtail, black and grey opossums. It was a far cry from the neat fields, the banked hedgerows, the small undulations of Tolpuddle. or even the less tame heaths and strange primeval lump-hills of Dorset. But Loveless also recorded a feeling of 'gloom and dreariness' that enveloped the whole country. This was partly nostalgia, but it also stemmed from Loveless's character. He was not a romantic. He preferred the smallness and tidiness of the English countryside, the panorama the eye can easily encompass, to the wildness of a landscape that stretched endlessly beyond the vision and hinted at dark and dangerous forces.

During the many months he spent on the 'gloomy' island, Loveless also listened and thought. He listened to the first-hand experiences and horror stories of his fellow-convicts, some of the many that lay behind the statistics of fifteen thousand summary convictions, fifty thousand lashes inflicted. Later he recounted what had happened to two men he met, Greenwood and Pocock. Greenwood absconded from a bad master and was caught. In the struggle to recapture him, Greenwood slightly wounded a constable. He was sentenced to a hundred lashes for absconding and then to death for having attacked the constable, and he died 'while the maggots were crawling in the wounds inflicted by the lash'. According to Loveless, Greenwood was as 'fine, aspiring, strong a young man as any one would wish to set eyes upon'. Pocock absconded not once, but four times – 'a most determined runaway' the records would have noted him – and four times he was flogged. Finally he pleaded with the magistrate not to be sent back to his master but to be reassigned, but this request was refused and so he absconded a fifth time. On being captured he was sentenced to fifty more lashes and to work on a road gang. When he came to be tied to the flogging triangle the last time his back was in such a dreadful state that the doctor ordered him to be flogged over the breech. On his release Pocock was yet again returned to the bad master in whose service he was when Loveless met him. Governor Arthur would doubtless have said that the system worked – for had not a determined runaway learned his lesson *and* who were his masters? Pocock himself said 'I used to think I should not mind being hung for him [the master]. But I should not like to go to hell for him, and this prevented me shooting him.'

George Loveless also met a survivor of the *George III* which struck a rock and sank off Van Diemen's Land in 1835. He recounted this story to illustrate the fate of convicts trapped in shipwrecks. The young survivor told Loveless that when the vessel began to sink the hatches were battened down. As the water started to fill the holds, a fearful panic and terror gripped the convicts. Eventually, they rushed the hatches and managed to break them open, but many were shot or hacked to death as they scrambled up on to the decks and only a few were saved. Shipwrecks were frequent, and the loss of life was high, whether from the reasons given by the young survivor or not. Within a few months of 1835 the *Neva* and *Enchantress* also sank off the island. The *Neva* was carrying 150 female convicts with 33 children, and nine free women with 22 children, of whom only 15 were saved. (Governor Arthur complained heartily about the loss of despatches in the three ships.)

Loveless did not record the horror stories for their own sake (though doubtless they helped the sales of his pamphlet *The Victims of Whiggery*). He related them as the products of an evil system, and went on to question the validity of transportation. Did it contain any real hope of reformation, of turning convicts into useful members of society? In his opinion, and from his own experience, the opposite effect was the more likely to be true. If people were bad when they arrived, they were tenfold more the children of hell after a few years as convicts. Their hearts were hardened, their feelings stultified and they became heedless of the consequences of what they did, plunging into an uncaring abyss from which extrication became impossible. His conclusion was that 'Nothing can be more absurd than to suppose that you can keep down the conquered for any length of time, by pouring out upon them judgement without mercy.' Mercy combined with justice was already being effected for Loveless in England. Before the end of 1835 he received the first intimation of its workings, but the progress towards final justice was inevitably slow.

13: 'The Question of the Dorchester Labourers Is Not Finally Disposed Of'

After April 1834, little happened during the rest of that year to further advance the cause of the Dorchester Unionists. There were no more mass demonstrations or meetings, or petitions submitted to Parliament, although the *True Sun* continued to stir the pot from time to time. At the end of July, for example, it noted that Mr Baron Williams was again trying men for administering illegal oaths, this time at Oxford, a task 'which seems regularly assigned to him by his brother Judges'. But the prisoners at Oxford were, rightly in most people's opinion, discharged and as a corollary the *True Sun* asked why the Dorchester Unionists were not brought home. The Oxford case emphasizes the fact that for Lord Melbourne the Tolpuddle men had no particular significance. In May 1834 he had again written to his law officers with reference to oaths and trade unions and by May he had actually obtained a copy of an oath. It was similar to that printed by the *Dorset County Chronicle* earlier in the year and read as follows: 'In the awful presence of Almighty God I promise and solemnly declare to maintain the [whatever] Trades upon any just and lawful occasion; and also *not to betray* this our most worthy order; and I further promise not to write or cause to be written upon wood, stone, sand or paper, anything purporting to betray this our most worthy order.' Melbourne's query to the law officers was whether this oath came within the meaning of 37 Geo. III, c. 123. By May he should have learned that while legally such oaths could be brought within the meaning of the Act, morally the country at large considered they should not be. After the dismissal of the Oxford case, coupled with the Exeter dismissals, the 1797 Mutiny Act was finally abandoned as a weapon against the unions. On their side the unions ceased to administer oaths – in some trades slowly, in others immediately after the Tolpuddle trial – so that they could not again be accused of barbarism or be trapped by this particular snare.

The general tenor of political life was not in the Tolpuddle favour. In June 1834 Lord Grey resigned, without any sorrow on his part, over the perennial Irish question – O'Connell had been campaigning for the repeal of the Act of Union, and the King would not hear of it. The post of Prime Minister was offered to Melbourne who typically said, 'I think it's a damned bore. I am in many minds as to what to do', but eventually he accepted it. He tottered on until November 1834, when he too resigned, leaving the King 'in a great state of excitement, occasioned by what, is not known, unless the visitation of God'. In November the Houses of Parliament burned down which put Melbourne into a melancholic mood. The fire was symbolic of the end of an era, and to the new age he neither wished to nor could belong. By December, as the *Morning Chronicle* acidly recorded, 'the Peel Cabinet is at last matured, after a month's painful travail. It consists of the last remains of Toryism. A more abortive, ridiculous or insulting Ministry was never presented to a free nation.' Sir Robert Peel's 'insulting Ministry' did not last long either. He too fell over Ireland, this time the question of church revenues. In April 1835 there was a general election and the Whigs, with the unenthusiastic Melbourne as Prime Minister, were returned to power. The political yo-yoing, and the loss of the building itself, had not created a climate conducive to petitions for remission of sentence. With the return of some stability (though nobody expected Melbourne's administration to last as long as it did), the pressure on behalf of the Tolpuddle men was resumed.

With the opening of the new Parliament, Thomas

Wakley presented sixteen petitions from Ipswich, Rochester, Norwich, Stoke-on-Trent, Ashton-under-Lyne, Warrington and eight from the Dorchester area. The different parts of the country from which the petitions came – Norfolk, Suffolk, Kent, Staffordshire, and Lancashire – emphasize the nation-wide spread of the agitation. With reference to the petitions from the Dorchester area, it has been said that there was no agitation for the men's release in their own locality; that the furore was induced by urban Radicalism and trade unionism; that within Dorset the majority of people either disapproved or did not care. Certainly the savage sentences produced the desired effect on agricultural workers in that no more Dorset unions were formed. Obviously it required a very bold spirit to swim against the tide of magistrates and landowners. But sufficient numbers of people were found to support eight petitions, and shortly after the trial Frampton had written to Lord Melbourne regretting to inform him that the windows of Tolpuddle vicarage had been broken during the night in protest against the sentences, which is again evidence of some emotion in the neighbourhood.

In all, the sixteen petitions presented by Thomas Wakley contained 13,448 signatures praying for remission of sentence. Wakley is a newcomer to the scene. In fact he only became an M.P. in the April 1835 elections but he was a long-time reformer, mainly in the medical field. He was born in Membury, Devonshire, in 1795, coming to London in 1815 to study medicine, a profession which was then filled with bribery, corruption and nepotism. Wakley was a simple, direct man who saw life in terms of good and evil, and he decided to declare war on the medical evils. As one weapon he founded the *Lancet*, with the primary aim of disseminating medical information, but the secondary intention was to attack the intrigues surrounding the elections to lucrative jobs. Single-handed at first, he fought the Royal College of Surgeons as then constructed and eventually he won. But the fight involved him in politics because he had to get petitions presented to, and questions raised in, Parliament and he thus became friendly with William Cobbett and other Radicals. His decision to try and enter Parliament came from a desire to further the cause of medical reform and better fight the Royal College of Surgeons. At the third attempt at election as a Radical, in March 1835, he succeeded. The reasons he became the final, main champion of the Tolpuddle men were varied. Firstly he believed in their cause. Secondly he had a reputation for being a fearless man who would fight to the end – witness his battle with the august body of surgeons. Then he was a new M.P. uncommitted to any clique, and he was a good orator. Finally he was himself a West country man. In the House of Commons on May 27th, 1835, Wakley said that the working classes of the country now felt that if the Dorchester Unionists were not pardoned and brought home they, the working classes, could expect no protection under the law, as they had no vote and were not therefore represented in Parliament where the laws were made. He also officially raised the matter of the wives and dependants having been refused parish relief (it had of course been raised at earlier meetings and in the Radical newspapers). Most important, he gave notice that he would bring a motion before Parliament, for a full debate, on June 25th. Apart from parliamentary procedure, the month's delay was to give the government time to consider, in the light of the continued agitation and the strong feeling throughout the country, what their action should be. The government was considering, deeply, or at least the new Home Secretary was. With this appointment a member of the government was at last on the Tolpuddle side, for the new Home Secretary was Lord John Russell.

Russell came from the old Whig aristocracy, being the third son of the sixth Duke of Bedford. He was born in London in 1792 but spent his childhood at Woburn Abbey.

He was educated at home, at Westminster School, and at Edinburgh University which was selected because Tory Oxford was out of the question for a good Whig, and his father considered Whig Cambridge to be decadent and useless. The aura of the city of Knox could well have helped develop the young Russell's serious, earnest, uncompromising nature. He entered Parliament in 1813, being elected when under age, and his reforming activities started in 1819 after 'The Peterloo Massacre' when he lobbied for the transfer of seats to the unrepresented city of Manchester. Throughout the 1820s he supported most of the reforming Bills. But his finest hour up to 1834 was the moment in 1831 when he rose in the packed House of Commons and, in a speech lasting two hours, introduced the first reading of the Reform Bill. The passing of the Bill owed much to the courage, persistence and determination of Russell.

However, in this connection, Russell remained an old-fashioned Whig. For a long time, he believed the 1832 Reform Bill was the ultimate in Parliamentary reform, and in consequence earned the nickname of 'Finality Jack'. In other respects he continued to be radically minded. If Melbourne belonged to the eighteenth century, the age of the dilettante, the amateur who could afford to be detached and amused, Russell was of a newer, nineteenth-century breed of politician, earnest and involved. Physically Russell was a complete contrast to the tall, handsome, relaxed Melbourne. He was small, almost dwarf-like, with a head slightly too large for his body – Carlyle described him as 'The ninth part of a tailor'. He was precise of speech but fidgety of manner – 'He wriggles around, plays with his hat, and seems unable to dispose of his hands or feet.' The physical contrast between the two men was captured in a contemporary cartoon in which Russell was shown sitting in Melbourne's lap, little Red Riding Hood and Grandma, to the wolf of Daniel O'Connell.

Russell himself was of the opinion that the Dorchester

Unionists had been severely treated and by June 25th, the day set for Wakley's motion, he had arrived at a major decision. Before Wakley could present his motion Russell rose in the packed House, and asked him to postpone it. The Dorchester case, he said, was one to which he had given a great deal of attention. Having given it careful attention, he had recommended that all six men be granted pardons on condition that they remained in the colonies. Four of them would be allowed to return to England after a period of two years from their arrival in the colony, but 'two of those persons named Loveless' could not be allowed to return to England as they had been the ring-leaders, although they would obtain full benefit from the conditional pardons. In view of these facts did the Honourable Member for Finsbury (Mr Wakley) intend to pass the motion?

While the Honourable Member for Finsbury was deciding whether to press or withdraw, further petitions for remission of sentence were presented, including one from Manchester and Salford signed by twenty-one thousand people, and a debate ensued on the major announcements Russell had just made. Most members welcomed them wholeheartedly and the division of opinion was mainly between those who viewed them as a necessary act of mercy and those who considered them as the first step on the road to justice. For the former, the Attorney-General said without doubt the men had broken the law, and therefore the sentences had been legal. Supporting him William Ponsonby said that as a foreman of the grand jury who had found the True Bill he could assure the House that there had been no difference of opinion among the grand jury as to the legality of the case. Another M.P. said he would be happy if all six men had received the same pardon, and this was the argument on which Wakley rose to say he regretted he could not postpone his motion. If all the men had been similarly pardoned he might have considered postponement, but he could not accept the singling out of the Lovelesses. Wakley spoke for nearly an hour. His facts were well marshalled, he blended reasoned argument with emotion and passionate pleading and the House listened without interruption (not a common occurrence). As this speech of Wakley's was the major one delivered on behalf of the Dorchester Unionists and did much to effect their eventual release, we will examine it in some detail.

Wakley started by attacking Ponsonby for 'interposing between the sufferers and the seat of mercy' with his comments about the findings of the True Bill. He begged that the House would not be influenced by the Honourable Member from Dorset's remarks before they had heard other facts. He moved on to the activities of the Grand National Consolidated Trades Union, established in London in 1833, with which the government had not interfered, and by not interfering had sanctioned its existence. Four months after the establishment of this major union in London, the Tolpuddle Society was started with the object of trying to increase wages which had been reduced to the pitiable sum of six shillings a week. As the unions in London had been unmolested, how could the Tolpuddle men have imagined that they were committing an offence in starting their Society? It was true that a warning about the penalties of administering secret oaths had been found in the pocket of one of the men. But when had the warning been posted? The day before the men were arrested, and (according to Wakley) they had intended to break up the union as a result of reading the warning but they were not given the opportunity. When they were arrested they were not brought into open court to be charged but depositions were taken from them, and their accusers, in gaol. Wakley agreed that societies bound together by secret oaths were an evil, but he also stressed that men must know of the laws before they were prosecuted. The laws against the unions, as they stood, were to

181

say the least unclear and undefined. He then went into the details of the trial, quoting in full Mr Baron Williams' address to the grand jury, *before the trial had started*. And he could not, he implied, think of anything more calculated to influence judgment than such an address as Williams'. He agreed that there might have been a case for prosecuting the men under 39 Geo. III, c. 79 (the 1799 Act against the administration of illegal oaths); but the penalties contained therein were only three months' imprisonment. 37 Geo. III, c. 123 (the Mutiny Act) had to be used because of the severer penalty of transportation. He then dealt with the repeal of the Combination Laws which had made unions legal, and quoted various earlier cases 'when the unions did not create such agitation and excited no such morbid feeling', where the verdicts had been that secret oaths only came within the meaning of the 1797 Mutiny Act when the intention of the society was obviously and definitely illegal or seditious. The intention of the Tolpuddle Friendly Society of Agricultural Labourers was neither, as the reading of the rules at the trial had shown.

Wakley then turned to the characters of the six men, and his tone became more emotional. It was generally agreed that 'six more honest, peaceable and industrious men were not to be found in the county of Dorset'. He read a letter from Mrs Northover, in whose employ the Lovelesses and Standfields had been, testifying to the excellence of their characters. Two of the men were Methodist preachers, though on the score of Methodism Wakley hinted darkly there was 'something behind the scenes which would not, but ought, to come out'. Further to show the stamp of mind and estimable character of George Loveless he read extracts from the letters to his wife written from the hulks, and from which we have earlier quoted. Betsy Loveless had given her permission for the letters to be read and Wakley said, 'Never shall I forget with what trembling hands she gave me those documents, her countenance denoting almost insupportable agony, scarcely mitigated by an unceasing flow of tears, and her little children witnessing and partaking of the sorrows of the scene.' This excellent man Loveless, and his brother, were the two selected by the government to be left in New South Wales which was demonstrably unfair. Wakley made a further emotional plea on behalf of Diana Standfield who 'had taken from her two brothers, her husband and her elder son all at one fell swoop'. At one point he turned directly to Lord John Russell and said, 'This, my Lord, is your boasted England. This is your country of equal laws and justice. I do appeal to your Lordship . . .' whereupon he was called to order for being personal and duly apologized.

In his lengthy peroration Wakley begged that all the men be allowed to return home. He personally would stand security for the good behaviour and financial stability of the Lovelesses. He had no wish to press the House to a division, but the working classes of England felt most deeply on the subject and were without representation in the House. There might be no precedent for bringing the six men home, but there was no precedent for the case either. Let precedent not deter the House. The six men had committed no moral offence. The law, from which they were unwitting sufferers, had been fully vindicated. Gratify the thousands of Englishmen who had petitioned in the cause of the Dorchester Unionists. Let justice and mercy now prevail.

A debate followed Wakley's speech in which other members begged for equal treatment for all six men and/or full remission of sentence, while Mr Harvey, the Radical member for Southwark, made a lengthy speech in which he attacked the legality of the sentence and was rebuked for his passion by the Solicitor-General. For the government, Lord Howick congratulated Wakley on a speech 'no less distinguished by its moderation than its respect for the feelings of the House' but he defended the initial sentences on the grounds that revolutionaries might possibly have noble aims but for the good of the society they had to be put down, and oaths of secrecy could and would lead to the tyranny of the unions (and presumably revolution). Regarding other societies who took similar illegal oaths the government, Howick said, would not shrink from prosecuting if it could obtain evidence. As for the six men, they were already exempt from penal labour in the colony and their wives were free to join them. If the House overruled the government on the question of the conditional pardons already granted, and demanded full pardons, it would establish 'a precedent fraught with the highest danger'. Daniel O'Connell then rose. He too congratulated Wakley on his speech which had produced an effect such as he had never seen exceeded in his life. He also offered Wakley his advice, which was not to press for a division. It would not succeed because the House of Commons was not the proper place to appeal against the decision of the courts of law. Wakley would serve the cause he had advocated so excellently by now withdrawing, leaving matters to the government, and by not forcing the House to vote on an issue of law. Several other members supported O'Connell in this contention, notably Sir Robert Peel who said he would vote not on the individual issue but on the question of leaving government in the hands of government. While Serjeant Wilde, who had prepared the actual indictment for the government, said there were now two distinct issues: the question of legality and the claims of mercy. The former must be established as valid, whatever the claims of mercy. However, another M.P. proposed that those who were ignorant of the 1797 Mutiny Act at the time of the Dorchester trial should vote in favour of Wakley's motion, while those who were aware of it should vote against the motion. For Wakley did press for the division and it was defeated; those in favour of complete remission numbered 82, those against 308.

The London Dorchester Committee later presented an analysis of those who had voted in favour, including Daniel O'Connell whatever his feelings about the wrongness of place and certainty of defeat. The Committee concluded that from a full House of 390 members, only 7 Whigs had been found to vote 'for this act of mercy'. The other 75 noble members who voted in favour had included 12 Tories, Radicals and independent Liberals, the latter being 'something more than Whigs'.

Apart from the fact that the agitation had pushed the government into its first major concessions – and without the weight of the agitation even the sympathetic Russell would have been unlikely to act – the change of atmosphere occasioned by the pressure was notable. On June 25th only one M.P. said categorically that the sentences were legal, justifiable and should not be remitted (Ponsonby's defence of the grand jury and the True Bill was limited to that while others clung only to the initial legality). This one member was howled down. June 25th, 1835, with Russell's concessions and Wakley's important speech, was the turning point in the Tolpuddle drama but there was still a long, long way to go before any of the men would see England again. Lord Howick's assertion that the men already had been exempted from convict labour in the colony and that their wives were free to join them was a considerable jumping of the gun. It was true that letters were en route to the Governor of New South Wales, Sir Richard Bourke, and the Lieutenant-Governor of Van Diemen's Land, Colonel Arthur, but letters took four months to reach their destinations. Enquiries about the wives joining their husbands were only just being initiated.

On June 12th (i.e. before the debate) the Colonial Secretary, Lord Glenelg, had dictated letters to Governors Bourke and Arthur. With reference to Glenelg, it was as well for the Tolpuddle men that Russell was a strong-minded, liberal Home Secretary, equipped and prepared to push a cause, for Glenelg was a weak, vacillating man. Indeed, he and Russell were later to come into direct and bitter conflict. But Glenelg at least did what he was told in this instance. The letters, similar apart from the names involved, informed the Governors that

> His Majesty's Secretary of State for the Home Department, having had under his consideration the case of [names inserted] who was/were convicted at Dorchester March 1834 of administering unlawful oaths and transported to Van Diemen's Land/New South Wales for seven years in the *William Metcalfe/Surrey* – has requested me to authorize you to grant a pardon to [names inserted] provided his/their conduct had been good since his/their transportation, on condition . . .

The conditions, of course, varied. For George and James Loveless it was that they remained permanently in the colony; for Brine, the Standfields and Hammett that they could return home after two years from the date of their arrival. Governor Arthur was told, 'You will accordingly grant a pardon to the Prisoner on those terms and conditions', while Sir Richard Bourke was requested 'to take measures for carrying His Majesty's gracious intention into effect'.

However, there was a legal difficulty affecting conditional pardons which was pointed out to Lord John Russell, a bit late in the day, by his law officers. In 1832 and 1833 an Act had been passed (2 and 3 Will. IV, c. 62) which prevented any pardon or ticket-of-leave being granted to a transported convict until he had completed a minimum of four years as a convict on a seven-year sentence, six years for a fourteen-year sentence and eight years if serving a life sentence. So legally none of the men could be granted conditional pardons under four years. But in the meantime, Russell had announced in the House of Commons that he had recommended immediate conditional pardons for all six men, and that four of them could return home after two years. It was his personal desire that these measures should be carried out, and letters had already been despatched to the Governors ordering them to be effected. Russell was in a quandary. He did his best to find a way round the problem. On June 29th, he wrote to Glenelg saying that he had become aware of the difficulties raised by 2 and 3 Will. IV, c. 62. He therefore requested Glenelg to write to the respective Governors of New South Wales and Van Diemen's Land and ask them to report upon the conduct of the six men. If it should prove to have been excellent, Russell had hopes that 'his Majesty's gracious intention of extending mercy to them might be carried into effect under the Royal Sign Manual'. By this he meant he hoped to be able to persuade the King to use his prerogative of pardon, which overruled statutes. At this moment he had not obtained it, and William IV was the most obstinate of men. So the best he could suggest in the meantime was that the Tolpuddle men should receive the benefits which had been intended for them, as expressed in the earlier June letters to the Governors.

Accordingly, on July 8th Glenelg wrote further letters to both Governors, enclosing copies of the letter from Russell. The situation was complicated and equivocal as Glenelg admitted in 'private and separate' letters accompanying the official news. To Governor Arthur he wrote, 'I therefore do not conceal from myself that I impose upon you a duty which may possibly be in some degree at variance with the terms of the statute to which I have referred' (i.e. 2 and 3 Will. IV, c. 62). To Sir Richard Bourke he wrote, 'I trust, however, that it may be in your power to accomplish the immediate release of these Prisoners from Penal Labour without involving yourself and the Government in a responsibility which, it must be confessed, is not lightly to be undertaken.'

While the various letters were starting on their slow passage to the antipodes, Lord John Russell was engaged in other matters connected with the Tolpuddle men. He had to contend with the indifferent Melbourne and the obstinate King. At the beginning of October 1835 Russell himself was 'not disposed to do more than I have done, for then we should be in their power, instead of their being in ours. What say you?' The question was asked of Lord Melbourne who stated emphatically, 'I am certainly against doing anything more in the case of the Dorsetshire labourers. I thought the matter had been considered settled.' In his next letter, Russell had changed his mind about doing anything further. He wrote that fresh facts had come to light, regarding George Loveless's Van Diemen's Land protestations that he had acted on the advice of other trade unionists and was unaware that he was doing anything illegal. As for the illegality of the offence itself, 'it required putting together two Acts of Parliament to prove that the thing was unlawful . . . and no proclamation warned them that what was notoriously done all over London was illegal. Secondly, it appears that the Duke of Cumberland and Lord Wynford have been doing the same thing only with more cunning, and deserve at least a more severe punishment.' These mitigating facts had now just come to light within the week from Russell's first letter, so it would be more accurate to say that the implications had suddenly struck him hard. He assured Melbourne that, 'Certainly if I stay in office I shall not keep the sentence in force for the whole seven years,' whereupon Melbourne more or less gave him a free hand with the words, 'I do not care much what is done respecting the Dorsetshire Labourers.' In his first October letter, Melbourne had also written, 'Perhaps if it will tend to prevent the revival of the question you might facilitate their being joined by their families.' The suggestion was out of date. It had occurred to Russell immediately after the major parliamentary debate of June 25th. He was doubtful whether pardons, conditional or full, could be wrung from the King, and certainly did not know how long this would take. If the wives and children, particularly of the Lovelesses, who were the main problem, were interested in joining their husbands this might solve the difficulties. Accordingly he instructed the local Tolpuddle vicar to interview the Loveless wives. The vicar was still Doctor Warren who had so disgusted George Loveless in 1832 by denying his vow to see wages righted (although in Warren's favour, at one of the early London protest meetings it was stated that he had written to Mr Baron Williams on behalf of the Lovelesses). On receipt of Russell's instructions which had been delayed because the full, correct address of Tolpuddle, *Blandford*, Dorset had not been included, Doctor Warren visited the two wives and it is interesting to note that they remained in their cottages. The pressure of the general agitation had prevented the local magistrates-cum-landlords from exercising their right to evict discontented, or disapproved-of tenants. After the interviews Doctor Warren informed Russell that George's wife, Elizabeth, was anxious to join her husband in Australia, but James's wife, Sarah, was not, although she would go if her husband so desired. Wisely, neither was prepared to accept the offer until they had written to their respective husbands and ascertained whether the men wanted them to go. As a result of this information, transmitted by Russell to Glenelg at the Colonial Office, Glenelg despatched further letters to the Governors of New South Wales and Van Diemen's Land, asking them to enquire whether the two Lovelesses wished their wives to join them.

Russell's efforts for 1835 were not finished. By November he had obtained conditional pardons from the King, under the Royal Sign Manual, which allowed the Standfields,

Brine and Hammett to return home at the end of two years and – this was a new concession – the two Lovelesses to return at the end of three years. However, to complicate the situation further for Governors Bourke and Arthur, two letters were sent, in October and November. The October letters announced that Russell was recommending the new conditional pardons to the King, while the November ones actually enclosed them.

By the end of 1835, the campaigners at home were feeling reasonably pleased with themselves, and a dozen letters had left England for Governors Bourke and Arthur whose intent was to ameliorate the lot of the Tolpuddle men. Intentions, particularly when they are muddled, are not the same as effects.

14: 'The Real Difficulty Raised by the Act 2nd and 3rd William IV, c. 62'

By the end of 1835 three of the letters from Glenelg had reached Governor Arthur: the one recommending the conditional pardon for Loveless, that about the difficulties raised by 2 and 3 Will. IV, c. 62, and the third asking if Loveless wished to have his wife and children join him in Van Diemen's Land. Governor Arthur went into action immediately, though George Loveless was in no position to appreciate the Governor's promptitude.

Loveless recorded three interviews at the end of 1835 and the beginning of 1836, with the conversations again appearing in suspicious and too literary detail. On December 29th, 1835, Loveless said he was called to the police office in Hobart Town where he was interviewed by Mr Spode, a magistrate according to Loveless, in fact the Principal Superintendent of Convicts. The following conversation took place:

SPODE: I have sent for you, Loveless, to know if you wish your wife and family to be sent to join you in this colony, if the government will grant them facility.

LOVELESS: I hope you will allow me to ask a question before I say anything about my wife and children.

SPODE: What is it?

LOVELESS: Am I to obtain my liberty?

SPODE: Liberty! What do you mean?

LOVELESS: Is there a prospect of my obtaining my free pardon?

SPODE: Not that I know. That depends upon the ministry at home.

LOVELESS: Then, Sir, I can have nothing at all to say on the subject while I am a prisoner.

Spode called him an audacious, obstinate rascal, and said he would have him charged and given a damned good flogging for insolence. Loveless adhered to his position, and Spode sent him back to work on the government farm. On January 7th, 1836, Loveless was again sent for by Mr Spode, and a similar conversation ensued:

SPODE: I want to know if you have any objection that your wife and family should be sent over to you, and let me tell you, before you answer me, it is intended for your advantage.

LOVELESS: Nothing could give me more satisfaction as to join my wife and children had I my liberty, but I do not want them here while I am a prisoner.

SPODE: You want to be above government, and tell them what they must do.

LOVELESS: No, Sir, I do not want to be above government, nor tell what they must do, but I tell you, rather than be the instrument of bringing my wife and children into the distress and misery of this colony, such as I feel it, I will remain as I am as long as I live.

He was again ordered back to work. On January 24th Governor Arthur personally visited him on the government farm, interviewing him in the field where he was working, and Loveless recorded the conversation at length. When Arthur asked him what his objections were to having his family brought out Loveless replied:

LOVELESS: I should be sorry to send for my wife and children to come into misery.

ARTHUR: Misery! What do you mean?

LOVELESS: Why, Sir, I have seen nothing but misery ever since I came into this country.

192

Arthur enquired how long he had been in Van Diemen's Land. Loveless told him and Arthur then asked why he had seen nothing but misery.

LOVELESS: Because the food and clothing allowed to the government men only renders them miserable. It is no better than slavery.

ARTHUR: Oh, no, there are no slaves under the British dominions. You are only prisoners.

Loveless said Arthur could call it by what term he chose, but that was how he viewed convict life. Arthur pressed the matter of his family coming out, and said the colony could offer a good living. Loveless replied that he had no knowledge of good living because he had been shut up since he had arrived, and that he would be a monster to bring his family out while he was still a prisoner. Arthur then said that he had no doubt but that Loveless would have his liberty as soon as his wife arrived. Personally he would give Loveless his freedom immediately but he did not dare on account of the Act of Parliament that had been passed forbidding the issue of tickets-of-leave under four years. Arthur finished the conversation by urging Loveless to consider writing to his wife and asking her to join him. Loveless did consider, and on January 27th he wrote to his wife requesting that she come to Van Diemen's Land. He said he did so because he feared that otherwise he would become a marked man. From what other convicts had told him and from what he himself had observed, if you were singled out by authority you might as well abandon hope. He sent the letter to Governor Arthur for forwarding to England. On February 5th, 1836, he was again called to the police office in Hobart Town whereupon Mr Spode gave him a ticket-of-leave exempting him 'from every penal observance'.

Loveless's account of the sequence of events and general

reporting of what was said was undoubtedly true. He was later to regard the sequence in a fairly bitter light, with justification considering that Lord John Russell had announced his conditional pardon in the House of Commons in June 1835. Loveless considered he was brow-beaten into writing to his wife before he knew of his ticket-of-leave. To an extent he was. Governor Arthur had three confusing letters in front of him, one of which stressed the solution of the family being reunited, therefore if he could get Loveless to write to his wife first it made it easier for him to issue the ticket-of-leave. Viewed in comparison with what happened to the five men in New South Wales, Governor Arthur's actions were surprisingly fair and lib-eral. The ball had been put squarely into Arthur's court by the letters from London. He caught it neatly and gave Loveless as great an indulgence as he could, i.e. the ticket-of-leave, officially issued on February 3rd, 1836.

On February 13th, 1836, Arthur wrote to Glenelg to thank him for the various letters relating to the case of George Loveless, and to inform Glenelg that he had accorded Loveless 'all the benefits of the Pardon, which will be subsequently confirmed to him under the Sign Manual'. He also enclosed Loveless's letter to his wife and 'a memorial on the subject'. He noted that Loveless was desirous of remaining in the colony 'where he had come to the conclusion that by honesty and industry a person may obtain a far better livelihood than can be procured in England'. Arthur's memorial is missing, but presumably it referred to his personal interview with Loveless. If it was as a result of this interview that he decided that Loveless was desirous of remaining in the colony, remembering Loveless's own account there is evidence of a distinct lack of communication.

By February 1836 Loveless was a comparatively free man. On May 23rd his conditional pardon was granted; Governor Arthur again acting quickly on receipt of the autumn letters from London. Loveless himself makes no reference to the conditional pardon, so whether he was officially informed or read of it in a newspaper (pardons were gazetted), we do not know. He was already enjoying the benefits of the pardon anyway, so its official announcement made little difference to him. The only extra news was that he would be able to return home when three years from his arrival in the colony had expired. Being a ticket-of-leave man or conditionally pardoned was not, as Loveless discovered, necessarily a happy lot. The freed convict had no friends and no money, nor were settlers over-eager to employ him – partly because they had to pay wages whereas they could buy a convict for a pound, partly because of the bad reputation all convicts had. It was for these reasons that so many ticket-of-leave men got into trouble, as stealing something to eat or falling in with rogues was often the only means of survival. After tramping the Hobart area, growing more convinced that he had come to the wrong end of the world, Loveless himself finally found a safe harbour.

The man who employed him was a Major de Gillern who farmed at Glen Ayr, near Richmond, and who had experienced troubles of his own with government departments. William de Gillern was born in Germany, but served in His Majesty's Britannic forces from 1807 until 1815 when he was put on half pay. He married an English girl, and in 1827 sold his commission, obtained a grant of land and emigrated to Van Diemen's Land. Later, Governor Arthur introduced a denizenation, or naturalization, law – one of his many stringent regulations – and de Gillern found himself in difficulties. His name was erased from the jury list because he was not a British citizen, and other rights were threatened. After repeated delays in obtaining denizenation papers from Arthur's minions in Hobart, de Gillern took up the matter with the Colonial Office in London. In his letters he pointed out that he had faithfully served in the British army and had been granted the land as a result of that service, and referred to the injurious effects and the injustice of his inability to obtain denizenation papers. In October 1835, not long before Loveless applied to him for work, de Gillern finally obtained a satisfactory reply from Lord Glenelg. But it had been a lengthy, time-consuming business and cannot have increased his respect for Governor Arthur or the wheels of government. When a man such as Loveless, patently of intelligence and good character, came asking for work, de Gillern was in the right frame of mind to offer it. In addition to a job Loveless was given his own stone cottage on the Glen Ayr estate, most beautifully situated against a backdrop of wooded hills. He himself had little to say about Major de Gillern, but he did record that his master allowed him to read his newspapers – a fact which was to prove of great importance – and this plus the allocation of a cottage indicates a tolerable relationship.

Meanwhile, in New South Wales at the end of October 1835, Sir Richard Bourke had received Glenelg's letters, announcing the conditional pardons and then outlining the difficulties presented by 2 and 3 Will. IV, c. 62. The reaction of the liberal Bourke was the opposite to that of the dictatorial Arthur. He took the view that it was not possible to implement the intentions of the conditional pardons until the pardon under the Royal Sign Manual had been granted. He did not exempt any of the men from 'every penal observance' as had Governor Arthur with George Loveless. Bourke's caution is understandable, for all he knew the King's pardon might not be obtained for years. But Glenelg, prompted by Lord John Russell, had asked him to effect the immediate release of the prisoners from convict labour, if possible. It was possible, because Governor Arthur did it for George Loveless. It is curious that it was the liberal, more humane Bourke who felt he could not involve himself in the responsibility of releasing the men. Perhaps it was the soldier in Arthur that reacted. Here was a dilemma. Could it be solved? Yes. Whereas the lawyer in Bourke – he had trained for the bar – said: here is a legal dilemma, let us wait and see, time will solve it.

However, Bourke took certain measures. He did not just leave the men where they were, scattered throughout the country at their various convict tasks. At the end of October 1835 he sent a memorandum to his Colonial Secretary requesting that the latter obtain information on the conduct of the five men since their arrival in the colony 'with as little delay as possible'. The pardons were dependent on their behaviour having been good and their avoidance of summary convictions. Some of the subsequent delay stemmed from the facts that there were five men involved, that they were hundreds of miles apart, and that New South Wales was a much larger place than Van Diemen's Land. Much of the delay can be laid at the doors of bureaucracy. There were infinitely more levels of administration in New South Wales through which the buck had to pass and could be conveniently mislaid than in Governor Arthur's neat dictatorship. Arthur could ride out of Hobart and interview George Loveless personally for Loveless was, fortunately, working near the capital; had he been at the other end of the island Arthur might not have bothered. The idea of Sir Richard Bourke riding hundreds of miles to Woodlands and St Vincent and up the Hunter and Williams Rivers to interview Hammett and James Loveless, the Standfields and Brine was not feasible.

The wheels of bureaucracy started their grinding course on November 9th, 1835, when Bourke's Colonial Secretary wrote to the Principal Superintendent of Convicts, transmitting the Governor's request and asking for the information to be returned to him 'as soon as possible'. On November 29th having had no reply, the Colonial Secretary sent another letter to the Principal Superintendent asking him to expedite the report on the men's conduct. Then there was silence until January 13th, 1836, when Sir Richard Bourke issued a further memorandum to the Colonial Secretary 'Let the Principal Superintendent of Convicts be desired to order these men, viz. James Loveless, Thomas Standfield, John Standfield, James Hammett, James Brine, to Hyde Park Barracks to await further instructions, and to report their arrival. This to be done *immediately*.' Before the Colonial Secretary could transmit these orders, he received a reply from the Principal Superintendent which explained the reasons for the two months' silence. The Superintendent had received answers to his queries regarding the conduct of the men from the masters, with the exception of Hammett's master, E. J. Eyre (who was probably off exploring the hinterland). He had been waiting for Mr Eyre's report but as it had still not arrived he felt he should communicate what he already knew, namely that the conduct of Brine, J. Loveless and J. and T. Standfield had been excellent. By return, on January 15th, the Colonial Secretary transmitted the next set of orders – to bring the men forthwith to Hyde Park Barracks. These the Superintendent expedited, or tried to, for by February 3rd, 1836, he was pleased to be able to inform the Colonial Secretary that John and Thomas Standfield had arrived at the Barracks and were being held pending further instructions.

By this time Bourke had decided what to do with the men. Having got them together he would keep them together, so that as soon as the pardons arrived from London he would be able to extend the benefits. Dismissing the fact that Bourke could have implemented the intentions of the original conditional pardons and allowing him his cautious legality, this was a sensible move on his part. Unfortunately, the place to which he decided to send the men in the interim waiting period was Port Macquarie. From this decision the even greater subsequent delays partially stemmed because Port Macquarie had been a notorious penal settlement with all the miseries that entailed (although by 1836 it was being used as a selected base for educated convicts on arrival and for suspended, though not vicious, ticket-of-leave men). Having transmitted his decision to the Principal Superintendent of Convicts via his Colonial Secretary, Bourke wrote to Glenelg in mid-February explaining his actions and motives in connection with the five men:

> I have directed that they be severally withdrawn from the masters to whom they have been assigned and removed to Port Macquarie where the magistrate will be instructed to allow them every indulgence consistent with their situation. I have considered this as the most convenient way of disposing of them during the interval which must elapse before His Majesty's pardon can be received, so as to accomplish as far as the law will admit the intentions expressed in your lordship's several communications regarding these persons.

When 'these persons' heard that they were to be sent to Port Macquarie their reactions were, understandably, of horror because news had not circulated on the convict grapevine that the function of Port Macquarie had changed. Its reputation as one of the nether regions of hell remained. Neither had the experiences undergone by 'these persons' en route to Hyde Park Barracks in Sydney put them into a relaxed frame of mind. Those of John and Thomas Standfield were shared, fortunately for the older man, who once again had his son to sustain him. On January 25th, 1836, they were both ordered from their respective farms on the Hunter and Williams Rivers to appear before the Maitland Bench. There they were put in the lock-up, chained, put on a boat for Newcastle and left in prison in Newcastle for three days, most of the time without food, all of the time without bedding. Next they were placed on board a boat for Sydney. The passage was rough, most of the convicts were sick and being chained had to lie in their vomit. In Sydney they were taken to the common gaol in George Street, then handcuffed to a long line of chained prisoners and 'marched through the streets of Sydney like a lot of wild beasts', as John Standfield recorded, to Hyde Park Barracks. This treatment was not on Bourke's command, it was just a routine measure. Orders had been sent for two convicts named John and Thomas Standfield to be conveyed to Sydney. Why they were being sent there none of the guards or officials knew or cared. Chains, lock-ups, lack of food were the way things went.

Soon after his arrival at Hyde Park Barracks on February 3rd John Standfield demanded to see the Barrack Superintendent to ascertain why he and his father had been brought into Sydney in such a rough manner, and what the charge against them was. Having succeeded in his demands, further proof of his persistence of character, he was told there was no charge. They had been brought in on the orders of the home government. That was all the Superintendent knew, which was true. The letter informing the Principal Superintendent of Convicts that the five men were to be sent to Port Macquarie at the first opportunity, there to remain until His Majesty's pleasure had been made known, was not despatched until February 15th and the news would then have had to have been relayed from him to the Barrack Superintendent. It is of interest to note that at this interview John Standfield also recorded that he was told that on their initial arrival in the colony the home government had sent orders for them all to be worked in irons on road gangs. This would seem fairly conclusively to corroborate George Loveless's statement that he was to be worked in irons on Van Diemen's Land. In this instance, unlike that of the conditional pardons, Governor Arthur and Sir Richard Bourke both acted to reverse the orders. It can only be repeated that the orders were an example of Whiggery at its most vindictive, and of the deep-rooted fear of trade unionism.

Shortly after the Standfields' arrival at Hyde Park Barracks, Brine and James Loveless arrived too. Loveless did not record any particular sufferings en route, although he experienced the same fear of not knowing why he had been brought in. When he first asked the question he too was told that the Superintendent had no idea. James Brine's account of his experiences en route to Sydney was extraordinary. He, too, was called before the Maitland Bench, put in a cell, chained and sent by boat to Newcastle. But Brine stated that at Newcastle he was put on a ship for Norfolk Island, that hell upon earth, a thousand miles off the mainland from whose shores no man returned alive. It was only by the grace of God that a storm blew the ship back into Newcastle whereupon he protested so vigorously, he was released, and put on another ship bound for Sydney, finally ending up at Hyde Park Barracks with the others. One has no wish to disbelieve Brine's story but why he should have been put on a ship for Norfolk Island is impossible to understand. If he made sufficient fuss to be taken off after the ship had been blown back into port, why could he not have done so before it left? Or did he not know of its destination before it set sail? Once knowing, did desperation and the second chance presented by the storm give him extra eloquence? Or was an appalling clerical error made and Brine put on the wrong ship? Without doubting that young Brine had a nasty experience, the destination of Norfolk Island must be regarded with some suspicion because there was absolutely no reason why he should have been sent there. Bourke's orders down the line had been explicit, the five men were to be brought in to Hyde Park Barracks forthwith and to stay there pending further instructions.

By the end of February the Standfields, James Loveless

and young Brine were all at Hyde Park Barracks. Before March 12th they had learned what Bourke's further instructions were, namely their despatch to Port Macquarie. On that date the Standfields submitted a petition to 'His Excellency, Major-General Sir Richard Bourke, K.C.B., Governor General of New South Wales and its dependencies'. It ran thus:

Thomas and John Standfield, father and son, prisoners of the Crown per *Surrey* humbly sheweth that your Petitioners have learned with sincere gratitude that His Majesty has been pleased to promise Your Petitioners a free pardon, provided Your Excellency shall see proper, on examination into the past conduct of Your Petitioners to recommend the same; and having moreover learned that Your Excellency having seen grounds to remit home the case of Your Petitioners favourably, to the Secretary of State, has been pleased to order that in the meantime, Your Petitioners shall proceed to Port Macquarie, there to remain till such time as the further pleasure of His Majesty shall be known, most respectfully solicit that instead of thus transmitting Your Petitioners, to a distant and unknown part of the Territory where they may be subjected to unforeseen temptation or casualties, Your Excellency will be pleased to remit Thomas Standfield to the service of his former master Mr Nowlan to whose kindness he is indebted for the restoration of his health, which had been much impaired, and being still very feeble he humbly entreats that his son may be allowed to accompany him to the same service, and Your Petitioners pledge themselves that till the arrival of His Majesty's further pleasure regarding Your Petitioners, their conduct in every respect shall correspond with the favourable account which has already been certified before Your Excellency. And Your Petitioners as in duty bound will ever pray etcetera.

(Signed) Thomas Standfield. John Standfield.

John Standfield's own brief account of submitting the petition is more indignant in tone than its actual terms – the idea of being sent to Port Macquarie, a hell on earth little better than Norfolk Island, was monstrous. Sir Richard Bourke granted their petition, and on March 17th his Colonial Secretary sent a letter to the Principal Superintendent of Convicts informing him that in compliance with their own wishes, the Standfields were 'to remain both in the service of Timothy Nowlan, until the commands of His Majesty shall be received respecting them'. John Standfield said they left Hyde Park Barracks on March 16th, but they certainly both returned to Nowlan's farm up the Hunter River and had the comfort of being together. Incidentally, Mr Jones, John Standfield's previous master, objected to the reassignment of young John. He thought he should have been informed of the petition before it was submitted, and when it was granted that he should have been allowed to have John back. A note in the margin of the complaint dismissed it: 'The Standfields' Petition sufficiently explains the grounds upon which their application has been acceded to.'

Whether James Loveless and James Brine also petitioned against being sent to Port Macquarie is unclear. There is no record of their having done so, but equally they were not sent there. At the beginning of March, the Colonial Secretary had not been informed of their arrival at Hyde Park Barracks. He sent a letter to the Principal Superintendent asking whether they, and Hammett, had arrived. The letter also asked the Superintendent to ascertain whether James Loveless was desirous of having his wife and children sent out. (This request being the result of the further letter from Glenelg.) Loveless himself recorded that while at the Barracks, the Superintendent called him into the office and informed him that Sir Richard Bourke would probably grant him a pardon if he sent for his family. He was given two days to consider the offer but he, unlike his brother, refused it although his reason for refusal was similar to that initially offered by George. He had seen nothing but misery in the colony and it was his intention to return to England once he was free, however long the freedom took. Loveless also recorded that he stayed in the Barracks for three months, after which time he and young Brine went to work on a government farm outside Sydney. For what reason or by what means they found themselves there remains unknown. The work was probably not too arduous, as Bourke had earlier ordered that none of them was 'to be sent to labour'. But they were still convicts.

There remains the fifth man, the regrettably silent James Hammett. All that has been recorded to date is that he landed in Sydney with the Standfields, James Loveless and James Brine on the convict ship *Surrey* in September 1834, then he disappeared 'into the hinterland' of New South Wales, and nothing more was heard of him until he finally arrived back in England in August 1839. The lack of knowledge has stemmed from Hammett's failure to write his memoirs, and the implication has been that he was forgotten, that he remained oblivious of his conditional or free pardons for over five years. Examination of the English and Australian archives has proved that Hammett was assigned to E. J. Eyre at Woodlands on the Molomglo Plains. Further examination of the New South Wales records shows that in fact he was not forgotten. Along with the other four men he was included in Sir Richard Bourke's round-up. By May 6th he, too, had arrived at Hyde Park Barracks because on that date the Principal Superintendent of Convicts was happy to be able to inform the Colonial Secretary that Hammett had arrived 'from Woodlands in Argyle, the residence of his Assignee, Mr Edward John Eyre'. On May 24th the Colonial Secretary, acting on previous orders from Sir Richard Bourke, instructed the Superintendent that Hammett was to remain on the barrack list 'but not taken out to labour, until an opportunity offers of sending him to Port Macquarie'. Although Bourke intended holding to his original decision, Hammett did not go to Port Macquarie, nor did he remain permanently on the barrack list because when next heard of he was in Windsor.

By June 5th, 1836, Sir Richard Bourke had received the further letters from Glenelg in London enclosing the conditional pardons under the Royal Sign Manual. On June 17th he informed his Colonial Secretary who on June 22nd duly had a notice inserted in the *Government Gazette* to the effect that James Brine, James Hammett, John and Thomas Standfield were pardoned provided they resided in New South Wales 'for the term of two years from the day of their arrival', and for James Loveless three years from the day of his arrival. Even then Bourke did not grant the pardons immediately. He directed his Colonial Secretary to ensure that the men received the full benefit of the pardons 'as soon as the respective periods fixed on the warrant shall have transpired'. This meant they must remain convicts until, in the case of the four men, September 1836, in the case of James Loveless until September 1837 (their arrival was counted from the moment they actually set foot on Australian soil).

James Loveless and young Brine, working near Sydney, heard of their conditional pardons, though whether the Standfields, 150 miles up the Hunter River, or Hammett did, was not clarified. But the men accepted the conditions as fact, which they had to. James Loveless's only form of protest was to ask why he had been singled out for three years. He was told by the farm superintendent that it was because he was one of the ring-leaders. When he asked what he was a ring-leader of, he was further told, 'Of your secret combination; and you may think yourself well off not being hung, as I believe you were bordering on High Treason.' With that comforting thought, he and the others continued to work as assigned convicts.

15: 'His Majesty Has Been Pleased to Grant a Free Pardon'

For the first nine months of 1836 George Loveless was receiving the benefit of a conditional pardon in Van Diemen's Land, while in New South Wales his brother, brother-in-law, nephew, James Hammett and James Brine were still working as assigned convicts. But by spring of that year, absolute free pardons had in fact been granted to all six men. It was an irony they must often have deliberated upon in later life – except for Hammett who never deliberated upon anything connected with those years with anybody.

June 25th, 1835, which saw Wakley's mammoth speech and Russell's concessions, was the turning point, but the campaigners continued to work for absolute free pardons. Whatever Daniel O'Connell might have said about Parliament not being the place to appeal against the decisions of a court of law, Parliament was the place where the offensive continued. However, the main line of attack shifted to the Orange Lodges. The move was implicit in the earlier tactics and it did much to effect the release of the six men. Even William IV was made to realize that (a) the pressure for their release would not die while it was patently obvious that members of the Orange Lodges, of which his brother the Duke of Cumberland was the Grand Master, could be prosecuted under the same Act and for the same offence as the six men had been and (b) that the Tolpuddle prosecutions had stirred a serious hornets' nest in which sat the members of the Orange Lodges, the nest itself was now under direct attack and one way of salvaging it was to release the six men.

Although the subject of the Orange Lodges was initially raised by the Dorchester prosecutions and although the

Radicals continued to link the case of the Dorchester Unionists to the Lodges, the frame of reference was widened. The matter of secret and illegal oaths had brought the Orange Lodges into the spotlight but the Radicals wanted to ensure they stayed there, while the whole question of their organization and activities, particularly within the army and apart from the administration of oaths, was examined. For if the trade unions presented a menacing force for the right and middle of the road men, the two-hundred-thousand-strong Orange Lodges had the same aspect for the Radicals. Their arguments against the Lodges ran on the following lines: trade unions were supposed to threaten the security of the country and were legally suspect; the Radicals did not agree; but if these two points were admitted, was not another threat, quite as serious, presented by a two-hundred-thousand-strong body, deeply rooted in the army, participating in secret oaths and secret meetings? Having established the seriousness of the threat, the Radicals proceeded to expand it. The secret army within the army, the possibility of a *coup d'état*, were implied. The arguments were strong and the threat was a real one, although all the supporters of the Lodges protested their undying Protestantism and loyalty to the personage of the king. The arguments and threats attracted the support and suspicion of the middle of the road men and thereby they undermined the very existence of the Orange Lodges which, with so many illustrious persons among their members, would never do.

The *Radical* newspaper's assessment of the effect the onslaught on the Orange Lodges had on the release of the Dorchester Unionists was thus:

The indictment, against His Royal illustrious Highness the Duke of Cumberland, for being at the head of an illegal Society, were all but prepared and would have been sent to the next Grand Inquest of Middlesex, had not Ministers, in a quiet way, interfered . . . His Royal Highness would have been tried by Petty Jury. Ministers, all bewigged as they are, were not radical enough to avoid a shudder at the thought of even the possibility of indicting a Prince of the Blood Royal, and as to transporting His Royal Highness, only imagine a Whig so much as thinking of such a thing. As it was an awkward affair, the labourers were pardoned to save the Prince.

The assessment was lurid, but possessed truth. Three years later, during the Chartist agitation, the *Globe* which was no friend of Radicalism (although it was a faithful supporter of the Tolpuddle men), made similar allegations, if from a different angle. The Chartist uproar had again brought to a head questions of which bodies were loyal to the King and Country, mass demonstrations and the maintenance of law and order. *The Times* spoke of the loyalty and obedience of the Orange Lodges which had disbanded 'at the mere suggestion of the sovereign'. In reply the *Globe* said, 'Now, as far as our recollection goes, the Orangemen continued their lodges and attempted their processions long after both had been declared illegal; and it was not until after the Dorchester Labourers had been convicted, till the same law was found to be applicable to the Orange Lodges, and till a pretty strong intimation had been given to the Grand Master that an experiment might be made upon him, that the Orange Lodges dissolved.'

Back in 1835 and 1836, the agitation against and condemnation of the Orange Lodges, together with the demand for full pardons for the Dorchester Unionists, mounted to an alarming degree. The sequence of events was as follows. On August 4th, 1835, there was a debate on the Lodges, in fact those in Ireland. Joseph Hume quickly introduced the matter of members of trades associations who had been severely punished for taking illegal oaths, who were at this minute undergoing punishment in New South Wales, and who were not one-thousandth part as guilty of criminal acts as those perpetrated by members of Orange Lodges. He moved a resolution for a Select Committee to be appointed to enquire into the Irish activities in the Lodges. The resolution was accepted. Two days later there was further parliamentary discussion about the Lodges. On August 10th, Hume moved that a Select Committee should also be appointed to enquire into the English Lodges, paying specific attention to their activities within the army and the Duke of Cumberland's connection with them. The motion went to three divisions in the House, but in the end Hume won. The next day Hume was back at the attack. He understood that the Duke of Cumberland had personally signed the warrant for the institution of the Orange Lodges within the army.[1] Surely this needed investigating? The following day Thomas Wakley initiated the next move. He presented a petition from Bristol on behalf of the Dorchester Unionists, but linked it directly with the Orange Lodges. He said categorically that every member of a Lodge came within the meaning of the 1797 Mutiny Act and was liable to its maximum penalties and that it was time an end was put to one law for the rich, and another for the poor. Three days later a message from the King was read to Parliament. Although deploring all secret societies, basically it supported the Lodges and their loyalty to his personage, but that the King should have been persuaded to send a personal message was an indication of how seriously the hornets' nest had been stirred. In September, Joseph Hume presented the report of the Select Committee to Parliament. It was not favourable. In February 1836, Hume again raised the matter of the Orange Lodges and forced a debate. In the meantime, as a

---

[1] The Orange Lodges had had a chequered career, being suppressed and revived. They were suppressed in 1825, and it was to the Duke of Cumberland's subsequent revival of the Lodges that Hume referred.

result of the Committee's report, the King had issued orders making membership of a Lodge within the army a court-martial offence. But Hume contended that the Lodges were still illegal societies, and also accused the Duke of Cumberland of trying to circumvent the orders within the army. In reply Lord John Russell agreed that *all* secret societies were a bad thing, and should be suppressed. In Parliament on March 3rd, a Radical neatly asked Wakley whether he intended to renew his motion for free pardons for the Dorchester Unionists now that the Orange Lodges were being disbanded? Wakley's reply was that in the light of all that had been revealed about Orange Lodges he hoped the government would adopt a course which would render further application by him unnecessary. Whereupon Lord John Russell rose and announced that he had now recommended that the Lovelesses be allowed to return home when three years had expired. He had, of course, sent these instructions to the respective Governors in 1835, but this was the first official announcement of the fact and was a further step forward. However, at the moment, he could not recommend full pardons as nothing had occurred to justify such remission; by which Russell meant that he had not yet been able to obtain the full unconditional pardons from the King. But eleven days later, on March 14th, 1836, Wakley presented more petitions for remission of sentence, and asked whether further investigations into the case of the six men had been made? They had. Once again Lord John Russell rose in the House and announced 'with great satisfaction' that His Majesty had been pleased to grant a free pardon to the whole of the persons who had been convicted on the occasion to which the Honourable Member for Finsbury (Wakley) had just referred. Undoubtedly it was with satisfaction that Russell made the announcement. Undoubtedly making it gave him much pleasure. Undoubtedly the letter he received from the wives, on March 18th, 1836, also gave him pleasure. The wives wrote from Tolpuddle:

May it please your Lordship, My Lord, We whose names are hereunto fixed with feelings of our warmest Gratitude and of our most humble acknowledgements Return to you our Grateful thanks for your Kindness shown towards us by Procuring for our husbands, the son and relatives His Majesty's most Gracious Pardon viz. on the Dorchester unions. But those especially by procuring Pardon for the two Lovelesses to return with the others at the end of two years and Hearing of your unworried diligence for them and us. We will as in duty bound pray for your Lordship's health, Happiness and prosperity.

(Signed) Elizabeth Loveless. Sarah Loveless. C. Brine. Dinniah Standfield. H. Hammett.

It was victory. Almost two years exactly from the day of sentence, the six men and the trade unions were vindicated. The government, implicitly, admitted misjudgment and defeat. Victory had been won by left, middle and right, notably by a member of the government, Lord John Russell, in large part by a nation-wide sense of justice as opposed to legality. But the driving force came from the Radicals and trade unionists, and they had reason to be jubilant.

Right and justice had triumphed, but the six men for whom the battle had been fought continued to suffer for a long time. First, there was the time-lag between the full pardons being granted and the time when they arrived at their destinations. Despatches were sent to Governors Bourke and Arthur on March 24th, 1836, in which Glenelg informed them that:

I have now the honour to enclose [*transmit*] to you a copy of a letter which had been [*I have*] received from the Home Department, together with [*enclosing*] a Free Pardon which his Majesty has been fully pleased to grant to George Loveless [*those persons*], and to desire that you will give him [*them*] the benefit thereof. I have further to desire that if George Loveless should wish [*request in the event of all or any of them wishing*] to return to this country, that you will provide him [*them*] with a free passage [*s*] by the first favourable opportunity, the expense of which will be defrayed from [*chargeable on*] the funds applicable to Convict Service.[2]

The wording of the enclosed free pardons was suitably grand. It is to be hoped that George Loveless read his, for he had a feeling for words and their usage.

Whereas G. Loveless was at the Lent Assizes 1834 holden for the County of Dorset tried and convicted of administering Unlawful Oaths and sentenced to be transported seven years for the same – We in consideration of some circumstances hereby represented to us are Graciously pleased to extend Our Grace and Mercy unto him and to Grant him Our Free Pardon for his said crime provided his conduct has during his residence in our Island of Van Diemen's Land been satisfactory to the Governor thereof. Our Will and Pleasure therefore is that you do take due notice hereof. And for so doing this shall be your Warrant. Given at our Court of St James's the tenth day of March 1836, in the sixth year of our reign.

William IV.

[2] This is the text of the despatch to Arthur. The amended wording for Bourke is given in brackets.

When the pardons finally arrived in Van Diemen's Land and New South Wales little happened. Governor Arthur had the free pardon and instructions to afford G. Loveless a free passage home at the earliest opportunity in his possession by the end of July 1836. He did nothing about them. The reason later offered by his Colonial Secretary was that the authorities did not know where Loveless was. A feeble excuse, as Loveless pointed out, his address being registered by law at the police-office. Governor Arthur may have transmitted the orders and they may have become entangled in the downward administrative path (which existed, even in his neat dictatorship). There was good reason why Arthur did not leap into personal action as vigorously or fairly as he had done in connection with the conditional pardon. He had his own problems. From 1835 onwards he had been under a mounting attack from newspapers and individual colonists, with criticism reaching a crescendo in 1836. Apart from a dislike of his stringent regulations, there was a general outcry for a wider franchise, electors currently being 'confined to a limited number of individuals in Hobart Town'. This was linked to the strong feeling that Van Diemen's Land must soon have its own government and that it could not remain dependent on England. Printed letters were in circulation 'shewing the oppression and Tyranny of the Government', and demonstrating the unlikelihood of any lessening of the oppression or tyranny while Governor Arthur held the reins of the colony in his hands. Arthur was personally attacked for his 'black book', in which he marked the names of the opposition, and for being possessed of 'so arbitrary a spirit, and such unmitigated severity'. From January 1836 the *Colonial Times* mounted an all-out attack on him, persistently calling for his resignation. By September 1836 the small faction of his supporters were saying that, having served a twelve-year term of office, he had been recalled, while his many opponents were saying he had been sacked. He was due to leave Van Diemen's Land at the end of October, so in the preceding months he had other things to occupy his mind than the matter of G. Loveless.

On July 29th, the *Tasmanian* ran a leading article headed 'Convicts!!!' in which it reported both Joseph Hume's attack on the Orange Lodges and their link with the case of the Dorchester Unionists, and the fact that Lord John Russell had given them all free pardons and free passages home. It said, 'What self-condemnation does not the British Government here pronounce. What a hateful system must not that be which can be capable of working such execrable justice.' Unfortunately, George Loveless did not see this article, and it was not until the beginning of September when Major de Gillern handed on the recently arrived March copy of the London *Weekly Dispatch*, that he knew he was a free man and had been awarded a free passage home. (A free passage, incidentally, was not usual, it was an extra concession for the Tolpuddle men. Normally the pardoned convict had to make his own way home.) Loveless waited to see if anybody would inform him of his freedom. Nobody did. Then, on September 16th, the *Tasmanian* ran another long article on the dual subject of the Dorchester Unionists and Colonel Arthur's conduct. It was in this article, in partial defence of Arthur, that it printed its information about his refusing to work Loveless in irons on a road gang. After a résumé of the case it noted that 'it was wrung from the Government, by the force of public opinion that the men should be pardoned'. It did not know whether the orders for their release had yet been received but, again defending Arthur's character, it was convinced that the Governor would not hesitate to effect the orders the minute he received them, indeed he may already have done so. This article Loveless read, but again he waited to give Governor Arthur time to act. Again nothing happened. Finally he decided to write to the editor of the *Tasmanian* and his letter was published on September 30th. In it Loveless said, 'I do not know whether Governor Arthur has received orders from home; I should like to know. If His Excellency has received intelligence to that effect, I hope he will have the goodness to communicate that knowledge to me before he leaves these shores.' Loveless then thanked the newspaper for its efforts on behalf 'of some half-dozen humble individuals who, in 1834, were transported to these colonies for unwillingly and ignorantly giving offence', spoke of the torment of being torn from his wife and family and signed himself 'A Dorchester Unionist'. Beneath the letter the *Tasmanian* said, 'We repeat our former statement, that Lord John Russell, the British Home Secretary, stated explicitly in the House of Commons that free pardons had been sent out for the Dorchester Unionists, with orders to provide them with free passage to England.'

Shortly after the publication of Loveless's letter, Major de Gillern received a communication from the authorities asking if Loveless was still in his employment. He told Loveless of this enquiry, whereupon Loveless himself wrote to the Governor assuring him that he was at Glen Ayr. On October 6th Loveless received a letter from Mr Spode, the Principal Superintendent of Convicts, which finally and officially informed him of his pardon. The letter also said he could have a free passage home on the *Elphinstone* if he wished to return to England. This presented a problem, as Loveless indicated in his reply. Nine months ago he had 'been persuaded' to write to his wife, asking her and the children to join him in the colony. He had received no answer as yet and for all he knew she might be on the high seas at this very moment. 'It would be a dreadful thing for me to leave before I have heard from my wife, to know if she intends coming or not, for her to find, when she arrives in Hobart Town, I had gone to London.' Therefore he asked to be allowed to remain until he had heard from

Elizabeth, and if she were not coming, then to claim his free passage. He received a curt note from Spode in reply to this request: 'I have to inform you, that unless you go by the present opportunity, the government will not be able to give you a free passage.' Loveless was not the man to withdraw at this stage of the fight. He went into Hobart and obtained an interview with the Colonial Secretary which again he recorded at length. The Secretary's argument was that Loveless did nothing he was told – 'it appears you altogether treat the authorities with disrespect'. Loveless's counter-argument was that it was very difficult to do what he was told when he had been told nothing about his free pardon. In answer to this the Secretary brought out the excuse that they had not known where Loveless was, whereupon Loveless mentioned the registration of his address at the police-office. He might also have mentioned the fact that the authorities managed to find him at Glen Ayr after the publication of his letter in the *Tasmanian*. But Loveless's main plea, regarding the awkward situation of his wife, was, 'I was sent out a prisoner, contrary to my wishes, and with a free pardon, I am to be sent back a prisoner, contrary to my wishes.' He begged the Colonial Secretary, whom he knew was a husband and father, to imagine himself in the same situation. Either the plea to head or heart won the day, for the Colonial Secretary asked, 'Well, Loveless, what do you want?' Loveless told him exactly what he wanted. On October 24th he got it, a written undertaking from Mr Spode, the Principal Superintendent of Convicts, which ran thus:

Memorandum, with reference to a former notification addressed to you from this office, relative to a free pardon having been ordered for you from England, I am now to inform you that His Excellency, the Lieutenant-Governor, is pleased to approve of that indulgence being issued to you immediately; and I am further to acquaint you, in consequence of your having expressed your disinclination to embark for England, by the *Elphinstone*, from having written some months ago to your wife, to join you with your three children in this colony, and that you are therefore anxious to await the result of that communication, that in the event of your expectation not being fulfilled, as it regards the arrival of your family, and which an interval of three or four months may determine; His Excellency has been pleased to direct that a free passage is to be then offered you by the government that you may return to England – Josiah Spode.

Having won yet another battle, Loveless returned to Glen Ayr and continued to work for Major de Gillern. It was not until the end of December that he finally heard from Elizabeth who was not en route for Van Diemen's Land because she was well aware of the agitation for the release of her husband and his friends. Indeed, from the time-lag, she should have known of his free pardon before she received her husband's request to join him, in which case she would obviously not have wished to set sail for the convict quarters of the British Empire. Having received Elizabeth's letter, George Loveless immediately wrote to the Colonial Secretary to inform him that his wife was not en route and to request his passage home. By January 20th, 1837, he had heard nothing. Once more he went into Hobart Town. At the police-office he was told that a letter had that very day been sent to him at Glen Ayr. This stated that he had been offered a berth on the *Eveline*, in the forecastle with steerage passage allowance. This, after inspecting the accommodation offered and seeing the captain, Loveless accepted. On January 30th, 1837, the *Eveline* weighed anchor and sailed down the Derwent River towards the open sea. George Loveless's days as a convict were ended. Ahead lay England, and most important of all, Tolpuddle, his dear Betsy and the children.

In the meantime, the full free pardons and the request to furnish the five men with free passages home if they so desired had arrived in Sydney on August 31st, 1836. Sir Richard Bourke absorbed the news and on September 4th duly informed his Colonial Secretary; on September 6th the free pardons for the five men were printed in the *Government Gazette*; on September 13th the *Australian* also carried the information. But still nobody notified the five men. John Standfield said, 'Not the slightest communication was ever made to me or my companions by any government officer of our free pardons having been received.' Young Standfield and the others had reason to be aggrieved, because in their case notification should have been given. Normally, the onus for obtaining conditional or free pardons lay with the convict. Assuming his conduct had been good and the statutory time had elapsed, it was up to the convict or his relations in England to petition. There were official forms and a set method of application. Having petitioned it was also up to him and his relations to keep lobbying and, to a degree, discover if the pardon had been granted. The Tolpuddle men came into a special category. It was not, for instance, normal for half a dozen letters within a few months to be received from the Colonial Office in London by the Governor-General on the subject of the same five convicts. They had not themselves petitioned. They knew that conditional pardons had been granted, and that full pardons might be, but thousands of miles from England they were not fully aware of the agitation on their behalf. Neither were they, as assigned convicts, subscribers to the *Government Gazette* or the *Australian*. Sir Richard Bourke should have seen that his Colonial Secretary and the superintendents down the line were less dilatory in their actions. But Bourke, like Arthur in Van Diemen's Land, had far greater troubles besetting him than the fate of the men from Tolpuddle. He was involved in a serious dispute with his Colonial Treasurer, and as a result of the controversy offered his resignation in January 1837.

However, in mid-November 1836, Bourke did instruct his Colonial Secretary to ascertain from the Principal Superintendent of Convicts whether the five men wished to receive the benefit of the free passages and return to England. As the free pardons and notification of free passages had been received by Bourke at the end of August, his instructions cannot be termed over-hasty. The Colonial Secretary duly transmitted Bourke's orders, then for eight months absolutely nothing happened. It was not until July 24th, 1837, that the Principal Superintendent replied to the November letter and in those eight months there were no requests from the Colonial Secretary's office to expedite the matter. In the July 1837 letter the Superintendent said that the five men, Hammett included, were anxious to return to England, and accordingly he requested that the Colonial Secretary authorize the free passages. At the end of the letter he added that the delay in replying 'was at the express desire of the prisoners themselves'. The prisoners, with the exception of Hammett told a very different tale. James Loveless and James Brine said they heard of their free pardons from another convict who had seen the report in a newspaper, while the Standfields received the news from George Loveless in Van Diemen's Land. To emphasize the sluggish manner in which authority acted, if George Loveless could send the news from a thousand miles away, it should have been possible to have transmitted it 150 miles from Sydney to the Hunter River. There is no excuse for James Loveless and young Brine not being informed, for they were in direct government employ only a few miles outside Sydney.

On being given the news by his friend, James Loveless recorded that he 'instantly proceeded to Sydney to learn the truth'. There he said he was told that he was a free man, but that he was not entitled to a free passage back to England. This interview occurred at the end of December 1836. The superintendent who gave Loveless the information was either lying or this proved the lack of communication between the various departments, for notification of the free pardons and the free passage had been sent to the Principal Superintendent of Convicts in mid-November. The official may have been lying, because Loveless recorded months of half-bullying, half-persuasive action from the superintendent of the government farm on which he and Brine were working. The superintendent had, apparently, decided that Loveless and Brine were good men and workers and urged them to stay in the colony, continuing to work for him, though as emancipists, not convicts. Loveless either knew or sensed that a free passage had been granted, and evinced the family persistence and determination. Finally, the farm superintendent admitted that a free passage had been granted but continued to urge the men to stay in New South Wales, and applied delaying tactics by saying all ships were booked and there was no passage available for months.

Meanwhile, at the end of November 1836, John Standfield had learned of his Uncle George's address in Van Diemen's Land and accordingly written to him. He received his uncle's reply, written on January 21st, the week before he left the island forever, in February 1837. The letter told John that full pardons had been granted, that his uncle was already a free man and was shortly to sail for England. It also told him how to set about obtaining a free passage for himself and the others. John then wrote to his Uncle James 'informing him of the good news'. To a degree, James Loveless already knew, though presumably the information that his brother was en route for England gave him extra ammunition in his battle to obtain his own passage.

Thus, on the one hand, there is the official version that the delay was 'at the express desire of the prisoners', on the other the prisoners' version that they were never officially informed of the pardons at all, and were subsequently obstructed in their efforts to obtain free passages. The brevity of the Principal Superintendent's explanation – 'at the express desire of the prisoners themselves' was all he said – and the eight months' silent gap between notification and reply would seem to uphold the Tolpuddle men's version. The likelihood of their wanting to stay in the country where they had seen so much misery was remote and if they had been desirous of remaining in New South Wales, as the Superintendent's words implied, they would surely have made enquiries about their families joining them. James Loveless had been expressly asked to bring out his wife and children and had refused. John Standfield said flatly that none of them was officially informed of their free pardons, and equally firmly asserted that it was only due to his Uncle James' persistence that the free passages home were finally obtained.

However, once the Principal Superintendent had informed the Colonial Secretary that the men wanted to go home, the wheels finally started to move. On August 12th, 1837, the Superintendent was instructed by the Colonial Secretary to contact the harbour master with reference to the free passages to England. The letter was marked *immediate*. On August 23rd the harbour master wrote to the Colonial Secretary informing him that Captain Robson of the *John Barry* was willing to take the men to London, via New Zealand, for the sum of £25 a head. If the Colonial Secretary agreed to the arrangement, Captain Robson 'intended to make them each a present of five pounds, either to provide themselves with necessaries here, or given to them on their arrival in England'. This was a nice gesture on the part of Captain Robson who presumably was aware of the identity of his passengers and shared the view of many people in England that they had been cruelly and unjustly treated. On August 30th Sir Richard Bourke wrote a note in the margin of the harbour master's letter which read 'By a *free passage* any obligation to work as seamen is of course excluded. This being the case (and it should be clearly so understood) I do not think £20 a large sum to pay for each of the persons concerned; but the £5 may be perhaps better expended in supplying their requisites before they embark, reserving if expectant a small sum to be available on their landing in England.' Underneath was written a further brief note: 'the Pl Supt of Convicts should be requested to expend the £5 for the men.' It can be assumed that the Principal Superintendent effected this request, as the four men themselves praised the kindness and generosity of Captain Robson.

It was on September 11th, 1837, that James Brine, James Loveless, and John and Thomas Standfield finally sailed from Sydney on the *John Barry*. It had taken just over a year from the time the free pardons and authorization of free passages had arrived in Sydney for them to be effected. In *Injustice Within the Law* the Honourable Mr Justice Evatt suggested that had Sir Richard Bourke's original intentions been implemented, had all five men gone to Port Macquarie and remained together in one place, the free pardons might have been effected more quickly. This is possibly, if ironically, true. However, Port Macquarie was hundreds of miles from Sydney. In view of the slowness with which the news travelled in the Sydney area, it is equally possible they might have been forgotten for as long a period. Bourke's major difficulties within the Legislative Council, his being on the brink of resignation from January 1837 (he finally resigned in December), surely had some connection with the delay. His involvement in the major battles left him little time to be concerned about minor details such as the fate of the Dorchester Unionists. Therefore the necessary prodding reminders to expedite the matter, and queries as to whether the instructions had been effected (of which there were many in connection with the conditional pardons), were not issued.

What of the fifth man, the silent Hammett? His name was included in the Principal Superintendent's letter at the end of July 1837, which had stated that the men wanted to return to England and requesting their free passages. So either he was actually contacted by authority, or more probably, like the others, heard of his pardon in a round-about manner and asked for a free passage. Certainly he wanted it in July, equally certainly he was not on the *John Barry* when it sailed from Sydney. Suddenly, by September, he was on an assault charge at Windsor. Whom he assaulted, or why, or if he did assault anybody (for a charge was not the same as a fact), how he got to Windsor, or what he was doing there, we do not know. But Windsor, an early convict settlement and by the 1830s a thriving small town, is situated on the Hawkesbury River only thirty-four miles from Sydney, so Hammett had not travelled far. One can only assume that, as in the case of James Brine and James Loveless, the orders for him to be sent to Port Macquarie were not effected and that Hammett obtained permission to remain in the Sydney area and found work at Windsor, either as an assigned convict or as a ticket-of-leave man. There his temper frayed and whether he actually hit or attacked somebody his behaviour definitely came to the authorities' notice, and he was consequently charged with assault. The fact that he was on the charge was the reason why he did not leave the colony with the Standfields, James Loveless and James Brine.

Hammett lost all contact with the other four men from the moment of his arrival in New South Wales. No effort appears to have been made on either side to make contact, not that it would have been an easy matter to have done so, even had they wished to. Hammett was the most isolated, the one assigned the furthest distance from

Sydney. He was, therefore, the last to arrive at Hyde Park Barracks and consequently missed the others in the round-up. John Standfield recorded in his narrative that Hammett had not arrived at the barracks before he and his father returned to Mr Nowlan's farm up the Hunter River, which was true. They left in March and Hammett arrived at the beginning of May, but he can only have missed Loveless and Brine by a hair's-breadth. James Loveless said he and Brine stayed at the barracks for three months before going to work on the government farm outside Sydney. One assumes it must have been less because Hammett was definitely at the barracks by the beginning of May. When they all became separated for the second time, and during the long efforts to obtain the free passages home, presumably neither the Standfields nor Brine and Loveless attempted to trace Hammett's whereabouts, as they had done with each others'. This is understandable as they had their own problems and battles to fight. However, the story that Hammett was left up-country, somewhere hundreds of miles in the hinterland, when the others were brought into Sydney and finally obtained their free passages, was started by the other four. On their arrival in England they gave this explanation, for the good reason that they did not know where Hammett was. To date, this picture of Hammett languishing up-country, working as a convict for a further three years, unaware of his free pardon, has been the accepted explanation. In fact he was not left at Woodlands, but was brought, following Sir Richard Bourke's orders down the bureaucratic line, to Hyde Park Barracks in May 1836 (and further to corroborate this, his master, E. J. Eyre's request for a replacement convict is also extant). Hammett was then ordered to be sent to Port Macquarie until His Majesty's gracious pleasure should be known, but did not, for whatever reason, go. There the trail ends, until September 1837 when he reappears having been detained on the assault charge at Windsor. The charge, not his being stranded up-country, was the reason for his failing to leave the colony with the others.

16: 'The Poor Dorsetshire Labourers Restored to Their Cottages'

George Loveless was, obviously, the first to arrive back in England. The *Eveline* docked in London on June 13th, 1837. He was welcomed by members of the London Dorchester Committee, but whether the committee also paid and arranged for Elizabeth and the children to be at the dockside is not known. His return attracted no newspaper attention, even from the Radical ones. This was probably partly because he was the only one to have returned. What had happened, or was happening, to his fellow-victims was unknown. It was also because Loveless landed in a week when national attention was focused on the King. William IV was gravely ill and a week later, on June 20th, he died. The newspapers were then filled with obsequies for the dead, whom they were all able to love now he had departed, and hopes for the reign of the young, unknown Victoria.

Loveless returned to his cottage in Tolpuddle. It must have been an extraordinary sensation to be back there with Elizabeth and the three children; to walk down the quiet High Street to the village green and to stand under the sycamore tree where he and his friends had discussed and planned their society. Fortunately the human mind is capable of enormous erasures and stupendous adjustment and, to assist nature, George Loveless immediately set to work on a task which would nowadays be called self-therapy. He sifted and clarified his experiences, and expunged some of the bitterness by writing *The Victims of Whiggery*. It was on the suggestion of the London Dorchester Committee, particularly of the secretary Robert Hartwell who wrote an introduction to the finished work, that Loveless embarked on the task. One assumes the committee continued to make a weekly allowance to the family while

George wrote the pamphlet. It was in print by September 1837, which means Loveless, not a professional writer, must have worked hard and fast. The continuing financial assistance was well worthwhile from the viewpoint of the London Dorchester Committee and from the Radical viewpoint in general, for Loveless had been, in the words of the felicitous title, a victim of Whiggery. What had happened to him was the sort of thing that would continue to happen until the people had a voice in the government of their country.

The pamphlet was issued as *The Victims of Whiggery; being a statement of the persecutions experienced by the Dorchester Labourers; their trial, banishment, etc. Also reflections upon the present system of transportation. With an account of Van Diemen's Land, its customs, produce, and inhabitants, dedicated (without permission) to Lords Melbourne, Grey, Russell, Brougham and Judge Williams.* (It seems a trifle unjust to have included Lord John Russell among the culprits.) The pamphlet's price was fourpence and the profits were devoted to the relief of the families of the Dorchester Labourers. It sold extremely well, and was much quoted at the Chartist meetings that were beginning to assemble throughout the country. It was indeed a good pamphlet, remarkably free from bitterness. There was some, understandably, but it was neither corrosive nor reeking with self-pity. It also contained a great deal of information, as the full title indicates. After the account of his experiences[1] and a brief outline of the customs, laws and climate, produce and inhabitants of Van Diemen's Land, Loveless warned free emigrants that the country was not 'the garden of Eden' that the deluded people of England imagined, of the difficulties and stringent regulations facing them (which was true under Arthur's régime). His conclusions on transportation were that it was not only arbitrary and cruel but

[1] On which I have drawn in preceding chapters.

self-defeating, a view upheld by most witnesses before the Select Committee on the subject held in the same year of 1837. His political conclusions – and they were political whether he considered them so or not – were that 'England had for many years been lifting her voice against the abominable practice of Negro slavery. Numbers of great men have talked, have laboured and have struggled until at length emancipation has been granted to the black slaves in the West Indies. When will they dream of advocating the cause of England's white slaves?' By that he did not just mean transported convicts because he continued, 'When will they attempt to raise working man to that scale in society to which he can lay claim from his utility? Never, no never will (with a few honourable exceptions) the rich and the great devise means to alleviate the distress, and remove the misery felt by the working men of England. What then is to be done? Why, the labouring classes must do it themselves, or it will for ever be left undone.' He further urged that, 'Every working man come forward, from east to west, from north to south; unite firmly but peaceably together as the heart of one man; let them be determined to have a voice in, and form part of, the British nation.' His final cry was, 'Arise, men of Britain and take your stand! Rally round the standard of Liberty, or for ever lay prostrate under the iron hand of your land and money-mongering taskmasters!'

It will be readily understood that such pleas and cries lit up Chartist meetings like fireworks. What people such as James Frampton thought of them will be equally readily appreciated. Nothing specific is known of Frampton's activities in 1837, although he was to burst briefly into recorded life in 1838, but Frampton was very much alive and George Loveless had returned to a Tolpuddle that had changed not one whit. Magistrates still possessed their great powers; farmers were still paying appallingly low wages; there was still a glut of labour. With the new Poor

Law of 1834 in operation, the situation for the destitute was even more harsh and humiliating. Into this unchanged situation returned a man who had successfully cocked a snook at authority. He might have suffered in the process but he was the victor, hence his return. Moreover he had written a rabble-rousing, republican pamphlet which was being used by agitators, for their own ends, to rouse the rabble up and down the country. It was not a situation that could continue. Loveless, an intelligent man, must have appreciated this fact. How much courage it took to remain in Tolpuddle, what pressures were applied to him and his family by the local hierarchy, whether some villagers ostracized him through fear, we do not know. But once the initial joy of being home had evaporated, life cannot have been very pleasant. However, he stayed in Tolpuddle for the rest of 1837 and part of 1838.

On March 16th, 1838, the *John Barry*, with his brother, James Brine and the Standfields on board, docked in Plymouth, almost four years to the day of the trial that had sent them across the world. March was a significant month for the men: tried and sentenced in March 1834, free pardons granted in March 1836, the final return home in March 1838. They were welcomed by local trade unionists in Plymouth, and stayed in the house of one of them. The Devonshire newspapers reported their homecoming, but there was little metropolitan or other provincial coverage. On March 22nd a public welcome and meeting was held in the Mechanics' Institute in Plymouth. Captain Robson of the *John Barry* attended, and spoke highly of the men's conduct and character while on board his ship, particularly of James Loveless. Of Hammett it was variously reported by the newspapers that he had been left in New South Wales, 'his companions not being able to ascertain his residence', and that he remained in the colony from choice. James Loveless was the spokesman at the meeting. He recounted his experiences, and he also complained about the delays in communicating the news of the free pardons. The view he expressed was that the delays were definitely due to the inefficiency or obstructionism of officialdom, not to any 'express desire' of the men to remain in New South Wales. Extracts from brother George's pamphlet, *The Victims of Whiggery*, were read which 'excited much interest' and a penny collection was made at the door. How much was contributed was not recorded. From Plymouth the men proceeded to Exeter where another public welcome was organized by local trade unionists. Finally, on March 26th, they reached Dorchester where they stayed overnight at the Antelope Inn. There was no public welcome at Dorchester, not from lack of enthusiasm or fear imposed by local authority, but for the inefficient reason that the organizers had muddled their dates. The next day the men were driven the seven miles from Dorchester to Tolpuddle, the distance they had walked in the charge of Constable Brine four years previously. Reunited with their families, they stayed in Tolpuddle for a fortnight.

On April 16th there was an official welcome home in London, organized by the London Dorchester Committee. George Loveless had already seen the capital city on his return to England, but for the other four it was their first visit. The assembly point for the public welcome was Kennington Common and from 8 A.M. the crowds began to gather. Observers commented on the gaiety of the display – there were whitesmiths, bricklayers, blacksmiths, tinplate workers and glass blowers, cordwainers, wood-sawyers, silk latters and gold beaters, all in their Sunday best, with the farriers providing a band. Observers also commented – and this procession and the dinner following it were well covered by the Press – on the general decorous behaviour which could be taken 'as one of the many proofs of the advancement of the people'. The Lovelesses, Standfields and Brine arrived just before 10 A.M. They stepped into an open carriage, and the procession, about six thousand strong, set off. Its members carried trade union and other banners, one of which bore the words 'The Queen's Guards – The People'. It proceeded over Westminster Bridge, through streets thronged with spectators. As it entered Whitehall and passed the Home Office, the farriers' band played the national anthem, 'See The Conquering Hero Comes', 'We'll Fight and We'll Conquer Again and Again', and 'Hurrah for the Bonnets of Blue'. Presumably the band stationed itself in front of the Home Office for this recital, while the procession marched by. From Whitehall it proceeded to Charing Cross and Pall Mall, up Regent Street, into Oxford Street and Tottenham Court Road, along Grays Inn Street, through Pentonville to Copenhagen Fields. It was the mammoth procession of April 21st, 1834, in the reverse direction. The actual destination was White Conduit House, where a public dinner had been arranged. The guests of honour – six hundred notables including Thomas Wakley, Doctor Wade and members of the London Dorchester Committee – were accommodated in a room of the House. In the garden two tents had been erected, one capable of holding a thousand people, with a dais for the guests of honour once they had finished inside the House, the smaller one for two hundred people. The cost of the dinner was 2s. 6d. a head, and the fare included cold veal, ham, roast beef, with innumerable dishes of hot potatoes, pies and plum pudding. As the Tolpuddle men ate it is possible that they thought of the rations in New South Wales and Van Diemen's Land. Doctor Wade said grace before and after the meal, but he mixed the blessing of the Almighty in with thanks to Him for the safe deliverance of the Tolpuddle men which the *Globe* thought was 'extraordinary'. After the meal came the speeches. Thomas Wakley asked the most pertinent question of the hour: If the people of England had their political rights, could such things happen as had happened to these five men? The answer to this was most definitely not. He then proposed a toast to

'The People', five splendid representatives of which stood beside him on the platform. The *Globe* described them as 'all unaffected labourers' and having the appearance of respectable farmers rather than labourers. It was shortly after this reception that *Cleave's Penny Gazette* published the drawings of the five men in which they looked extremely respectable. The two young men, James Brine and John Standfield, have a dandified air, with their hair cut à la mode. The most interesting face is that of George Loveless with its high wide forehead, determined mouth and chin and calm thoughtful eyes. At the April reception, it was George Loveless who thanked everybody on behalf of the unaffected, respectable-looking farmers for their kindness and concern. He said he had suffered in the cause of truth, and by truth he would always stand. After Loveless's speech, the launching of 'the Dorchester Labourers' Farm Tribute' was announced. It was felt that the men had earned the right to something better than remaining labourers for the rest of their lives, and it was proposed that a farm be bought for them. The fund was officially opened in May 1837 and the subscriptions, mostly penny ones, started to pour in.

The connections with Tolpuddle were not yet severed. After the reception at White Conduit House, the men returned to their birthplace to await the results of the Farm Tribute. As *The Victims of Whiggery* had been such a success, the Standfields, James Loveless and James Brine were also persuaded to record their experiences.[2] Their pamphlet, written in Tolpuddle and published in 1838, was briefer and eschewed comments upon transportation or the working classes. It also lacked the narrative drive and style of Loveless's, and it is doubtful that it was as successful. But it provided additional first-hand accounts of suffering and injustice and added ammunition to the

---

[2] On which I have also drawn in preceding chapters.

Radical and Chartist cause. It was issued as *A Narrative of the Sufferings of Jas. Loveless, Jas. Brine and Thomas and John Standfield. Four of the Dorchester Labourers. Displaying the Horrors of Transportation. Written by Themselves. With a Brief Description of New South Wales by George Loveless*. The notes on New South Wales were added, it was explained, because of the success of Loveless's notes on Van Diemen's Land in *The Victims of Whiggery*. The explanation was presumably considered necessary because George Loveless's qualifications to write about New South Wales were not obvious. They were probably added as publishing bait. *The Victims of Whiggery* had been a success, George Loveless's name was known and with its inclusion on the new pamphlet more people would be induced to buy. As further bait the pamphlet was advertised by its most eye-catching words, namely *Horrors of Transportation*.

The Victims of Whiggery was not the only pamphlet George Loveless had printed. In February 1838, while still living in Tolpuddle, he also had published *The Church Shown Up*. This was a reply to a direct attack on him by a Church of England vicar, the Reverend Henry Walter. However uncomfortable the atmosphere may have been in Tolpuddle, Loveless had resumed his preaching as a Methodist layman and doubtless the word of God was mingled with the experiences of George Loveless. At one point he visited the village of Haselbury Bryant (now spelt Hazelbury Bryan), where the Reverend Walter heard him speaking and as a result of the speech launched his attack. Loveless's reply, *The Church Shown Up*, is worthy of examination for several reasons. It demonstrates that Loveless was a writer manqué, that he had a command of words and an urge to explain and reform by verbal attack.[3] The content of *The*

---

[3] On the subject of whether he actually wrote the pamphlet, which has been queried, my opinion is that he did. He may well have received editorial assistance, but if he did not write *The Church Shown Up* neither did he write *The Victims of Whiggery*, for the style is consistent.

Church Shown Up seems to be the essence of George Loveless. It is more passionate in tone than *The Victims of Whiggery* and it shows how completely Loveless believed in, and drew his strength from, Methodism.

The Church he showed up was the Church of England. Catholicism was outside Loveless's range. Indirectly, at the beginning of the pamphlet, he attacked Catholicism when he accused the Church of proclaiming the vanity of worldly goods for centuries while amassing wealth itself, of teaching peace while perpetrating the most savage wars, of claiming to possess the key of knowledge and locking up the human mind. He had no direct knowledge of the workings of the Catholic Church whereas he had of the Church of England. (Doctor Warren of Tolpuddle was surely as much in his mind as the Vicar of Haselbury Bryant when he wrote the pamphlet.) Inasmuch as Loveless directly regarded Catholics it was with a degree of sympathy, for they too had suffered from the restrictive practices and discriminations of the Church of England. He took the Anglican argument that the Church of Rome was the mother of harlots and asked what then were her daughters, specifically the Church of England, but prostitutes? His main attack was on the Church of England as a State religion. He confused the issue by asking: Was religion first established in pomp and mummery? Was an unbaptized child, were infidels, less human beings, less children in the sight of God? For a dislike of pomp and mummery, and a concentration on individual worth in the sight of God, in opposition to other Christian religions, not just the Church of England, were part of Methodist belief. But he then returned to the attack on that Church and its vicars. They were part of the framework of the State, owing their first allegiance not to God but to the State, thereby propping up the rottenness of the State, oblivious of the practical and spiritual needs of their flocks. Their perpetual cry that the Church was in danger surprised him not, because their Church was of the State and had forgotten its God. Moreover, what intelligent person would wish to join a Church that was in perpetual danger? Then he came to chapter and verse, namely Church of England clergymen opposed to all measures of reform, notably the 1832 Reform Bill when their record had been disgraceful. He ended on a political note. The poor were rapidly becoming their own teachers. They could see that labour was the source of wealth, that all men were born naturally free, that all had 'an unalienable right to receive sufficient maintenance from the land that gave them birth'.

For a poor Dorsetshire labourer the lines of the arguments were well marshalled. Above all they showed the God in whom Loveless believed, Who had sustained him in his years of trial. He was a fair, just God, concerned for every individual who cared to search for Him directly, without intermediaries, without pomp and circumstance. He was a hard God to find, but once you discovered Him He was the perpetual anchor. He was the God of the English Dissenters. One final comment on both pamphlets – they demonstrate how greatly Loveless had responded to the radical side of the Methodist coin. The demonstration is unconscious, the response inherent in Loveless's character. What emerges from both *The Victims of Whiggery* and *The Church Shown Up* is how very much Loveless did not know his place. He was a human being, with a good brain and a strong character, both of which he used un-selfconsciously and without regard for hierarchic ladders.

The five men's last connection with Tolpuddle occurred in the middle of November 1838, after they had left the area. By the end of 1838 the Chartist agitation was in full swing. The 'People's Charter' with its famous Six Points – Manhood Suffrage; Voting by secret ballot; Payment of M.P.s; Annual Parliaments; Abolition of Property Qualifications for M.P.s; Equal electoral districts – had been drafted.[4] Meetings to demand the implementation of the Six Points were being organized and held throughout the country. In November one was held on Charlton Down near Blandford, only a few miles from Tolpuddle. Placards were posted in the area announcing the meeting and stating that Robert Hartwell, the secretary of the London Dorchester Committee, would attend. There was also, to quote the *Dorset County Chronicle*, 'an accompanying placard, signed by George Loveless, one of the returned convicts, calling on his labourers to join the Working Men's Association'. In the event Robert Hartwell did not appear, neither did George Loveless, but John Standfield did. The meeting, again according to the *Dorset County Chronicle*, was badly attended, 'the number at any period could barely have exceeded 1,500'. The Radicals put the figures much higher, and the Radicals also spoke of intimidation by local farmers and landlords who tried to prevent the labourers from attending. The *Dorset County Chronicle* further recorded that 'the speechifying was of the usual ranting incendiary description'. The ranting included one speech in which it was said that the labourers stood in fear of the farmers, and their only hope for the future lay in uniting to obtain political justice which would, in due course, bring them practical justice, although the speaker stressed this must be done by bringing moral pressure to bear, not by the use of physical power. He also noted the current wages in Dorset, which were still around seven shillings a week, in comparison with the Queen Mother who had recently complained that £20,000 was not sufficient for a single lady to live upon. Another speaker said that he would now point out Standfield (one assumes it was John, not Thomas), whereupon 'Standfield stood on the rail of the waggon,

[4] The indefatigable Francis Place laid claims to drafting the Six Points but William Lovett's claims are stronger. The Six Points were based on an original four drafted by Feargus O'Connor.

received three cheers, and again sat down'. Then the speaker continued, 'The bloody Whigs had sent that good man across the seas, but in three years they [the people] had him back again; and had done more in giving him and the others a freehold farm each.' Among the resolutions taken was one to support the aims of the People's Charter, and another which said, 'That, in the opinion of this meeting, Mr George Loveless, late of Tolpuddle, is the most fit and proper person to represent the working men of Dorset in the forthcoming General Convention of the Industrious Classes.' This referred to the Chartist Convention in London which was to be held in February 1839, on the lines of the early assemblies of the French Revolution and intended as a direct challenge to Parliament. It did not work out that way, though why it failed is not within the scope of this book. Briefly English legality and dissension within the Chartist ranks between the advocates of direct action and moral pressure played their part. In any case, although elected as the Dorset delegate, George Loveless did not attend.

The *Dorset County Chronicle* had a leader on the Blandford meeting in which it said, 'We need not make an observation on the speeches delivered. Their violent, seditious, and mendacious character needs no comment.' The leader also asked, revealingly, why Messrs. Hartwell and Company should interest themselves in the conditions of Dorsetshire Labourers *unless they were paid to do so*? A genuine reforming zeal, a sincere belief that men and women were entitled to some basic rights, were beyond the *Chronicle*'s comprehension. It was in connection with this meeting that James Frampton's name entered the records once again when he forwarded a copy of the *Chronicle*'s report to the Home Office. He also stated that a further meeting had been held in Tolpuddle itself which was 'attended by a considerable number of persons' and that the situation was again grave and fraught with dangers. The comment written in the margin of his letter by somebody at the Home Office was, 'All that can be done at the moment is for the magistrates to be watchful.' Doubtless Frampton continued to be most watchful. However, five of the men who had given him the greatest cause for anxiety had left the area. There is no record of their again visiting Tolpuddle which, but for the combination of character and fate, they might never have left and which but for them would have remained simply the name of a Dorset village known only in the area.

17: 'They that Sow in Tears Shall Reap in Joy'

The Dorchester Labourers' Farm Tribute was a success, although the speaker at the Blandford meeting was not strictly accurate in saying that a freehold had been bought on a farm for the men. However, sufficient money was contributed to put a large deposit on leaseholds of seven years on two farms. They were in the county of Essex, near to London, but far from Dorset. One was Fenners Farm with forty-three acres in the village of Tilegate Green, High Laver, a reasonable-sized community of nearly a hundred houses and just under five hundred inhabitants. The other was New House Farm with eighty acres in the village of Greensted, a smaller-sized community comprising only twenty-nine houses and 150 inhabitants. The farms were about five miles apart in good rich farming land and the men and their families presumably decided who should live there. In the event the Standfields with their six children, including John, moved into the smaller Fenners Farm, while the two Lovelesses and their families, and young James Brine moved into the larger New House Farm. The London Dorchester Committee also provided them with the necessary capital to stock the farms.

By August 1838 they were installed in their new homes, which as the fund was only opened in May, indicates how quickly and generously the public responded to the call to compensate them. All seemed set fair for a happy life in England. Right and justice had not only triumphed, but the sufferers in their cause were actually and materially benefiting. The large timbered New House Farm, with its comparatively spacious rooms, was a far cry from the cramped cottages of Tolpuddle, and eighty acres of land to work yourself was a different matter from toiling all day for a master. The same was true for the Standfields at Fenners

Farm. In June 1839, the bonds between the families were further cemented when Elizabeth Standfield married James Brine at Greensted's charming wooden parish church. The happy occasion was witnessed by John, Susan and Charity Standfield and Brine's younger brother, Joseph, who had come to live at New House Farm. Brine was able to describe himself as a farmer, which was a considerable step up the social scale from an agricultural labourer, and the final vindication for a transported convict.

The men continued to uphold the view that George Loveless had expressed in *The Victims of Whiggery*, namely that he had returned from his bondage in Van Diemen's Land with his beliefs and principles not weakened but strengthened. As has been noted, he supported the Chartist upsurge in Dorset and was nominated as the delegate for the Blandford district to the National Convention. The reason he did not attend was the pressure of work on the Essex farm, but as he now lived there his nomination for Dorset was more symbolic than actual, the imprimatur from a renowned victim of Whiggery whose pamphlets were freely and frequently quoted at Chartist meetings. The families kept in touch with the London Dorchester Committee for as long as it existed and in Essex they formed their own Chartist association whose meetings were held in New House Farm. When the response proved large, the meetings moved into the spacious barn in the field adjoining the house. Delegates from other Essex and Hertfordshire villages, such as Waltham Abbey, Epping, Harlow, Hatfield and Broad Oak, attended. As New House Farm was the centre of this activity it is reasonable to assume that, as before, George Loveless was the driving force.

Their activities, as before, brought them to the notice of the Essex hierarchy who reacted in much the same way as had the Dorset establishment, though with less firmness, there being no Frampton amongst them. The Vicar of Greensted, the Reverend Philip Ray, preached a sermon in which he strenuously objected to a group of convicts being brought into his parish. He also wrote to the magistrates at Chelmsford and to the Lord-Lieutenant of Essex complaining about the Chartists who were invading his parish. In Ray's defence it should be noted that he was a most energetic parish priest, in the days when many Church of England vicars tended to be lethargic in so far as the needs of their flock were concerned. It was also during his tenure of the living that the parish church (which lays claim to be the oldest wooden church in Europe dating back to A.D. 845 but which had fallen into disrepair) was carefully and lovingly restored. Ray's reaction was merely typical. Chartism was threatening the whole country, the foundations of decent society were again tottering, and paternal, beneficial order where everybody knew his proper place must be restored. The introduction of ex-convicts into the calm and peace of the Essex countryside was not likely to produce the desired effect. Ray was by no means alone in his fears and indignation. The Chartist activities of the five ex-Tolpuddle families and the Essex counter-reation refocused metropolitan attention upon them.

In mid-December 1839 the *Morning Post* ran a lengthy article which started with a résumé of the just punishment meted out by Mr Baron Williams, 'a Judge whose liberalism had been the cause of his elevation to the Bench', to the Dorchester Labourers. It attacked Lord Melbourne's 'squeezable and squeezed' administration for granting the pardons, whereby 'the cause of Radicalism and unlawful oaths had gained a splendid victory over social order'. It outlined the 'extraordinary lengths' to which the welcome home, organized by the Radicals and backed by Lord John Russell himself, had been taken, namely in buying the men farms in Essex. It then asked, 'what was the effect of this Ministerial counter-colonization from Botany Bay to the rural parishes of Essex?' With the answer to this question it came to the nub of its article – Chartism was rife in Essex. 'The hitherto quiet and well-conducted population of these parishes' had been stirred into agitation and ill-conducted meetings by the advent of the Dorchester Labourers. To a degree, they probably had. 'Quiet and well-conducted' can be interpreted as demoralized and apathetic, and in need of a George Loveless to prod them into action. But Chartism was a nation-wide movement, sweeping through the country like a bush fire, fanned both by poverty and spreading education into the realization that politics was power, that without political rights the improvement of economic conditions (which was what most Chartists were basically interested in) would not be effected. It could have taken hold in the rural calm of Essex with or without the Tolpuddle men.

However, this was not the opinion of 'a conservative magistrate for the county of Essex', nor of the Vicar of High Rooding (a nearby parish). At the end of December, the *Morning Post* published a long, indignant letter from the conservative magistrate headed *Chartism in Essex*, in which were incorporated his views and those of the vicar. The Chartist poison was not being widely diffused among the labourers of Essex, as the *Post*'s earlier article had inferred. Their labourers were honest peasantry who knew that 'those who complain without cause will soon have cause to complain; that no one is to be entrusted with power in the guidance of others or can command respect, who has not first learned to obey'. The eyes of the honest Essex peasantry were opened to 'the pernicious designs of evil-minded fomenters of sedition' and were aware of 'the empty, subtle boasts of "patriotism, freedom and liberty".' It was true that 'those little pets of my little Lord John [The Dorchester Labourers]' were resident in the vicinity, and that they had tried to stir the honest peasantry into agitation. But it was also true that 'those firebrands, the dreaded Dorchester

Labourers, are four poor ignorant creatures, who literally do not even know how to plough the land they occupy'. The idea of their succeeding in rousing the happy, contented Essex peasantry was risible. Would the *Morning Post* be so kind as to make these facts known to its readers so that they would realize that Essex remained the loyal county it always had been?

With reference to the four ignorant creatures mentioned by the conservative magistrate, which one he did not consider to be a firebrand is open to speculation. Thomas Standfield, too old and out of the fray? Young James Brine, not nominally part of the caucus? That they literally did not know how to plough their land was a surprising statement. They had been farm workers all their lives and George Loveless's trade was that of a ploughman – there were earlier references to his being the best ploughman in the Tolpuddle area. What the conservative magistrate surely meant was that four (or five) farm labourers could not possibly know how to run a farm, because all such creatures were ignorant and lacking in those qualities which were his by tradition and birth, and which gave him the knowledge of how to run his farm. The local paper, the *Essex Standard*, also printed the articles and letters. Thus, once more, for doing what they thought was right and just, the Lovelesses, the Standfields and Brine were, in the words of the magistrate, 'marked men'.

There remains, as always, Hammett. In September 1837 he was on an assault charge at Windsor. The next time he was heard of was in February 1839, when he presented a memorial.

To His Excellency Sir George Gipps, Governor of New South Wales and the dependencies, etcetera, etcetera – The Humble Memorial of James Hammett sheweth that your memorialist is one of the Dorchester Labourers tried in 1834 and arrived in this Colony by the Ship

Surrey under sentence of transportation. That Memorialist received his pardon in 1836 with other labourers sent here under the same circumstances who obtained a free passage to England. That Your Memorialist would have obtained the same indulgence but he was unfortunately detained at Windsor charged with an assault when the other labourers left the Colony.

That Your Memorialist is now anxious to return to his native land and he trusts Your Excellency will take his case into your humane consideration and order your Memorialist a passage to England which he unfortunately lost on the former occasion and your Memorialist in duty bound will ever pray.

(Signed) James Hammett.

On February 20th, 1839, Sir George Gipps was presented with Hammett's memorial and an accompanying memorandum which read, 'A passage to England is authorized by the Secretary of State Despatch No. 131, March 24th, 1836, to be provided for this applicant and charged to the funds applicable to the Convict Services. Four other prisoners alluded to in the same despatch have been already found a passage at an expense of £25 each. See 37/7954.' Underneath Sir George Gipps wrote, 'Let the Commissary General (or the proper office) be authorized to procure him a passage. G. G. Feb 21st.' The whole memorandum was marked *Urgent*. On February 23rd the Colonial Secretary wrote to the Deputy Commissary General transmitting Gipps' orders. On February 27th the Commissarent Office replied, informing the Colonial Secretary that 'In compliance with the directions of His Excellency the Governor contained in your letter of the 23rd instant, the Prisoner named in the margin (James Hammett) has been provided with a passage for England in the ship "Eweretta" under an agreement which I had already made for the conveyance of invalids. She is expected to sail on the 8th proximo.' On March 2nd a note was written in the margin of this letter – 'Inform the Pl. Supt. of Convicts' – and on March 8th Hammett duly sailed from New South Wales on the *Eweretta*.

Once Hammett had submitted his memorial, the matter of his passage was treated with urgency, but the surviving correspondence does not clarify what happened to him in the eighteen months between being 'unfortunately detained at Windsor charged with an assault' in September 1837 and the submission of the memorial in February 1839. The most likely explanation is that he was convicted on the assault charge – charges against convicts were rarely dismissed as we have already noted, and Hammett was not George Loveless, able to talk his way out of difficulties – and spent the eighteen months sentenced to some form of secondary punishment (such as working on a road gang). February 1839 was, therefore, the first opportunity he had to present his application for the free passage. The wording, 'Your Memorialist is *now* anxious to return to his native land', would seem to indicate that previously he had been unable to show such anxiety. On receipt of the memorial and the information about the granting of the free passage, Sir George Gipps presumably decided that the lapse of time, over three years, was too great to instigate enquiries into Hammett's conduct during the eighteen months. Or perhaps the fact that Hammett was one of the Dorchester Unionists was sufficient reason to expedite the matter without further enquiry, their case being a hornets' nest it was wiser not to reagitate. Whether if Hammett had not presented his memorial, any government officer would eventually have examined the past despatches, discovered that the free passage awarded to James Hammett in 1836 had not been implemented, and been sufficiently curious to ascertain why not, remains an interesting but unanswerable point.

By August 1839 Hammett was back in England, five

years and four months after he had been transported, three years and five months after his free pardon and free passage had been granted. His wife and child had presumably remained in Tolpuddle – there is no mention of them on the farms in Essex – with the London Dorchester Committee continuing to supply them with a weekly income. Reunited with his wife, Harriet, and his son, now six years old, Hammett did not return to Tolpuddle but went to live with the Lovelesses and Brines at New House Farm, Greensted.

On October 8th, 1839, the London Dorchester Committee organized the final 'Farewell Benefit' for the Dorchester Unionists, although the reason for this benefit was not solely in order to honour the last man home, James Hammett. Prior announcements in *Cleave's Penny Gazette* explained what the main reason was: the benefit was necessary because a further sum was urgently required to complete the purchase of the leaseholds on New House and Fenners Farms. Previous contributions to the Dorchester Labourers' Farm Tribute had been heart-warming and generous but they had not been quite sufficient. Friends of the London Dorchester Committee, trade societies and the public in general were, therefore, begged to buy tickets (dress boxes 2s., boxes 1s. 6d., gallery 6d.) in order that the money previously subscribed might not be rendered useless. According to *Cleave's Penny Gazette* the money still required amounted to £100; according to the *Globe* it was the higher sum of £160. The benefit was to be held in the Victoria Theatre[1] which 'during the recess had been splendidly fitted up and embellished, with every attention to comfort and convenience', and the audience was promised a favourite farce, an historical play and a variety of other entertainments, in addition to the presence of the Dorchester Labourers.

[1] Later to become famous as 'the Old Vic'.

On the night of Tuesday, October 8th, the public responded and, as *Cleave's Penny Gazette* recorded, 'the house was literally crowded to suffocation'. The audience watched an historical play *King Harold*, followed by a favourite farce *Family Friends* and an operatic drama *The Lass O' Gowrie*. A comic song was then announced but the singer did not appear and the audience started to grow restive, so the Dorchester Labourers were quickly brought on to the stage to be greeted, again according to *Cleave's Penny Gazette*, 'by one of the most enthusiastic bursts of approbation ever heard within these walls since the memorable appearance of Macready as "Virginius".' In fact, only four of them appeared, Hammett, George Loveless, James Brine and John Standfield, the other two sending a letter which was read, apologizing for their absence and explaining it was due to the pressure of work on the Essex farms. George Loveless was first introduced to the audience, then 'a thin, pale-looking individual stepped forward' who had obviously not recovered from 'the base and brutal treatment' meted out to him in New South Wales. The thin, pale Hammett was so overcome by the occasion that he could hardly voice his thanks to the audience, and even George Loveless was so overwhelmed by the reception that he gave vent to his feelings in a flood of tears. It was left to John Standfield to thank everybody for the support given since he, his friends and their families had fallen into 'the claws of the oppressors'. Young John then embarked upon the subject of unionism and of the people joining together, peaceably of course, to obtain their just rewards. Immediately there were loud noises offstage whereupon, as *Cleave's Penny Gazette* further reported, Loveless tapped John Standfield on the shoulder 'as much as to say – "don't say any more".' The Chairman also whispered something to young Standfield and he stepped backwards just in time to save himself from being crushed by 'the heavy curtain which descended with great velocity, to the astonishment and indignation of all present'. However, despite the theatre management's lack of enthusiasm for Radical politics on their boards, the occasion was a success. Hammett was given his public welcome home and the vital £100 to complete the leasehold purchase on the farms was raised.

Thereby, the task of the London Dorchester Committee was completed. Just over five years from the date of its inception the committee had accomplished all it had set out to do. It had sustained the wives, morally and financially, during the long years of separation. It had maintained pressure throughout the fight for full free pardons. It had organized the welcoming committee and dinners which made the men realize they had not suffered in vain and been forgotten. It had raised the means of compensating them for their suffering. If by so doing it had also furthered the Radical cause that was a fair exchange, one which the men in any case upheld. Without doubt the members of the London Dorchester Committee were motivated by feelings of the injustice done to the men and their families, apart from the wider context of Radicalism. They deserve praise, for five years is a long time to maintain pressure and retain interest.

After this final public welcome, Hammett returned to New House Farm with the Lovelesses and Brine who by now had a baby daughter, Mary Jane, born at the end of December 1839 (the result of some fine summer evenings in the Essex countryside, or a very premature birth). By modern standards the farm must have been crowded, with four separate families and their children, and James Brine's brother, and only three bedrooms, but they were good-sized rooms and it was probably due to personal temperament, rather than an overcrowding unremarkable for the 1830s and '40s, that Hammett left New House Farm and Essex. The Standfields and Lovelesses had long been a close-knit clan into which James Brine fitted with ease.

Hammett had increasingly become the odd man out as events unfolded. By 1841 he was back in Tolpuddle where he stayed for the rest of his life, mainly silent and anonymous. The London Dorchester Committee may have asked him to record his experiences, as they had the other five men. If they did, he refused. The 1841 census returns list Hammett as an 'agricultural labourer' but he did not remain long in his old line of employment. As in Essex Hammett found himself a marked man, an ex-convict trade unionist who had caused so much trouble in the past. Fortunately he was given employment by a wealthy builder who was a member of another Nonconformist sect that had suffered at the hands of the Anglican squirarchy, the Congregationalists. Working as a builder's labourer for a sympathetic employer, Hammett was able to slip from the limelight he had never courted.

By his first wife Hammett had four more children, two girls and two boys, but in 1860, when he was nearly fifty, Harriet died and two years later he remarried. The second marriage produced a tragically short-lived baby girl (infant mortality remained high) and another son named William, so he had at least seven children. In 1870, however, his second wife died and the same year, an unhappy one for him, his son James died, aged only eighteen. Later he married for a third time, although in what year is not certain. The first two marriages are recorded in the Tolpuddle parish register but the third is not (he could, of course, have married in another parish). The evidence for his third marriage comes from two sources, a local genealogist and William Hammett, the son of the second marriage. The local genealogist informed me that some years ago he had met 'a very difficult individual in Tolpuddle' who claimed relationship to James Hammett and who insisted that James had married three times. In 1934, the centenary year of 'The Tolpuddle Martyrs', William Hammett was still alive and he told several reporters that his father had 'married a second time – my mother. When she died he married again – a third time.'

In the year 1875 Hammett had one last brief exposure to the limelight. By that year there had been a resurgence of agricultural unionism, but the movement was fighting for its existence and it was decided that a presentation to one of the earliest of agricultural unionists would be a good idea. The occasion would remind the country of the forces that had always been ranged against agricultural unionism and to what lengths they had gone in the Tolpuddle case. It would also honour the man who had suffered for the cause, if belatedly. As the *Bee-Hive* 'the people's paper', reported, 'On Wednesday last, March 17th, being the forty-first anniversary of the conviction of the Dorchester-Labourers, a great demonstration was held in a large tent, capable of holding 2,000 persons, erected at Briantspuddle, the occasion being the presentation of a testimonial to James Hammett, one of the men transported.'

In the afternoon of March 17th local unionists gathered in Briantspuddle, a village about a mile and a half from Tolpuddle, 'wearing the blue ribbon of the union', and marched through the village with a band at their head, to the large tent where tea was served. At six o'clock labourers who had finished their day's work swelled the meeting, and Hammett was introduced. The *Dorset County Express* reported that 'there was no self-consciousness of heroism. He was a simple-minded, plain old man who had done his duty according to his light in the past, and now rather shrank from the prominence in which he was placed.' In one of the first speeches 'the singular fact' that Hammett was not present when the fatal oath was administered in December 1833 was mentioned, and it was on this occasion that Hammett himself said that it was his brother John who had been present. Brother John, who was also at the Briantspuddle ceremony, confirmed this. A hymn, especially composed for the occasion, was then sung, of which the following are a few lines:

No brute hooves on our union tread
No evil laws our free speech mar.

We meet today to pay our grateful debt
To those who bore the felon's lot
Their unjust judges names forgot
The memory of the vile shall rot.

No stone may mark the exiles' graves
In distant lands beyond the sea
Who wore the clanking chains of slaves
Because they struggled to be free.

The chairman spoke of the 'necessity for a union of agricultural labourers to place them on equal terms with the employers when making bargains for service'. He gave a résumé of the Tolpuddle case, which had been one of the first attempts at performing this necessity, and hoped that celebrating this anniversary would be 'the beginning of a new era in Dorset', and that henceforward 'all working men would do their duty to one another', i.e. join the union. The next speaker said they were gathered 'to do honour to the stainless memory of George Loveless, and to recognize the worth of James Hammett', which was a somewhat back-handed compliment to Hammett. He further said that bad men had always put good men in prison and that agriculture had always had its martyrs, such as Wat Tyler and Jack Cade, not to mention those of Tolpuddle. Like the 'stainless' George Loveless before him, the speaker then attacked the Anglican clergy who 'by their conduct were alienating the people from the church and from religion itself'. He concluded by exhorting the labouring man to remember that benefits had been effected,

251

that they were reaping what James Hammett had sown in suffering, which applied to non-unionists as much as unionists, but that the situation would only continue to improve by a show of solidarity. At this juncture the Vicar of Dorchester, who was in the crowd, was asked to say a few words and briefly he expressed his sympathy with the labourers' present conditions.

The final speaker was Mr Cox who had come from Belper in Derbyshire. He resurrected the matter of the Dorchester Unionists having only been released because of the pressure on the Orange Lodges, and also spoke of the need for the county franchise. Until the agricultural workers obtained the right to vote, he urged them to exercise all the influence they could as churchmen, by attending parish and vestry meetings where decisions vital to their interests were taken. It was Mr Cox who actually presented the testimonial to James Hammett, in the absence of Joseph Arch, the Agricultural Labourers' Union leader, who had been unfortunately detained at a meeting in Norfolk. The testimonial was 'a beautifully illuminated address', to quote the *Bee-Hive*, and it read thus:

Dear Sir, We the members and friends of the National Agricultural Labourers' Union are desirous of testifying to the esteem and regard in which you are held by us as one of the Early Martyrs to the cause of Unionism. The blood of the martyrs is the seed of the church, and we all feel that the cause of the Union, the cause of true humanity, was hastened and gained strength by the outrageous penalties inflicted upon you and your comrades. We know full well in this country that the days of oppression are not yet over, and that we have many battles to wage in the future.

Reference was then made to the current evictions of tenants by the farmers, but it was hoped that Hammett would live to see the blessings of agricultural unionism. It concluded:

We are confident that your memory, when it shall please the Great Father in the Perfecting of His Plans to call you to Himself, will live in the hearts of our children's children, not as a Felon, but as Noble Pioneer of the righteous movement in which we are one and all toiling.

Mr Cox also presented Hammett with a purse of gold sovereigns and a gold watch on which was inscribed 'Presented to Mr James Hammett of Tolpuddle, March 17th, 1875, by the members and friends of the labourers' union in Dorset as a mark of great respect for his patience and courage while undergoing a sentence of seven years' transportation for belonging to a labourers' union in Dorset in 1834.' The sovereigns were given, Mr Cox said, because Hammett, unlike his friends, had not benefited from the money subscribed to the Dorchester Labourers' Farm Tribute.

Hammett then rose to express his thanks and said, 'It appears a great deal better than what I got 41 years ago.' It was during this speech that he related his experiences on his arrival in Sydney, and of finding his solitary way to Woodlands. He concluded by showing the watch to the audience and asking, 'Isn't that better than having seven years put on you, and that for a wrong cause? We only tried to do good to one another, the same as you're doing now.' According to the *Dorset County Express*, the old man was then greatly cheered, and a resolution for county franchise was proposed and carried. James Hammett retired to live the rest of his days in anonymity.

Sadly, he died in the Dorchester Workhouse in 1891, nearly blind, so he must have outlived his third wife, too. His relations always stated that he refused to be a burden on them and insisted on going into the Poor Law Institution. A Methodist Minister who, in the 1950s, was stationed in Dorchester, was of the opinion that this fitted Hammett's character. Always deeply interested in the

Tolpuddle men, the Minister made friends with Hammett's then few surviving direct descendants, particularly with Mrs Roberts, a grand-daughter who remembered the old man well. Mrs Roberts believed her grandfather to have been 'a quiet saint'. During the 1934 centenary celebrations, there were several descendants in evidence. From them the most quotable explanation for Hammett's silence about his years in New South Wales was obtained, and employed both in the T.U.C.'s book, *The Martyrs of Tolpuddle*, and Miles Malleson's play *Six Men of Dorset*. This sole explanation attributed by them to James Hammett was, 'If you'd been sold like a sheep for £1 would *you* want to talk about it?' The remark would also seem to fit a revised version of Hammett's character, though surprisingly it was not supplied to the press in 1934, eager as reporters were to extract anecdotes about father or grandfather or great-uncle Hammett's days as a pioneer of trade unionism and as a transported convict. Information then gleaned by the press was negligible. It consisted of the story of James accepting responsibility for brother John because the latter's wife was pregnant, and additional stories about James having never been officially informed of his free pardon, but one day reading about it in a newspaper as he languished in the New South Wales hinterland. In which newspaper he was likely to have read about his pardon in 1839, three years after it had been granted, and how he set about obtaining his passage home was not explained. Of the real reason he failed to leave the colony with the others, because he was on the assault charge at Windsor, no mention whatsoever was made. The silent Hammett of legend, like all good legends, had a base in reality, because obviously he had not discussed his convict years with his family. His son William, a child of his second marriage, was alive in 1934.

Samuel, one of the sons of his first marriage, was dead by the centenary year but he had served in the British

Army. It was a Victorian habit to present soldiers with literature to improve their minds, and Samuel Hammett was presented with a small book, which is extant, entitled *Morning Light – A Waking Thought for Every Day of the Year* published by the Society for Promoting Christian Knowledge. On the fly-leaf is written 'No. 40 Private Samuel Hammett. A Company 39th Regt Nougong Bundeland. East India.' On the same page in the same hand is written, 'Mr S. Hammett, Tolpuddle, Dorset.' Beneath this, in a different hand, is pencilled 'James Hammett' in what looks like Hammett's handwriting.

If Hammett read the waking thoughts for the most vital days of his life he should have been impressed by their appropriateness. The waking thought for February 24th, the day of his arrest, was, 'Eye hath not seen, nor ear heard . . . the things which God hath prepared for them that love Him (1 Cor. ii 9)'; for March 17th, the day of the trial, it was, 'They that sow in tears, shall reap in joy (Psalms cxxvi 5)'; for March 19th, the day of the sentence, 'Watch thou in all things. Endure inflictions (2 Timothy iv 5)'; for April 11th, the day he sailed for New South Wales, 'He is my refuge and my fortress; my God, in Him will I trust (Psalms xci 2)'; and for August 17th, the day of his return to England, 'Unto the godly there ariseth up light in the darkness (Psalms cxii 4).'

The evidence of family affection lies in what Samuel Hammett personally wrote inside the small book, and which can serve as our epitaph too:

In affectionate Remembrance of James Hammett who died November 21st, 1891, aged 79 years, and was this day interred in Tolpuddle Church Yeard [*sic*] with family's kind regards. Tolpuddle November 24th, 1891.

Adieu dear Father short farewell
What thou hast suffered none can tell

But thou art gone to endless rest
To be ever with the bless [*sic*]
How much he suffered Heven [*sic*] knows
But now he's free'd from all his woes
He's passed through Jordon [*sic*] swelling floods
And landed safe with Christ his God.

18: 'The Land Big Enough to Make a Lark a Sod'

While James Hammett returned to his native Tolpuddle, the other five men and their families remained in Essex. George and Betsy Loveless had two more daughters, Louisa born in 1839 and Sina in 1840. James and Elizabeth Brine also had another two daughters, Susannah Standfield born on Christmas Day 1841 and Charity in January, 1844. During this period the only unmarried member of the group, John Standfield, went to the altar. His bride was Elizabeth Thurgood and their first child was born in November 1841, and their second son who rejoiced in the name of Theophilus Washington, in 1843. For all the men and their families the scars appeared to have healed, but by the beginning of 1844 the Lovelesses and Brines had come to a major decision – to emigrate to Canada.

One good reason for the decision to abandon farming in Essex could have been the great depression that earned the 1840s the title 'the Hungry Forties'. Nowhere did the economic recession bite more deeply than in East Anglia, and 1844 in particular was a year of maximum despair among agricultural workers in that area, with echoes of the 'Swing' riots in widespread rick-burning and general arson. The centre of the disturbances was Suffolk, but the ripples spread southwards into Essex. Apart from the difficulties of trying to make a living in such a harsh economic climate, to support six families off the depressed land, none of them was a violent revolutionary. Their leader, George Loveless, most definitely was not. It was the legitimate, democratic, constitutional means of trade unionism that Loveless backed, not the desperation of Swing-type anarchy. It was the moral, not physical, force legions of Chartism that he supported. They had tried the ostensibly legal method of trade unionism and where had that landed them? As chained felons, wrenched from their loved ones, transported to the other end of the world and deprived of all their rights. Although Chartism was to be given a fresh impetus in the European revolutionary year of 1848, in 1844 the movement was at a low ebb, riven by bitter internal disputes and power struggles, the high hopes and dreams of 1838 apparently dying, if not dead. Loveless, indeed all of them except Hammett, may therefore have seen no way forward in their native land.

They also decided that once they had emigrated, the past would become a blank. The vow of silence was confirmed by a nephew of James Brine who years later visited the men in Canada, and later still wrote a pamphlet entitled *Christian Songs* in which their experiences were briefly outlined. Nephew Brine said, 'They appear to have made a compact among themselves that their story should be kept locked in their own breasts.' He also said he was warned not to tell the younger children of their fathers' past, as they knew nothing of the arrests, trial or the years as convicts in Australasia. The compact of silence suggests another motive for the decision. The families had endured sufficient notoriety. Fighting for their own and other people's rights had led across the seas to the penal colonies, but it had not stopped there. It had led on to sermons being preached against them, to hostile articles in newspapers, to antagonism from the Essex hierarchy, to their being permanently 'marked men'. Wherever they went in England, even if they tried to court anonymity, it was certain that sooner or later they would be recognized. The solution to all their problems was to emigrate, to start afresh in a new country where nobody knew them.

The decision to emigrate, and to stay silent, was in a way a rebuttal of all they had previously stood and fought for, a negation of so much that George Loveless had said or written in *The Victims of Whiggery*. Although, demonstrably, all six men, and the wives who backed them to the hilt, possessed extraordinary qualities which impelled them to form their Society in Tolpuddle, basically they were ordinary people. None of them had sought the limelight; they had been unwillingly thrust into it and then trapped in its glare. By 1844 it was more of a glow than a glare, but it was a constant glow, causing them to live in the daily knowledge that they were at worst detested and reviled, at best misunderstood and feared, and that the glare could be switched back. Should any trade union activity or threat of riot occur in the vicinity of Greensted or High Laver, whether responsible or not, they would be thought the automatic ringleaders. They may have wearied of the struggle themselves – and who can blame them? To a degree they may have been motivated by the very human reaction of not wanting to forfeit what had been gained. This time, if anything went wrong they and their children stood to lose far more than before. Probably both decisions, to depart and to remain silent about the past, were taken as much for the children's sakes as for any other reason. John Standfield had, in 1834, written of the stigma which was attached to all the families' names. By 1844 they may have finally decided to remove that stigma. The closeness of the group and the manner in which they clung together over the years is indicative of their strong sense of family responsibility.

Once the decision had been reached – and one senses George Loveless's sober, earnest, logical reasoning behind it – Canada was the obvious country. Australia lagged far behind in the great emigration rush of the 1840s. Gold had not been discovered, officially anyway, although the early convicts had found some when they were opening up the country, but they were flogged or threatened with the penal settlements to keep them quiet. Without the lure of gold, the distance and cost deterred the majority of emigrants, most of whom scraped together their last pennies to find a new life. The Tolpuddle men were not as poor as the majority of emigrants, but they were hardly likely to choose Australia. That continent they had already visited. Canada was British (whether the French-Canadians liked or accepted the fact), was woefully underpopulated and clamoured for immigrants. By the 1840s communication between the old and new worlds was increasing in both volume and speed (Cunard opened the first regular Atlantic steam service in 1839). Agents with land to sell were touring Britain and painting the virtues and opportunities of Canada in glowing colours. The newspapers were filled with similar glittering advertisements expounding the wonders of the new world. For those who had insufficient money to buy land before sailing, the opportunities on arrival were pointed out. There was some State-aided emigration and under the terms of the 1834 Poor Law, parishes were enabled to provide assistance from the rates (not that many of them did). There were charitable organizations, giving aid to the poor but honest, and information such as 'Families should take bedding, blankets, sheets, pewter plates or wooden trenchers, knives, forks, spoons, metal cups and mugs, tea kettles and saucepans, working tools of all descriptions. *Clothing* – a fur cap, a warm great coat, a flushing jacket and trowsers, a duck frock and trowsers, a canvas frock and trowsers, two jersey frocks, four shirts, four pairs of stockings, three pairs of shoes, a bible and a prayer book.' But the majority of emigrants – and some eight hundred thousand left Britain for Canada between 1815 and 1850 – with the main rush in the 'Hungry Forties' – made their own way to the land of opportunity, with virtually no possessions and very little clothing. We can assume that the Tolpuddle men and their families made their own way. With their background and desire to wipe the slates clean, it was unlikely that they would apply to a charitable organization for assistance.

Having reached the decision to go to Canada, the next step was to obtain passages. From what we know of the families in general, and George Loveless in particular, it is reasonable to assume that they would not embark upon such a momentous venture without making as thorough preparation as possible beforehand, including the prior booking of their passages. This was not true of many unassisted emigrants, thousands of whom simply packed up and arrived at their port of departure, Liverpool being the main one, where they often had to wait weeks for a passage, thus spending their limited money before embarkation. A race of middle men quickly stepped in and amassed small fortunes by employing touts and runners who persuaded the desperate emigrants that they could obtain passages quickly, induced them to part with a deposit, and were then seen no more. (By the 1840s legislation had been introduced to counter this malpractice, but it was not working very effectively.) With or without a pre-booked passage, once on board the boat the emigrants' troubles were by no means ended. The captains were supposed to supply bread and water, though not all did, but the emigrants were expected to bring their own food. Having already spent or lost their money in obtaining a passage, many boarded without sufficient food and were consequently less able to resist the fevers that swept the ships. For, apart from not being chained, conditions were often as gruesome as on the convict ships. There was a large timber trade between Canada and Britain, and the owners put their boats to excellent use on the return journey by cramming them with emigrants. This they could do as the laws relating to passenger traffic were extremely lax. When hundreds of men, women and children were jammed into old ships built to carry timber; when many were already undernourished or indeed starving – which applied particularly to the Irish emigrants – before they boarded and had insufficient food to see them through the journey; when sanitation hardly existed – it was inevitable that disease should ensue. In the 1840s the mortality rate on the emigrant ships rose from 5 in every 1,000 to 55 in every 1,000, while the numbers of those arriving in Canada seriously ill rose from 1½ in every 1,000 to 60 in every 1,000. There were accounts of people being thrown overboard into the Atlantic 'one after t'other', and of numerous orphans arriving, their parents having died en route. In the Canadian Legislature in 1847, 'an unprecedented influx of emigrants from Great Britain and Ireland, in a state of destitution, starvation and disease, unparalleled in the history of the Province' was spoken of.

Two dates have been given, 1844 and 1846, as the year in which the families left England to undertake the hazards of the Atlantic crossing. The earlier year of 1844 is the generally accepted one, partly because it seemed probable that the families should depart before the leases on the farms expired (which they did in 1845), but also based on more concrete evidence. It has always been agreed that Charity Brine, James's third daughter, was born at New House Farm and that she was a babe-in-arms when the families emigrated. At the time of her death in 1935, her birth date was given by the Brine family, and reported in various newspapers, as January 28th, 1844. An old Brine family Bible shows that the next child, John Thomas, was born in 1845 in Canada. The 1851 census returns for Ontario confirm the birth dates, and the countries of birth. The census recorded 'Age next birthday', and Cherry (or Charity) Brine's was given as eight, John Thomas's as five. Charity, being born in January 1844, would have been eight in 1852. Her country of birth was given as England, John Thomas's as Canada. There is, therefore, documentary proof that the Brines left England in 1844. The legend within the Loveless family has always been that George and his eldest son, also called George, acted as trailblazers for the families, arriving in Hamilton, Ontario, in the spring of 1844. There is no documentary confirmation of this, as George Loveless had no more children after his arrival in Canada. But as the Brines definitely left England in 1844, it seemed reasonable to assume that the Lovelesses and Standfields did, too. This, to date, has been the assumption – that all the families emigrated together.

However, examination of the Standfield family tree, painstakingly compiled by descendants, showed that the third child of John and Elizabeth Standfield, a girl named Charity Madeline, was born on September 8th, 1845, at High Laver, Essex. The date, and her country of birth, was confirmed by the 1861 Ontario census returns in which her 'age next birthday' was given as sixteen, and her country of birth as England. Obviously, Charity Standfield could not have been born in England in 1845 if all the families had emigrated to Canada in 1844. But the Lovelesses and Brines lived at New House Farm, while the Standfields lived at Fenners Farm. The solution to the problem of the two dates given for the emigration year is that both 1844 and 1846 are correct, and that the families in fact emigrated separately. The Lovelesses and Brines came to the decision to leave England in 1844, giving up the lease on New House Farm before it expired (and the knowledge that it was due to expire assuredly prompted the initial discussions). For whatever reason (perhaps Thomas's age, as he was in his mid-fifties by the 1840s) the Standfields were not so certain about the decision to uproot. They must have renewed the lease on Fenners Farm and followed their friends to Canada two years later, probably on receipt of favourable reports on the land of opportunity.

Exactly where the advance guard of the Lovelesses and Brines landed in the New World is a question that cannot be answered with certainty. The only solution to that problem would be the discovery of their immigration papers, and to date they have not come to light. One fact is known, that George Loveless's youngest daughter, Sina, was a victim of the cruel passage across the Atlantic. Her death must have been a bitter blow to him and Betsy, devoted parents as they were. The popular belief is that the families landed in New York. From there they travelled westwards to Albany, then on the Erie Canal to Buffalo, from Buffalo, across Lake Erie to Port Stanley, finishing the journey to their destination of London, Ontario, by ox-cart. The Loveless family legend, which has George and George Junior acting as trailblazers, says they arrived in Hamilton, from where they walked overland to London, Ontario. How they got to Hamilton, the legend does not reveal. They could have followed the westward trail from New York as far as Buffalo, crossing the border into Canada and Hamilton either by portage round Niagara Falls or by stage coach. Or they could have landed in Quebec, as many Canadian-bound British emigrants did, and travelled up the St Lawrence River, using the early Lachine and other canals. But London, Ontario, was definitely their destination. London Town was then a small place, with a population of less than three thousand including the British garrison, serving as a centre for the scattered farms and hamlets of London Township. Again, exactly why they chose this area remains unknown. It could have been from literature obtained in England before they sailed, but it seems more likely that they knew somebody living there. There is an unsubstantiated version that George Loveless was acquainted with a man named Storey, already settled in London Township. There is substantiated evidence that a William Loveless, believed to have been a relation, had emigrated from Dorset in 1828 and settled in Scarborough to the east of Toronto; George may have kept in touch with William Loveless. By 1844 land around Scarborough had been sold, but in the London area it was still available. William Loveless may have advised George to make for London and apply for land in the Township.

The first existing record of George Loveless in the

London area dates back to 1847. Exactly what he did in the previous three years is not known, but by that year he had acquired sufficient money to purchase, on October 15th, from one Francis Walden a hundred-acre property in the south half of lot 11 in the 12th concession of London Township (land was divided into concessions and sub-divided into lots). Loveless paid £25 down, and he and Betsy were jointly given a mortgage of £125. This 12th concession was situated half a mile west of the hamlet of Bryanston and somewhat over twelve miles from the centre of London Town itself. Here, near Bryanston, George and Betsy Loveless and their children, in true pioneering fashion, built a log homestead that they could genuinely call their own (New House Farm had been leasehold, and provided by the London Dorchester Committee). James Loveless also apparently first settled in London Township. Records to prove this have not been discovered as he does not appear to have owned any land in Canada, but tradition says he settled in the area and it seems reasonable that the two brothers and their families should initially have wished to be close in a strange land.

However, James Brine went farther afield. From a practical point of view he may have been a strong advocate of the decision to emigrate: he had a growing family; he wanted his own home; and the difficulties of striking out on his own and obtaining one were far greater in England than in Canada. Having arrived in the London area, he, his wife and young family travelled by ox-cart into nearby Huron County where they are believed to have farmed first at Homesville, near Clinton. For this journey across the wild land of Ontario, and against the dangers of settling into a country supposedly populated by bears and Indians, James Brine was well prepared. Before he left England he purchased a formidable weapon with which to defend himself and his family – a brass-barrelled blunderbuss with a spring bayonet. The Brines were duly driven out from their first Canadian home, not by the anticipated bears or Indians, but by a plague of grasshoppers which totally destroyed their crops. Their second attempt at farming in Ontario was at Bayfield, also in Huron County. The later arrivals, the Standfields, migrated to the London area and their first recorded home was on lot 8 in the 11th concession of London Township, to the south of the land farmed by George Loveless but again not far from the hamlet of Bryanston.

During those early years in Canada, for their own sakes and their children's, it was as well that the men had decided upon their vow of silence and to wipe the slates clean. For the Upper Canada in which they settled was in many ways less liberal and more despotic than the England they had left. It was still suffering from the after-effects of the abortive 'Mackenzie Rebellion'. William Lyon Mackenzie was born in Dundee, Scotland, in 1795, emigrating in 1820 to York (rechristened Toronto in 1834). Upper Canada had mainly been colonized by the loyalists who had fled from the United States during and after the War of Independence. Its hard-line Toryism and loyalty to the British flag – 'The people of Upper Canada detest democracy; they revere the Constitutional Charter and are staunch in their allegiance to the King' – had been further strengthened by the 1812 war between the United States and Britain, and an influx of ex-army officers. It was into this Province of die-hard loyalism that Mackenzie arrived, a small excitable man, 'Five feet nothing and very like a baboon, but the O'Connell of Canada' and of whom it was said, 'You could trust him with your life, but not with your secret.'

Mackenzie soon became obsessed with the need for honest, democratic government in Upper Canada. To propagate his passionate feeling for the necessity of change, he started a newspaper whose editorials burned with radical views previously unheard in the Province. Later, inevitably, he moved directly into the political arena and was elected as an independent candidate to the Legislature. Several stormy years ensued, culminating in a bitter campaign in 1836 in which the newly appointed Governor of Upper Canada, Sir Francis Head, campaigned lustily for the ruling party on a straight King and Country issue against Mackenzie and his radical reformers, and won, Mackenzie himself losing his seat in the Assembly. By November 1837, the defeated if not depressed Mackenzie drew up a constitution on the American model which stopped just short of being an outright declaration of independence. He then proceeded to try to effect his constitution by gaining control of Upper Canada. However, his rebellion never really got off the ground, although with a different man at its head it could have succeeded. The elements of a tight, closed circle of government, denial of rights, general frustration and the wish for a greater independence from Britain were present. If Mackenzie was a personal tornado who generated excitement and stirred havoc in his path, he was not the man to lead a revolutionary coup. His head was always full of too many ideas, he shot off at too many tangents and failed to keep a clear objective in view. Most vitally, he hesitated at the moment of decision, when the legislative forces were unprepared. He thought of linking with Papineau and the French in Lower Canada (who had even more lists of grievances and were in even more rebellious mood than Mackenzie and his British Upper Canada). He considered taking possession of the arms dumps, but in the event he wasted a week, achieving nothing in particular. The government forces, once alerted to the danger, acted swiftly and strongly. Most of the rebels were arrested, although Mackenzie himself and a handful of others escaped over the border into the United States. Throughout 1838 there were spasmodic border clashes between the supporters of the rebels and the Upper Canadian authorities, which the latter won handsomely. In the trials that were held after the rebellion many of those sentenced followed in the footsteps of George Loveless, being transported to Van Diemen's Land. Toronto had been the centre of the revolt, but the inhabitants of London had also been active. In 1839, as a result of a border clash, three Canadians and three Americans were hanged at London and eighteen others were sent to Van Diemen's Land. Mackenzie himself remained in the United States until 1850 growing yearly more disillusioned with American democracy as practised. In that year he was allowed to return to Canada but he was a broken, dispirited man, the hopes and the ideals of his youth having been shattered. In 1861 he died in the Canada he had wanted to build into a strongly democratic country, which would be a model for the rest of the world, an almost forgotten man.

The years after the Mackenzie rebellion, the period when the Tolpuddle men were settling into Ontario, were years of suspicion and fear. The failure of the revolt had strengthened the supporters of the status quo and dampened the spirit of reform. The immigrants from Britain, searching for a new life, feared to become involved in politics, and it was an era of narrow self-interest.[1]

In the 1840s after the two Canadas had been united, even in the 1860s after Canada became the first Dominion within the British Empire, the country was by no means a free or liberal society. However, there was greater opportunity than in Britain. If the immigrant was prepared to work hard he stood a better chance of breaking away from

[1] A life-long English trade unionist once said to me, 'If the Tolpuddle men had tried to form an agricultural union, which they should have done, and then got into trouble in Canada, they'd have met with a great deal less sympathy and agitation for their release than in England.' There is some justification for the remark, although the suggestion that they should have formed a union after their experiences asked a great deal of basically ordinary men, or any men.

class structures and of becoming his own master than he did in Britain. A folk poem of the time illustrates such an opportunity:

> We've got a tidy place, the saints be praised
> As nice a farm as ever brogan trod –
> A hundred acres – us as never owned
> Land big enough to make a lark a sod.

To this promise of a better, less rigid, society the Lovelesses, the Standfields and the Brines surely responded, even if the practice of the moment meant a non-radical form of government and a concentration on the survival of the fittest and ablest. Another factor of life in Ontario which as surely appealed to them was that the province was strongly Methodist. (It was in Canada that Brine became a Methodist.) It was the Jabez Bunting variety of the old school which said, 'Methodism is as opposed to democracy as to sin', and Mackenzie had been as much in conflict with it as with the High Church establishment. After the rebellion Methodism became a potent force, trying to steer a middle course between the radicalism of Mackenzie and the High Church/High Tory attitudes of the governing body. It was a slow cautious course, partly because it had to cope with the inevitable backlash of the upholders of the status quo, partly from the nature of orthodox Methodism. To the Lovelesses and the Standfields it probably seemed the sensible one. Methodism was their life-blood. They had always been law-abiding citizens, and they were growing older. That they participated whole-heartedly in the religious life of their creed, we know. They may also have worked to foster the political aims of Methodism, the slow road towards reform and tempered liberalism.

Nothing definite is known about George Loveless taking part in any political activities, but later in life John Standfield re-entered the political arena in a minor capacity.

John remained near Bryanston for several years. An 1862 map lists him as owning lot 10 in the 11th concession of London Township, the homestead he built on the land being named, nostalgically, 'Dorset Hall'. This agrees with local tradition which asserts that John built another house near the original homestead on lot 8 in which he and his family lived, while his father and mother remained in the first house. By 1862 John had four more children: Wesley Loveless born in 1848, Herbert Thurgood born in 1850, Evangeline in 1853 and Gertrude in 1856. Tradition next has John moving into Bryanston itself where he kept two stores, one in the south-east corner of the small community, another which he built himself in the south-west. Later still he moved to the outskirts of London Town where he became a hotel proprietor. He had always been a lively man, able to stand up for himself, as his endeavours in New South Wales showed. He made a success of his job as an hotelier, he made contacts and became involved in municipal affairs. For a time he was reeve (the equivalent of mayor) of East London which was then an unincorporated village independent of London Town. During those years of minor municipal power he must have thought back to his years as a convict on the other side of the world. His present life, the knowledge of what he had endured and that he was a triumphant survivor must have given him a great deal of inner satisfaction. John had always been musical and particularly enjoyed singing. He founded a choir in East London which gave concerts and became famous throughout Western Ontario. His wife Elizabeth died in 1883, but he lived until 1898, dying at the age of eighty-five. Both he and Elizabeth were buried in Mount Pleasant cemetery in London. The graves were marked by an elaborate white granite monument but there was no mention on it of the 'Dorchester Unionists'. The secrets of the past had been kept locked in his breast, and seemingly died with John Standfield.

His father and mother, Thomas and Diana, are believed to have spent their declining years at the home of their daughter, Elizabeth Brine. Until recently the dates of their deaths were unknown, but family examination of old bibles revealed that Thomas died on February 19th, 1864, aged seventy-four, while Diana, née Loveless, lived another year, dying in 1865. They were always believed to have been buried in Siloam cemetery, outside London Town, but in unmarked and therefore untraceable graves. Painstaking detection work in the 1950s, by descendants and amateur historians, among the old lists of plot owners and the original layout of Siloam cemetery finally pin-pointed the graves. Diana and Thomas Standfield lay buried in the plot adjoining that of Betsy and George Loveless, both plots having been purchased at the same time so that in death as in life husbands and wives, brother and sister, brother-in-law and sister-in-law could be together.

James and Elizabeth Brine, having gone farther afield into Huron County, returned to London Township to be nearer their old friends. They had one final move, to St Mary's, Blanshard Township, Perth County. Here James Brine built the log homestead in which he was to spend the rest of his life, and which still stands in St Mary's, a local landmark known as 'the old Brine homestead' and the only building connected with the Tolpuddle men remaining in Canada today. Along the line of their various moves the Brines produced seven more children, Louisiana (who died young), William, Evangeline, Charles, Elizabeth, Louise and Tillie, bringing their offspring to the grand total of eleven. At St Mary's, James Brine established himself as a farmer, a respectable pillar of the community, and he lived into the twentieth century, dying in 1902, aged ninety. His wife, née Elizabeth Standfield, survived him by six years, also living to be ninety. Both were buried in St Mary's cemetery, in marked graves, though again there was no mention of their past on the headstones.

James Loveless, who had shown so much of the family determination during the years in New South Wales and his fight to obtain the free passages home, evinced the least enterprise of the five men after their arrival in Canada. He was the only one who apparently never achieved the object of all immigrants – a piece of land to call his own. If, as is believed, he originally settled near his brother George in London Township he did not stay there very long. By 1856, he had moved into London Town itself. In the directory for that year (London's first), he is listed as sexton of the North Street Methodist Church. In that position he apparently remained until his retirement, faithfully serving his chosen creed. He had a further child, Emily, born in 1853, although whether she was the daughter of his first or second wife is not certain. His first wife, Sarah, died and it is known that he married a second time but the date is unrecorded. From the long gap (his two children by his first marriage would, by 1853, have been in their twenties), and the fact that he and Sarah had no more children after his return from New South Wales, it would seem probable that Emily was the daughter of his second marriage. James died on February 16th, 1873, aged sixty-five, and was apparently buried in Mount Pleasant cemetery, London, as the records of the cemetery have the cryptic statement, 'James Loveless, removal, Nov 23rd, 1874 to Sect B. Plot 263.' Discovering why the body was removed, if indeed it was that of *the* James Loveless, again involved painstaking detective work among old records. What happened was that James Loveless was buried in the Methodist cemetery in London Town, as one would expect, but this was sold in 1873, shortly after his interment. The next year Mount Pleasant cemetery was opened and the records of its shareholders' first annual meeting show that 'already over 400 "removals" from other places' for reinterment in Mount Pleasant had been effected, and that James Loveless's body was among those somewhat gruesomely 'removed'. Thus for many years the site of his grave, like that of Diana and Thomas Standfields', remained unknown and therefore unmarked as that of a 'Tolpuddle Martyr'.

Finally, there is George Loveless, the man who more than any other unwittingly set the drama in motion. He and Betsy did not stay on the first farm near Bryanston. In 1851 their son Robert bought a hundred acres of land in the south section of lot 10 in the 9th concession, somewhat nearer to London Town. The next year Robert transferred part of the property to his father who had, presumably, in the meantime sold the original land near Bryanston. Then in January 1856 George purchased land in the 4th concession and the frame house he built there is the one generally associated with him (it was standing in 1951, nearly a hundred years later, but has since been destroyed). This land in the 4th concession was situated at Siloam, just over five miles from the centre of London Town close to the intersection now known as Fanshawe. It was also at Siloam that George helped build a Methodist church. The original wooden church has been destroyed but a brick Methodist church stands on the same site, about two hundred yards from the Fanshawe intersection. It was at Siloam that George and Betsy Loveless lived out their lives, although later, in 1864, George transferred the deeds of the property to his son Robert, while the property given to him by Robert in the 9th concession he handed over to his eldest son, George Junior.

The amount of property owned by the Lovelesses, not vast as land in Canada went, but reasonable, indicates how well they prospered in their new lives. It was not only George and his sons who prospered. Other members of the Loveless family and their relations (including the eldest son of John Loveless, the flax dresser brother from Bridport who had supplied George with the information about trade societies in 1833, and Betsy's brother, Samuel Sprachlen) also came to Canada. (Incidentally, three of John Loveless's other sons emigrated to the United States during those torpid, dispirited years of English rural life in the mid-nineteenth century, and there are many Loveless descendants living in Ohio.) How close the five families remained is indicated by Thomas Standfield and George Loveless buying adjacent plots in Siloam cemetery, by Thomas and Diana Standfield going to live with their daughter Elizabeth Brine, and by John Standfield's naming one of his sons, Wesley Loveless.

Elizabeth Loveless died in 1868, aged sixty-eight. George lived a further six years, dying in 1874, aged seventy-seven. Despite their sufferings the men were a tough breed and lived to a good old age. Both Lovelesses were buried in the selected plot in Siloam cemetery, a short distance from the wooden Methodist church they had helped build. Their graves were from the start marked by a double headstone on which was carved the words, 'These are they which came out of great tribulation and have washed their robes and made them white in the blood of the lamb.' At the time of their deaths it was not known who the Lovelesses were, nor that they had suffered any particular tribulation. All the men had faithfully kept their secret locked in their breasts, and were regarded by their neighbours as hard-working, God-fearing, respectable families of British immigrants who had successfully found a new life in Canada. But George Loveless could obviously not resist the temptation to record the past with a suitable, albeit mysterious, verse from the scriptures. It was a gesture in character with the Loveless who so many years before had thrown the verses of 'God Is Our Guide' into the crowds as he was led, a chained felon, from the Crown Court in Dorchester. In the intervening years he had helped raise the watchword liberty, higher than he himself might have imagined and he had claimed the birthright of his sires, if not in his native land. For him, and for his dear Betsy, it had worked for the good and they had yet rejoiced, as Loveless had hoped in his farewell letter from the hulks.

Epilogue: 'Freedom! Gorgeous Is the Dawn'

In 1834 when the six Tolpuddle men endured the grue-some, grim routine of the hulks, convict ships and transpor-tation, it seemed to be in endless motion. In fact wholesale transportation was nearing its end. Nearly all the witnesses before the Select Committee on Transportation which had been appointed in 1837 to enquire into the system, were against it, although their reasons varied. Some objected from a moral standpoint. It was a form of slavery, however the references were phrased. More objected from a practical morality. The system was a total lottery, therefore hope was withdrawn and redemption unlikely. Others pointed to the soaring crime rates and widespread vice. One witness said that transportation had produced in New South Wales 'a fearful degree of immorality unparalleled, perhaps, in any age or country' and there were frequent references to 'unnatural crimes', homosexuality being rampant in the single-sexed penal settlements, where it was said 'many convicts went by the names of Polly, Sally, Bet etcetera'. Witnesses representing the Churches were particularly horrified by the breadth and kind of vice. Although in the main they showed little sympathy for the convicts themselves, they were in agreement that Christianity was unlikely to win the battle against evil while transportation remained. Nearly all witnesses pleaded for the colony's future. How could a decent class of person be encouraged to settle and the country be peacefully and prosperously expanded, in the face of such arbitrary misery, vice and crime? Others argued on economic lines. With the numbers of overseers, superintendents and magistrates needed to keep the convicts in check, in addition to the hundreds of clerks noting their details and keeping track of their movements and tickets-of-leave and pardons, it was a very expensive method of colonization. In 1838 the yearly cost of transportation to Australia was running at £250,000 and mounting rapidly. Even before this date Sir Richard Bourke had, in a letter to the Colonial Office in London, queried the building of a bridge by convict labour which he said was constructed for the sum of £10,000, whereas in England the same type of bridge would have cost only £7,000. Bourke himself did not give evidence before the Commission, but Governor Arthur did. Basically, he remained in favour of transportation, considering it a just version of crime and punishment that worked. However, his testimony was not so vehement as some of his previous public and written remarks. He admitted that the convict was 'deprived of liberty, exposed to all the caprices of the family . . . and subject to the most summary laws'. Certainly to be of use as a deterrent, he felt that a pamphlet should be issued and widely circulated in England warning people of the true horrors of transportation because he had noticed that on arrival many convicts seemed to be unaware of what lay in store for them.

Although as a result of the Select Committee's report, the volume sharply decreased after 1838, transportation lingered on for many years. By 1849 feeling against it in Australia was running so high that the citizens of both Melbourne and Sydney refused to allow a ship to dock and it had to sail to Brisbane before it could disembark its human cargo. By 1853 transportation to Van Diemen's Land was abolished and in the same year the island changed its name to Tasmania. Western Australia was the last bastion of convicted labour, but by 1867 it had finally ceased even there. Transportation had lasted nearly a hundred years.

The hulk system finally died out during the 1850s, before the end of transportation. Thereafter prisoners, whether sentenced to remain in England or to be sent across Her Majesty's high seas, were confined on dry land. When in

1854 orders were given to destroy the *York*, the hulk in which the Tolpuddle men and so many others had endured so much misery and degradation, the convicts themselves participated in its destruction. They worked at night by torchlight, and the breaking-up of the ship must have been a macabre spectacle. In a brief article describing this strange scene in Portsmouth harbour, the *Illustrated London News*, with commendable liberalism, hoped that the reformatory system under which the convicts were now placed would be attended by 'the most beneficial results', and believed that if care and interest were shown after the convict's discharge from prison that many would become 'useful and respectable members of society'. The *modus operandi* of the Tolpuddle case, the 1797 Mutiny Act, remains on the statute book, albeit in a curtailed version. The general words of Section 1 were altered by the Statute Law Revision Act of 1967; Section 3 was repealed by the Criminal Law Act of 1967; and Section 4 was repealed by the earlier Statute Law Revision Act of 1871. There has never again been confusion, deliberate or otherwise, between the intent and the provisions of the Act.

With reference to trade unionism, it has already been contended that the case of the Dorchester Unionists was of benefit to the movement as a whole, in providing a focal point at a crucial moment in union history, as a result of which the legal right to exist was firmly established. But the idea that trade unionism became an immediately viable force and that the upsurge of enthusiasm as demonstrated in the Tolpuddle protest meetings and countless petitions was a permanent manifestation, must be dispelled. In 1834, overlapping the Tolpuddle furore, a bitter struggle was being waged in Derby between trade unionists and masters. The strike lasted four months, but in the end the unions were beaten. Partly as a result of this bitter defeat, partly because the working classes were disillusioned when the millennium did not occur overnight, Robert Owen's Grand

National Consolidated Trades Union had virtually collapsed by the end of 1834. The next upsurge of mass working-class protest was Chartism which was a political movement. However, Chartism can be regarded as one of the first mergers between the economic and political forces of protest, in that while its motivation was economic, its programme was political. When trade unionism regathered momentum, there was a long, hard road ahead before it was able to effect benefits for its members or become a force to be reckoned with.

In the specific instance of agricultural unionism, the cause for which the Tolpuddle men suffered, the best-laid plans of Melbourne and Frampton did not go awry. The Dorchester Unionists may have attracted the attention of the urban Radicals, but the interest focused on the men themselves, on the injustice done to them, on the wider implications for trade unionism as a whole. It did not switch to the problems of the agricultural workers, to the rural conditions which had made the Tolpuddle men start their Society. Punishing them not so much for what they had done but as an example to others had the desired effect. Agricultural unionism was killed for close on forty years. 1797 Mutiny Acts might have been put into cold storage, but what other statutes could be brought to light? The fact that it was against agricultural workers, not the militant town trade unionists, that the Mutiny Act had been employed, did not, as Melbourne had hoped, escape the attention of the more intelligent farm labourers. All the circumstances which had made concerted political action so unlikely in the country, applied equally to agricultural unionism; the proximity and power of the local hierarchy; the total dependence on them for work; the isolation from the mainstream of activity, political and otherwise; the scattered nature of employment; and to an extent, the conservatism and fatalism of people who work on the land and are never entirely in control of the vagaries of climate.

The English countryside was not, however, entirely torpid in the years after 1834, although it was not until the 1870s that the banner of organized protest was finally raised by Joseph Arch and the National Agricultural Labourers' Union was founded.

At the time of their deaths, the six men themselves had managed to slip into obscurity, as they had desired, although George Loveless's mysterious graveside verse could be interpreted as a cry for future recognition. If it was such, the appeal was more than answered. As the twentieth century dawned and the struggle for decent wages and conditions for rural and urban workers continued, the Tolpuddle men were not only not forgotten but came into increasing prominence as pioneers of agricultural unionism and martyrs for the general cause.

In 1908 an appeal was launched to erect two cottages for the aged in Tolpuddle and to endow a scholarship to Ruskin College, Oxford, to be awarded annually to a bright, young Dorset agricultural worker. (Ruskin College had been founded by the Trades Union Congress in 1899 as a seat of higher learning for the working classes. Its finances were in the hands of Congress, and various unions or bodies sympathetic to Socialist aims endowed scholarships.) The appeal was organized by the Dorset Wesleyan Methodist Circuit, and the cottages and the scholarship were intended as a practical means of honouring the six men. Although the appeal aroused a reasonable amount of interest, it garnered little money. By 1912, when a sum sufficient to build the cottages and endow the scholarship had still not materialized, such money as had been contributed was put to a less practical purpose in erecting a memorial arch in front of the Methodist Chapel in Tolpuddle (although the balance was given to the Dorchester County Hospital). It is a pity that the dream of the scholarship to Ruskin College failed to be translated into reality. George Loveless would surely have given his approval to a scheme whereby a poor but intelligent young Dorset labourer, such as he himself had once been, would have been given the opportunity of stretching his talents to the full at Oxford University.

The memorial arch was unveiled on Whit Monday, 1912, in front of the Methodist Chapel which had been especially cleaned for the occasion. The chapel, an example of Methodist architecture at its most unaesthetic, had no connection with five of the men, the foundation stone not having been laid until 1861. But James Hammett's cousin William was a prime mover in the building, necessitated when the current Tolpuddle squire turned the Methodists out of their existing chapel which stood on land owned by him. (Persecution, it will be noted, still assailed the southern rural adherents of Wesley's creed.) The chapel was built at a cost of £192/3/4d – £192 17p in decimal coinage – which may have accounted for the starkness, and it is believed that Hammett himself worked on the construction. In 1961, when the chapel roof was being repaired, a workman found a piece of lead inscribed 'J. Hammett – 1862' which was thought to be the handiwork of the most famous member of the family. In 1912 the unveiling of the memorial arch was performed by Arthur Henderson, himself a staunch Methodist and one of the earliest of Labour M.P.s. On one column of the arch was inscribed 'Erected in honour of the faithful and brave men of this village who in 1834 so nobly suffered transportation in the cause of liberty, justice and righteousness, and as a stimulus to our own future generations.' On the opposite column were George Loveless's words to the packed Crown Court in Dorchester on April 17th, 1834, starting with, 'We have injured no man's reputation, character, person, or property.' The unveiling ceremony and the speeches were rounded off by the singing of Loveless's 'Song of Freedom'. Locally it was said this was the moment when the Tolpuddle men became respectable and when the name of the village, which had always been Tol*piddle*, was changed to Tol*puddle*, because nobody who came from such an irreverently named place could be treated seriously. So for the sake of respectability and the honour of the Labour movement and of Methodism, as Tolpuddle the village must henceforth be known. In fact, on the 1834 indictment of the six men it was 'Tolpiddle otherwise known as Tolpuddle'.

Although the *Dorset County Chronicle* recorded that 'char-à-bancs, brakes and motors' poured into the village at an unprecedented rate and created an incredible amount of noise, this pre-First World War ceremony was locally based. It attracted little national attention. At the time of the presentation to James Hammett in 1875, the *Bee-Hive* had spoken of the details of 'the prosecution, or rather persecution' as being 'somewhat obscure and not easily obtainable'. Despite the 1912 ceremonies, somewhat obscure they remained. The case of the Tolpuddle Martyrs was written about (and by 1912 they had become the Tolpuddle rather than the Dorchester Martyrs), but even in 1929, when the *Daily Herald* mentioned enlightening new material that had come into the possession of the British Museum (the Frampton/Melbourne correspondence), it merely referred to the letters as relating to six agricultural workers in Dorset rather than naming the men or using the now instantly identifiable label, Tolpuddle Martyrs.

Their 'canonization' did not occur until the centenary of their arrests, 1934, when somewhat late in the day, the labour movements recognized the propaganda value of the six men and decided to give them their full, due honour. This was perhaps not unconnected with the fact that the labour movements were living through internally strife-ridden and the externally dismal days of the 1930s Depression. The first Labour governments of 1923 and 1929 had come to power in unenviable circumstances and had unsurprisingly failed to achieve even a modicum of the millennium for their followers. By opting for a 'National' Government in 1931, rather than resigning or struggling on in a minority position, Ramsay Macdonald had split the Labour movement in two, with the majority regarding him as the great betrayer. What the T.U.C., which became the main disseminator of the Tolpuddle story, did with these unpalatable facts, at least in their popular propaganda, was largely to ignore them. They concentrated on the past, on reminding both their opponents and their disillusioned supporters of the conditions out of which trade unionism and Socialism had been born. Advances had been made and more than ever the weak-spirited must bear them in mind and keep right on to the end of the road, fighting until the new Jerusalem had been established in England's no longer entirely green and pleasant land.

The first of the many ceremonies organized by the T.U.C. in 1934 occurred in Plymouth where a gathering was held on the Mayflower Steps to commemorate the landing of the freed Standfields, James Brine and James Loveless in 1838. The main events obviously took place in Tolpuddle itself, at the end of August and the beginning of September. There was the unveiling of a shelter in the shadow of the sycamore tree, by then known as 'the martyrs' tree', under whose branches the six men had discussed some of their problems and plans a hundred years previously. There was the further unveiling of a headstone, which the T.U.C. had commissioned Eric Gill to carve, over the grave of James Hammett, the sole martyr to have been buried in his native land. On the simple slab of stone the figures '1834' are encircled by chains and the following words are carved: 'James Hammett, Tolpuddle Martyr, Pioneer of Trades Unionism, Champion of Freedom, Born 11 December 1811, Died 21 November 1891.' There was the dedication of a memorial plaque, attached to the wall of the Standfields' thatched cottage in the High Street. The ceremony was again performed by Arthur

Henderson and the plaque states: 'To the memory of six Agricultural Labourers of this village whose Trade Union meetings in this cottage led to their being sentenced to seven years transportation in 1834'. And there was the official opening of six cottages, each named after one of the 'martyrs'. The T.U.C. had adopted the idea that had collapsed in 1908 from lack of sufficient donations and had built not two, but six, cottages, for the use of retired agricultural unionists. Unfortunately, they did not adopt the other idea of endowing a scholarship to Ruskin College, Oxford. The results of these various centenary ceremonies remain visible in Tolpuddle in the mid-1980s.

Apart from organizing happenings and competitions up and down the country, the T.U.C. produced their literary tribute, *The Martyrs of Tolpuddle*, a large, lavishly illustrated and documented, if less than fully researched and far from infallible volume. It contained Walter Citrine's account of the story, pieces by illustrious Socialists on various aspects of the case, and a foreword from George Bernard Shaw in his most mischievous mood. He wrote: 'I am afraid I cannot say anything in praise of the Dorchester martyrs. Martyrs are a nuisance in Labor [*sic*] movements. The business of a Labor man is not to suffer, but to make other people suffer until they make him reasonably comfortable.' GBS finished his brief blast by embellishing the sentiments of Lord Ellenborough who, in a Penal Reform debate in 1810, had asserted that transportation was regarded by many of its victims 'as a summer airing by an easy migration to a milder climate'. Shaw wrote: 'There is this, however, to be said for the Dorchester men. They got transported at the expense of their landlords and employers. As they could hardly, if they were reasonable men, have desired to live in Dorset as slaves – for that is what it came to – they were lucky to be pushed out of it.' It can be said that GBS's perverse comments provided an antidote to the due seriousness of the rest of the book and the innumerable solemn tributes that occurred in and around Dorchester in 1934. The centenary year also spawned a clutch of plays about the Tolpuddle men, the best of which remains Miles Malleson's and Harry Brooks' *Six Men of Dorset*. Originally their play was performed by amateurs in the Corn Exchange in Dorchester during the commemorative week, but later in 1937 it had its professional premiere with a cast of high quality including Sybil Thorndike as Betsy Loveless and Lewis Casson as George.

If the T.U.C. in their celebrations eschewed the current 1934 political and economic situation, there was one person who did not. That was the old Welsh Wizard, Lloyd George, the first member of the working class to be Prime Minister. He could afford to be contentious as he no longer held high office nor did the Liberal party look like regaining their former ascendancy. Lloyd George climbed on to the band-wagon before the main T.U.C. activities were underway, in July of 1934, and the old magic was very much in evidence. On one of the hottest days of the year, with the temperature soaring into the nineties, the seventy-one-year-old war-horse first laid a wreath on the memorial arch in front of the Methodist Chapel in Tolpuddle. He then proceeded to the upper room of Thomas Standfield's cottage in the High Street, and from there to the 'Martyrs' Tree'. Under the tree he gave one of the impromptu speeches for which he was famous and told Hammett's son, William, who was present, that 'I would rather be descended from your father than from William the Conqueror', a remark which received nation-wide coverage. Lloyd George also said that the names of the Tolpuddle men would endure for evermore, whereupon a voice from the crowd said, 'So will yours, Sir.' From Tolpuddle he proceeded to Dorchester where in the afternoon, ·in the sweltering heat, he addressed a large crowd in the football ground for over an hour. He spoke of 'the only landless peasantry in the world' deprived of their rights by the Enclosure Acts, still a depressed segment of the population with too few rights. He attacked the current policies regarding agriculture, particularly the 'dumping' of Commonwealth produce (a development which would have intrigued the Tolpuddle men, as the main culprit was Australia). At the beginning of the meeting Loveless's 'Song of Freedom' was sung, but at the end it was 'Land of My Fathers', and all newspapers commented on the vastness and warmth of the crowds who turned out to see Lloyd George and of the spell he was still able to weave.

It was not only in England that the centenary was celebrated. It was widely reported in Western Europe, notably Germany, and the T.U.C. did comment on the struggles of their brethren in Adolf Hitler's Germany. Inaccurate parallels were drawn between the fight of the Tolpuddle men and the Whigs and that of the German trade unionists and the Third Reich; but then in 1934 no sane person could have imagined the depths of horror into which the Third Reich was to plunge Europe and by comparison with which even the system of convict transportation paled. In Canada the Trades and Labor Congress, similarly enmeshed in the Depression, seized the opportunity to remind their countrymen that they, like the Lovelesses, had come out of and intended to survive great tribulation. A ceremony was held at the Lovelesses' grave in Siloam cemetery which developed into an annual event when, on the Sunday before Labor Day, officials laid wreaths on the grave and a simple service was held. There was also a nicely romantic scheme to mingle the soil from the Loveless grave with that of Hammett's, but although the Canadian soil reached Tolpuddle on time, Hammett's was suspended somewhere in mid-Atlantic and did not arrive until 1935. Thereafter the desire to honour this segment of Anglo-Canadian history gathered momentum. In 1959 an impressive plaque was unveiled in Siloam cemetery. Surmounted by the coat-of-arms of Ontario it states:

> Within this cemetery lies George Loveless. He, with his brother James, John and Thomas Standfield, James Brine and James Hammett, were condemned to penal servitude in 1834 for organizing in Tolpuddle, Dorsetshire, England, a union of farm labourers. George Loveless was sent to Van Diemen's Land, the others to New South Wales. Public indignation brought about their pardon and return to England in 1837. The case of 'The Tolpuddle Martyrs' became a turning point in labour laws and practices in the United Kingdom. In 1844 all except Hammett migrated to this district. George Loveless died near here, May 6th, 1874.

In 1969 a Labor Memorial Park was officially opened on Queen's Avenue, London, Ontario, and dedicated to the memory of the Tolpuddle Martyrs. The five men, who in Tolpuddle owned neither garden nor allotted strip of land, would surely have liked the idea of a public park in their memory, one in which children could play, particularly as they were such devoted family men. The Canadians rightly claim that it was in their country that five of the 'martyrs' found a safe haven where they prospered, and died in peace.

In Australia in the centenary year there was nothing specific to celebrate, other than the demise of the British system of transportation. To an extent their interest then reflected an ambivalent attitude towards their days as 'the great gaol to the Empire'. In 1937, however, the identification of the stone cottage in which George Loveless had lived during his period as a ticket-of-leave man working for Major de Gillern attracted some attention. The estate had changed its name from Glen Ayr to Strathayr but it was still magnificently situated against the backdrop of wooded hills that Loveless had known. In recent years, as Australia has cut loose from the apron strings of the Mother Country and found her own identity, interest in the Tolpuddle men has grown rather than lessened. For the Australian labour movements too, they have become a symbol of past injustice and the need for present and future vigilance.

The ceremonies and celebrations were not confined to the centenary year. In July 1947, for no apparent reason other than that Britain had just emerged from the war with Hitler and in the austerity years was eager to grasp any opportunity for celebration, there was a further week of happenings in Dorchester. The festivities were opened by the Labour Chancellor of the Exchequer, Hugh Dalton, while the main event was the unveiling of a plaque on the wall of Dorchester County Hall by Alderman Gooch, long-time agricultural unionist and then president of the National Union of Agricultural Workers. The plaque states that 'In this building on March 19th, 1834, the six Tolpuddle men were sentenced to seven years transportation for their part in the founding of Rural Unionism.' Subsequently, in 1956, after the County Council had ceased to use the County Hall, the T.U.C. bought the old Crown Court and it is now preserved as a memorial to the Tolpuddle men.

The 150th anniversary of the arrest, trial and sentence of the six men followed a similar pattern to the centenary commemorations, with a ceremony in Plymouth early in 1984 to mark the triumphant return home, and a grand demonstration in Tolpuddle in July, though this was of one day's duration only. No new memorials were unveiled but a baby tree was planted, close by the old sycamore. The play *Six Men of Dorset* was also successfully revived, appropriately by the politically committed 7–84 company, though perhaps less appropriately, in view of GBS's comments on the Dorchester labourers, at the Shaw Theatre in

London. In one of England's long, hot summers, Sunday, July 1st was a particularly glorious day, with the heat shimmering along Tolpuddle High Street, past the Standfields' cottage and Hammett's grave, under the aged sycamore tree, over the sloping fields, the narrow lanes and banked hedgerows, and those lumpy Dorset hills that the six men had loved and longed for during their days as convicted felons. It was a day of proudly waving banners, a gathering of the labour clans from the three countries most connected with the Tolpuddle men: Britain, Canada and Australia. The mainly British crowd, some ten thousand strong, cheered the speakers, British, Canadian and Australian, including the newish Labour leader Neil Kinnock, mostly to the echo. The brown faces of the several contingents of Asian origin – though there were not many black ones evident – reflected the post-Second World War, post-Empire, multi-racial British society that none of the six men would have recognized.

Despite the pride, solidarity and apparent confidence displayed at this 150th anniversary, and enhanced by the beauty of the day, the grand demonstration took place in a context as externally dismal and internally strife-ridden as the centenary celebrations had been for the British labour movements. It took place in the middle of the 1984–85 miners' strike, the longest, most bitter and violent confrontation between trade unions and government within memory; though by no means, contrary to the loud assertions of those unaware of their British social history, of all times. Throughout this book the word 'Radical' has been correctly used with the capital 'R' to denote those loosely allied, early and mid-nineteenth century political forces of the left who were thus nominated. The basic definition of 'radical' is 'of the root' and there is nothing essentially, inherently, or fundamentally left-wing in the word. In 1984 the British trade unions were dealing with a radically right-wing government under the leadership of

Margaret Thatcher, one of whose election and re-election platforms was the curbing of their alleged power. Alleged because it can be strongly counter-argued that one of the problems of the world's first trade union movement has, from its earliest days, been that it was a *defensive* movement; merely uniting, as George Loveless said, 'to protect ourselves, our wives and our children from utter degradation and starvation'. The trade unions have seldom had the confidence to go on to the attack, which is the position from which to acquire real power. It was in the context of a radically right-wing political climate that the 150th anniversary was celebrated by the embattled British labour movements. With renewed emphasis the six men from Tolpuddle became the symbols of why the trade unions came into being and why they remain essential to effect any sort of just, equitable balance in any industrialized and technological society.

It has always been ironic that the six men now upheld as the pioneers of trade unionism, sufferers in the cause of liberty, justice and righteousness, should have been agricultural labourers. For the trade unions were born out of the industrial revolution; they were the concomitant urban development. It should therefore have been six men from Manchester, Leeds, Glasgow, or one of the northern towns that spawned the industrial revolution, who became the standard bearers, not a group of agricultural labourers, members of the last basic community to organize itself and one that has never been listed among the more militant. Having had the roles of 'martyrs' thrust upon them, the Tolpuddle men rose nobly to the fearsome challenge. So, in a different way, did their womenfolk, George Loveless's dear Betsy in particular, but Harriet Hammett, Diana Standfield, James Loveless's wife Sarah and James Brine's mother Catherine, all held their heads high in times of sore trial and tribulation. George Bernard Shaw in his capriciously provocative mood was wrong. Causes need, or at least are helped by, martyrs, so that the protagonists can point to the horrors and injustices that led to the martyrdom, and perhaps also because they provide a useful repository for vicarious suffering.

In the preceding pages an emphasis has been laid upon the sober, law-abiding side of George Loveless's character, but there was the other side, too, without which he would never have founded the Friendly Society in the first place. To the furious crusader who quoted John Milton in his tract *The Church Shown Up* thus, 'Give me the liberty to think, to speak, and to argue freely according to conscience, above all other liberties', and who himself wrote in the resonant language of nineteenth-century Methodism, shall go the last words, in his already quoted clarion cry:

'I would call upon every working man in England . . . to shake off that supineness and indifference to their interest. Arise, men of Britain and take your stand! Rally round the standard of Liberty, or for ever lie prostrate under the iron hand of your land and money-mongering taskmasters!'

Notes and Sources

My two main sources for manuscript material were the Public Records Office in London and the Archives Authority of New South Wales. The majority of the New South Wales material had not, to my knowledge, been previously printed. I have therefore given the sources clearly – and the convict records overlap between England and Australia – for those interested.

During my original research the Melbourne Papers in the British Museum had become unavailable, for reasons which were unclear, because they had previously been open to researchers. However, the T.U.C. had printed the Frampton/Melbourne correspondence in *The Martyrs of Tolpuddle* and of this I gratefully availed myself.

Chapter 1: 'RESPECTING THE CHARACTERS, ETC., OF THE SIX MEN'

The chapter heading is from Frampton's letter to Melbourne, written on 29.3.1834, when he had the honour to acquaint his lordship with the result of enquiries 'respecting the characters, etc., of the Six Men who were convicted at the Dorchester Assizes for administering unlawful oaths'. It is quoted from the T.U.C. book, *The Martyrs of Tolpuddle*.

Page 11. Regarding the weather, I tried to trace what sort of day February 24th, 1834, was. Official daily weather forecasts were not introduced until 1860, nor was I able to trace any local 1834 diaries describing the elements on the day of the arrests.

Page 11. The conversation between Loveless and Constable Brine is as recorded in *The Victims of Whiggery*.

Page 14. The assertion that Loveless was persecuted because he was a Methodist preacher appeared in the *Morning Chronicle*, 2.4.1834.

Page 17. The physical description of George Loveless in the 'Calendar of Prisoners for the Dorchester Assizes' is scant. I have followed that recorded on board the convict ship *William Metcalfe* (C.O.N. 18/22 Archives Office of Tasmania, Hobart).

Page 17. The statement that no less than seven persons of the name of Loveless were engaged in union activities was made in Frampton's letter to Melbourne of 29.3.1834. It is quoted from the T.U.C. book.

Page 18. The quotation about the Loveless brothers' mental capacity is from Thomas Wakley's mammoth speech to the House of Commons, 25.6.1834 (*Hansard Parliamentary Debates*, vol. XXXVIII).

Pages 18–19. For the physical descriptions of James Loveless, John and Thomas Standfield and James Brine I have followed those in the 'Calendar of Prisoners for the Dorchester Assizes', Lent 1834. They are much more detailed than those recorded for George Loveless. The 'Calendar' is in the Dorset County Records Office, Dorchester.

Page 20. James Hammett's physical description is also from the 'Calendar'.

Page 20. Owen Rattenbury, born into a well-known Methodist family and author of the romantic novel about the six men, *Flame of Freedom*, was among those who propagated the idea that Hammett was not a member of the Friendly Society. In the 1950 edition of his novel Rattenbury printed information, culled from Methodist registers, that there were the three James Hammetts probably alive in Tolpuddle in 1834; born 1785, 1801 and 1812 respectively; none of which dates fits *the* Hammett born in 1811.

Pages 22. Hammett's previous conviction is recorded in the 'Calendar of Prisoners for the Dorchester Assizes': folio 41, no. 50, 1829, for the committal; folio 42, no. 40, 1829, for the sentence (Dorset County Records Office, Dorchester).

Chapter 2: 'HOW DO YOU LIVE UPON HALF A CROWN A WEEK?'

The chapter heading is William Cobbett's question to an agricultural labourer. It comes from his *Political Register*, 29.3.1823.

Page 29. The reason for the Speenhamland meeting was reported in the *Reading Mercury*, 20.4.1795.

Page 30. The explanation about X and Y turning off their men was given in the *First Report of the Law Commissioners 1835*.

Page 31. The labourer's eloquent rhetorical questions were recorded in the *Annals of Agriculture*, vol. XXXXVI.

Page 31. Cobbett's question and answer to and from the poacher were recorded in the *Political Register*, 29.3.1823.

Page 31. The statement that 'nothing but the terror of human suffering can avail to prevent crime' was made by Sir William Dyott and is quoted from the Hammonds' *The Village Labourer*.

Page 34. Cobbett's description of the roadside dwellings is from his *Rural Rides*.

Page 34–5. The lack of concerted action among the peasants was reported in *The Times*, 17.11.1830.

Page 35. The magistrate's similar conclusion was written in a letter to the Home Office (H.O. 52/11).

Page 35. The contemporary diarist was Mary Frampton, and she gave her opinions about Charles X in her *Journal*.

Pages 35. The objective of the 'Swing' revolt was given in a letter circulated in Sussex. It is quoted from the Hammonds' *The Village Labourer*.

Page 35. The labourer's remark to Henry Hunt that they wanted full bellies for their children was reported in *The Times*, 23.11.1830.

Page 36. The admirable conduct of the peasantry was reported in *The Times*, 17.11.1830.

Pages 37. The Times correspondent's description of the scene at the Wiltshire Special Commission is quoted from the Hammonds' *The Village Labourer*.

Page 39. The sympathetic attitude of the magistrate, ibid.

Pages 39. The homily to the rich was delivered in *The Times*, 6.12.1830.

Page 39. That the 'Swing' insurrection was a dangerous precedent was reported in *The Times*, 17.11.1830.

Chapter 3: 'A KIND OF AGRICULTURAL SAVINGS BANK'

The chapter heading is from Mr Derbishire's defence speech at the trial, when he spoke of the Friendly Society as 'a kind of Agricultural savings bank'. It was reported in *The Times* and the *Dorset County Chronicle*, 20.3.1834.

Page 40. The sad song about Van Diemen's shore is quoted from Barbara Kerr's *Bound to the Soil*.

Page 40. The account of the meeting between farmers and men is as recorded by George Loveless in *The Victims of Whiggery*.

Page 40–41. Doctor Warren's promise, ibid.

Page 41. The remark about the reduction of wages causing great dissatisfaction and Loveless's description of the activities of all the villagers, excepting the two or three invalids, ibid.

Page 42–3. 'Eight Shillings a Week' is included in *Victorian Street Ballads*, edited by W. Henderson (*Country Life*, 1937).

Page 43. That it was impossible to live honestly on such scanty means was stated by George Loveless in *The Victims of Whiggery*.

Page 44. The fact that Loveless had seen accounts of Trades Societies, ibid.

Page 44. Francis Place's comment on the 1824 Repeal of the Combination Acts is from the Place Papers (Add. MSS. 27798/22, British Museum).

Pages 45. The discovery of the copy of the rules of the Flax and Hemp Trade in Loveless's locked box was reported by Frampton to Lord Melbourne in a letter written on 5.3.1834. It is quoted from the T.U.C. book.

Page 45. George Loveless's comment that it was his relation, Robert, who assisted him in forming the Friendly Society was made in his statement to Thomas Mason, the Assistant Police Magistrate, in Hobart on 15.9.1834 (C.O. 280/52, Public Records Office).

Pages 46. The 1841 census returns for Tolpuddle are contained in H.O. 107/286.

Pages 46–8. Details of the rules and regulations of the Friendly Society were taken from the material admitted in evidence at the trial, and reported in *The Times* and the *Dorset County Chronicle*, 20.3.1834.

Page 47. The password for the Tolpuddle lodge, 'Either Hand or Heart', was recorded by George Loveless in his statement made in Hobart, 15.9.1834 (C.O. 280/52, Public Records Office).

Page 49. Loveless's statement that the initiation oath was 'a form of prayer', ibid.

Page 49. His description of the delegates as 'a better sort of people', ibid.

Pages 49–51. The details of the initiation ceremony, the statement of John Lock and the description of the Lovelesses as being dressed in surplice-like smocks are from the trial as recorded in *The Times* and the *Dorset County Chronicle*, 20.3.1834.

The chapter heading is a line from 'Eight Shillings a Week', a contemporary ballad.

Page 52. A copy of *A Voice of Friendly Warning*, written by the Reverend Charles J. James, is contained in H.O. 40/33.

Page 56. The comment about the young Melbourne's ability to do anything if he chose was made by Lord Castlereagh. It is quoted from Lord David Cecil's *Melbourne*.

Page 56. Brother George's eleventh commandment, ibid.

Page 56. Melbourne's notes and aphorisms, ibid.

Pages 56–7. The comment about *Oliver Twist*, ibid.

Page 57. Lord Grey's comment on Melbourne's sudden activity is quoted in *Lord Melbourne Papers*, edited by Lloyd C. Sanders.

Page 57. Melbourne's comments about trade unions amounting to a conspiracy to control their masters was made in a letter to Sir Herbert Taylor, 24.11.1831, ibid.

Page 57. His belief that the unions were inconsistent and contrary to the laws of nature is quoted from Lord Cecil's *Melbourne*.

Page 57. The often-quoted letter about the unions being the most formidable difficulty and danger with which any government had to contend was also written to Sir Herbert Taylor (*Lord Melbourne Papers*).

Page 57. Professor Nassau Senior's assessment of the light in which trade unionists viewed themselves and their masters was made in his *Report on Trade Combinations 1831*.

Page 59–60. Edmund Burke's words are from his *Reflections on the Revolution in France* (1790).

Page 60. Charles Wollaston's comment that Frampton was in love with the Queen (Marie-Antoinette) was written in a letter to his mother in 1791, and is recorded in Mary Frampton's *Journal*.

Page 60. His comment on finding Moreton House barricaded like an Irish Mansion is quoted from *The Agricultural Riots in Dorset* by W. H. Parry Okeden.

Page 60. Mary Frampton's remark about the difficulties Portman occasioned by offering to raise wages is from her *Journal*.

Page 61. Her comments on her brother's spirited activity and consequent unpopularity, ibid.

Page 61. The description of Frampton as 'the Draco of the fields' is quoted from Barbara Kerr's *Bound to the Soil*.

Page 61. The description of Christmas dinner at Moreton in 1830 is from Mary Frampton's *Journal*.

Chapter 5: 'I HOPE YOU HAVE A COMPLETE CASE FOR CONVICTION'

The chapter heading is taken from a letter written by Portman to James Frampton on 1.3.1834. It is quoted from the T.U.C. book.

Page 62. Frampton's letter to Lord Melbourne regarding the dangerous combinations in the area and the employment of trusty persons to discover their activities was written on 30.1.1834. It is quoted from the T.U.C. book.

Page 63. Melbourne's reply, suggesting the use of the 25th section of 57 Geo. III, c. 19, was written on 31.1.1834 (H.O. 43/44).

Page 63. His earlier advice to the Duke of Wellington about the usefulness of this statute was written on 20.11.1832 (*Lord Melbourne Papers*).

Page 65. A photostat of the original Caution appears in the T.U.C. book. It bears the date February 22nd. George Loveless himself said in *The Victims of Whiggery* that the Caution was posted on February 21st.

Page 69. George Loveless wrote of being called before a bench of magistrates in *The Victims of Whiggery*.

Page 69. His comment about Edward Legg's testimony, ibid.

Page 70. His description of the discomfort of Dorchester Gaol, ibid.

Page 70. It was George Loveless, in *The Victims of Whiggery*, who said they were all in the gaol for striving to live honest.

Pages 72–3. Melbourne's letter to his law officers requesting their urgent opinion on the illegality of trade societies (H.O. 49/7).

Chapter 6: 'AN ACT FOR THE MORE EFFECTUALLY PREVENTING THE ADMINISTERING OF UNLAWFUL OATHS'

The chapter heading is taken from the 1797 Mutiny Act, 37 Geo. III, c. 123.

Page 75. Portman's letter to Frampton asking if he meant to proceed at the next Assizes is quoted from the T.U.C. book.

Page 76. (footnote). Serjeant Wilde's statement about the preparation of the indictment of 25.6.1835 is recorded in *Parliamentary Debates*, vol. XXVIII.

Page 76. George Loveless wrote of the fire and the foulness of the atmosphere in the Crown Court cells in *The Victims of Whiggery*.

Page 78. Lord Chancellor Brougham's wicked comment on Williams being made a judge is quoted from *Victorian Chancellors*, vol. II.

Page 78. The usual reading of His Majesty's most gracious proclamation was recorded in *The Times*, 18.3.1834. *The Times*, incidentally, was about the only newspaper to cover the grand jury hearing, in contrast to the many newspapers that covered the actual trial.

Page 78. Mr Baron Williams' speech calling the grand jury's particular attention to the case in the calendar where six persons were charged with administering unlawful oaths was reported in *The Times*, 18.3.1834.

Page 79. His comments upon the nature and quality of the offence, ibid.

Page 79. His comments on labourers refusing to join the societies at danger to life and limb, and having their common right obligations taken away from them, ibid.

Page 81. George Loveless's comment about the grand jury was recorded in *The Victims of Whiggery*.

Page 81. George Loveless's opinion of the petty jury as land-renters, ibid.

Page 82. The deep interest excited by the trial was reported in the *Sherborne, Dorchester and Taunton Journal*, 20.3.1834.

Page 82–3. The wording of the indictment is quoted from the T.U.C. book.

Pages 83 passim, 89. I have assembled the prosecution case from four contemporary newspapers, *The Times*, the *Dorset County Chronicle*, the *True Sun* and the *Sherborne, Dorchester and Taunton Journal*, all of which reported the trial on 20.3.1834. There is little discrepancy in the four reports. It is more a question of what they cut and what they covered. I selected these four newspapers as representing a fair cross-section: of the two local papers, the *Dorset County Chronicle* was the brightest of Tory blue, while the *Sherborne, Dorchester and Taunton Journal* was more liberal-minded and Whig (although it was, of course, the Whig administration that indicted the six men); of the two metropolitan papers, *The Times* was Tory but supported the government, and the *True Sun* was Radical.

Page 85. The comments on the actual nature of the charge appeared in the *Law Magazine*, vol. XI, May 1834.

Pages 85. George Loveless's comments on the evidence and the judge's interference were made in *The Victims of Whiggery*.

Page 85. The statement that the witnesses were not nearly so forthcoming in the witness box as they had been in their earlier depositions appeared in the *Law Magazine*, vol. XI, May 1834.

Chapter 7: 'WITHIN THE LETTER AND LEGAL SPIRIT OF THE LAW'

The chapter heading is from the article on the Dorchester Labourers that appeared in the *Law Magazine*, vol. XI, May 1834. The magazine considered that the indictment and convictions were 'within the letter and legal spirit of the law'.

Pages 91 passim, 96. The details of, and quotations from, Mr Butt's and Mr Derbishire's defence cases are from the same four newspapers as the prosecution case, namely the *Dorset County Chronicle, The Times*, the *True Sun* and the *Sherborne, Dorchester and Taunton Journal*, 20.3.1834.

Pages 96. George Loveless's written statement to the court is as recorded in *The Victims of Whiggery*.

Page 96. His accusation that Mr Baron Williams mumbled the statement so that nobody could hear it, ibid.

Page 97. His account of Williams' summing-up, ibid.

Page 97. Williams' contention that the precise nature of the oath was not a material subject for enquiry is from *The Times*, 20.3.1834.

Page 98. His statement that the drawings were intended to strike awe into the minds of the person to whom the oath was administered is from the *Dorset County Chronicle*, 20.3.1834.

Page 100. The details of the sentence, and Williams' observation that the intentions of the prisoners could be known only to themselves are as recorded in the *Dorset County Chronicle*, 20.3.1834.

Pages 100. The wording of the actual judgment, that each of the men be transported beyond the seas, ibid.

Page 100–1. The two verses of the 'Song of Freedom', are quoted from *The Victims of Whiggery*.

Page 101. It was Hammett's grand-daughter, Mrs Roberts, who said of course George had written the poem. I admit to not myself having tracked down the earlier evidence but to have accepted Walter Citrine's assertion in the T.U.C.'s book, *The Martyrs of Tolpuddle.*

Chapter 8: 'AN EASY MIGRATION TO A MILDER CLIMATE'

The chapter heading is from a remark made by Lord Ellenborough in a Penal Reform Debate in 1810. He said that transportation was thus regarded by its victims, as an easy migration to a milder climate.

Page 103. The *Memoirs* of James Hardy Vaux were first published in 1819, reprinted in 1827. They were not authenticated by the publishers, but were presented as a moral tract – what could or would happen to those who failed to keep to the paths of righteousness. The ebullience of Vaux's writing and character dissipated the morality. He emerges as one who would have fared splendidly if born rich, when he could have idled and gambled the years away. He did not believe in hard work or the just rewards of virtue. The book ends with his second transportation and return home. That he twice earned himself a free pardon and a free passage home is a tribute to his charm and plausibility. What happened to him eventually is not known. There are signs at the end of the book that even his ebullience was being worn down by the convict system.

Page 105. The sentence of fourteen years' transportation on a boy who had stolen some cheese, two ferrets and a tinder box is recorded in the 'Calendar of Prisoners for the Dorchester Assizes' (Dorset County Records Office, Dorchester).

Page 107. The records of the *York* and *Leviathan* hulks are contained in H.O. 9/8 and 9/9.

Page 107. George Loveless's description of the berth on

board the *William Metcalfe* is as recorded in *The Victims of Whiggery*.

Page 108. His comment that he had previously seen and heard but little, ibid.

Pages 108. John Standfield's horror at being confined with criminals is from *A Narrative of the Sufferings of Jas. Loveless, Jas. Brine and Thomas and John Standfield*.

Page 108. His comment on the rations, ibid.

Page 109. His agonized reflection that he had done nothing to deserve this punishment, ibid.

Page 110. George Loveless's conversation with Charles Wollaston is as recorded in *The Victims of Whiggery*.

Page 110. His astonishment at the sights that greeted him on board the *York*, ibid.

Page 111. The young convict's letter to his mother is contained in Appendix 21 to the *Select Committee on Transportation 1837*.

Page 112. George Loveless's letters to his wife, Betsy, were read by Thomas Wakley to the House of Commons in the debate of July 1835 (*Parliamentary Debates*, vol. XXVIII). Wakley in fact said that the first letter was headed 'Spithead, May 28th, 1834', which makes somebody's calculations wrong as Loveless said the *William Metcalfe* sailed from Spithead on May 25th.

Chapter 9: 'REFUSAL OF BILLY GUELPH TO PARDON THE UNIONISTS'

The chapter heading is from a column in *The Pioneer*, April 1834, a copy of which is contained in H.O. 64/19. 'Billy Guelph' was, of course, King William IV.

Page 116. That the trade unions were the most dangerous institutions ever legally permitted to exist was printed in the *Morning Post*, 29.3.1834.

Page 116. The view that the unions were the revenge of the working classes upon the capitalists appeared in the

Sunday Herald and was reprinted in one of the *True Sun*'s opinion polls on 7.4.1834.

Page 116. That the unions should not be attacked by a sidewind, and that the verdict showed the treachery of the law appeared in the *Morning Herald*, 2.4.1834.

Page 116. That people were not punished in England for that which they were found guilty was printed in the *Morning Chronicle*, 2.4.1834.

Page 116. The first use of the word 'martyrs' in connection with the six men appeared in a reader's letter to the *True Sun*, 5.4.1834.

Page 118. Doctor Wade was described as the chaplain to the metropolitan trade unions in *The Times*, 22.4.1834.

Page 118. The reader's letter asking whether Doctor Wade was *still* chaplain in Warwickshire appeared in *The Times*, 24.4.1834.

Page 119. The quotations from Robert Owen's speech are as reported in the *True Sun*, 25.3.1834.

Page 120. The wording of the Oxford petition is from *Parliamentary Debates*, vol. XXII, 1834.

Page 120. That the King had not been pleased to signify any commands upon the petition was reported in the *True Sun*, 3.4.1834.

Page 120. That the men were en route to Botany Bay was reported in the *True Sun*, 5.4.1834. It quoted an earlier report in the *Morning Post*.

Page 122. *The Republican* reported the decoration of its office windows with black stickers on 13.4.1834.

Page 122. The hour of trial being at hand was stated in the *True Sun*, 7.4.1834.

Page 122. The *Spectator*'s ironic query about the Dukes of Cumberland and Sussex was reprinted in the *True Sun*, 7.4.1834.

Page 123. The *Leeds Mercury*'s assessment of Daniel O'Connell was made later, in 1843, when he was at the height of his campaign for the repeal of the Act of Union. It is quoted from *The Life and Times of Daniel O'Connell*, a pamphlet printed in Dublin in 1846.

Pages 124. O'Connell's query about his slumbering statute is from *Parliamentary Debates*, vol. XXII, 1834.

Page 124. Mr Hutt's comment on the mischievous nature of trade unions, ibid.

Chapter 10: 'LABOUR PUT ITS HAT UPON ITS HEAD AND WALKED TOWARDS THE THRONE'

The chapter heading is from *The Pioneer*, 26.4.1834. On that day it ran an issue devoted to the Copenhagen Fields meeting and the subsequent procession. The front page carried a picture of the upper part of Copenhagen Fields in which it was estimated 'that no less than four hundred thousand persons were assembled on the occasion'. The text started with the words: 'Last Monday was a day in Britain's history which long will be remembered; for labour put its hat upon its head and walked towards the throne. Labour has been a thing of late which politicians thought possessed no soul; a thing of nerves and muscles without morality, and void of intellect.' The article proceeded to demonstrate that labour had both soul and intellect.

Pages 126–7. A copy of the letter from Lord Melbourne to Frampton, through the normal channels of the Under-Secretary, is contained in H.O. 43/45. The 'private and confidential' letter is quoted from the T.U.C. book.

Page 127. Frampton's letter reporting the anxiety of all classes and the great satisfaction derived by the Higher Classes from the sentence was written to Lord Melbourne on 29.3.1834. It is quoted from the T.U.C. book.

Page 128. The fact that Diana Standfield was told she should want and be shown no mercy was reported in the *True Sun*, 31.3.1834.

Page 128. The magistrates' cry to the wives and mothers, ibid.

Page 129. Frampton's letter of 8.4.1834, describing the well-dressed person who had arrived in the neighbourhood, is quoted from the T.U.C. book.

Page 129. His more detailed description of the person was sent to Lord Melbourne on April 11th, and is also quoted from the T.U.C. book.

Page 129. The purpose of Mr Newman's visit was given in a letter of April 19th and is similarly quoted from the T.U.C. book.

Page 130. Melbourne's request for information about the six men was contained in a private letter to Frampton and is quoted from the T.U.C. book.

Pages 130–31. Frampton's reply giving the unflattering character details of the six men was written on March 29th. Similarly quoted from the T.U.C. book.

Page 131. Melbourne's reply querying the grounds on which it was stated the Lovelesses had been involved in the 1830 riots was written on March 29th. This also was a private letter and is quoted from the T.U.C. book.

Page 131. Frampton's reply with the vague unsubstantiated information was written on April 2nd and is quoted from the T.U.C. book.

Page 133. The room at the Crown and Anchor being crowded to suffocation was reported in the *True Sun*, 19.4.1834.

Pages 133. That O'Connell contributed his mite in the name of God and mercy, ibid.

Page 134. His assessment that the English trade unions would provide an example to the world, ibid.

Page 134. His description of the House of Commons as an ugly house, ibid.

Page 134. Lovett's comments about the stimulus given to the Grand National Consolidated Trades Union by the Dorchester sentences are quoted from his autobiography, *The Life and Struggles of W. Lovett.*

Page 135. Francis Place's letter of 21.4.1834 is from the Place Papers (Add. MSS. 35154. British Museum).

Page 135. Place's references to the long holiday and the efforts of the discreet gentleman, ibid.

Page 136. Copenhagen Fields was described as the old rendezvous of disturbance in *The Times*, 19.4.1834.

Page 136. Lord Melbourne's accustomed courtesy was noted in the *True Sun*, 22.4.1834.

Page 136-7. Details of the troop detachments were reported in *The Times*, 22.4.1834.

Page 137. The descriptions of the various trades is quoted from an article entitled 'Traits of the Trades Unions' printed in the *Sherborne, Dorchester and Taunton Journal*, 1.5.1834.

Page 137. The different numbers of banners were reported in *The Times* and the *True Sun*, 22.4.1834.

Page 137. The *coup d'oeil* of the assembly on Copenhagen Fields was described in *The Times*, 22.4.1834.

Pages 138-9. Melbourne's refusal to accept the petition unless presented in a proper manner was reported in the *True Sun*, 22.4.1834.

Page 139. Lovett described the procession as one of the most remarkable ever to walk through the streets of London in his autobiography, *The Life and Struggles of W. Lovett*.

Page 139. Labour putting its hat upon its head is quoted from *The Pioneer*, 26.4.1834 (as chapter heading).

Page 139. The analysis of the numbers involved in the procession, and the report of the eye-witness, appeared in *The Times*, 22.4.1834.

Page 140. The demeanour of the participants, ibid.

Page 141. The Central Committee's receiving another 'evasive, and unmeaning answer' was reported in the *True Sun*, 28.4.1834.

Page 142. Mr Ewett's letter, as read by Daniel O'Connell, is from *Parliamentary Debates*, vol. XXIII, 1834.

Page 142. Lord Londonderry's inability to conceive for what object the trade unions congregated, ibid.

Page 142–3. The fact that Melbourne spoke in a low tone of voice was reported in *The Times*, 29.4.1834.

Page 143 (footnote). Melbourne's explanation of the torpor which overcame him in the House of Commons is quoted from Lord David Cecil's *Melbourne*.

Page 144. The comment that it was a little odd that nobody mentioned the monster petition, appeared in the *True Sun*, 29.4.1834.

Chapter 11: 'IN SHORT THE CONVICT IS, PROPERLY SPEAKING, A SLAVE?'

The chapter heading was a question put to a witness before the Select Committee on Transportation, 1837. The witness's answer was, 'Yes'.

Page 145. Cobbett's remark about the agitation being to the eternal honour of England was made in the *Political Register*, 5.4.1834.

Page 146. The various comments on the conditions on Norfolk Island were made by witnesses before the Select Committee on Transportation, 1837. It was a Catholic priest who said that those condemned to death there thanked God for His mercy; and Sir Francis Forbes, the Chief Justice of New South Wales, who said he would prefer death in any form to life on Norfolk Island.

Page 146. The young convict's remark about keeping a still tongue in one's head appears in Appendix 21 to the *Select Committee on Transportation 1837*.

Page 146–7. His comments that if you did not behave yourself you might as well be hung at once, ibid.

Page 147. The words of the convict who killed an overseer are quoted from *The Adventures of Ralph Rashleigh*. This book was published in 1929, and authenticated in an introduction by Lord Birkenhead. It is a curious book, dating back to the early days of transportation, full of hideous and horrifying descriptions of life in New South Wales; particularly in the lime pits at Newcastle (abandoned by 1834), where, as a punishment, convicts worked up to their necks in salt water, carrying lime immediately after being lashed, and where many walked into the water and drowned themselves rather than endure the agony. It is curious in that it ends with Rashleigh's redemption, thanking God for the virtues of the convict system which had shown him the true light. Or perhaps it is not so curious. Minor erotic-sadism needed uplift to be publishable in 1929. Lord Birkenhead, like Rashleigh and Governor Arthur, approved of the system. In his view it worked extremely well.

Page 148. The statement that the convict rarely sought and even more rarely obtained legal redress was made by a witness to the Select Committee on Transportation, 1837.

Page 148–9. The list of weekly punishments, ibid.

Pages 149. Details of the summary convictions and the number of floggings are from the *Report of the Select Committee on Transportation 1838*.

Page 152 (footnote). The relative criminal statistics were presented to the Select Committee on Transportation, 1837.

Pages 153–4. The details of the five Tolpuddle men on arrival in Sydney are contained in 'The Indent of the Convict Transport "Surrey", 17th August 1834' (A.O. 4/4018, Archives Office of New South Wales, Sydney).

Page 155. The brief details sent back to London are contained in H.O. 10/30.

Pages 156 passim 159. Details of the journeys of, and quotations from, the two Standfields, James Brine and James Loveless are as recorded by them in *A Narrative of the Sufferings* . . .

Page 160. Hammett's account of his experiences on arrival in Sydney was made when he was presented with the watch and illuminated address in 1875. It was reported in the *Dorset County Express*, 23.3.1875.

Page 160. His laconic conversation on how to get to Woodlands, ibid.

Chapter 12: 'THE GREAT GAOL TO THE EMPIRE'

The chapter heading was Governor Arthur's view of the Van Diemen's Land he ruled. It quoted from *Governor Arthur's Convict System* by W. D. Forsyth.

Page 164. Arthur's powers as a quill driver were noted by a contemporary. The remark is quoted from *Governor Arthur's Convict System*.

Page 165. The description of George Loveless on board the *William Metcalfe* is contained in C.O.N. 18/22, Archives Office of Tasmania, Hobart.

Page 166 (footnote). Arthur's observation on how deeply the 'Swing' labourers felt their transportation was made to the Select Committee on Transportation, 1837.

Page 166. Arthur's comments that Loveless had been deceived by more artful men were written on 20.12.1834 (C.O. 280/25, Public Records Office).

Page 167. Loveless's statement of 15.9.1834, ibid.

Pages 167–8. Loveless's own version of the conversations are as recorded in *The Victims of Whiggery*.

Page 168–9. Mason's comment that Loveless had been ordered to be worked in irons, ibid.

Page 169. The official returns to London for the *William Metcalfe* (C.O. 280/54, Public Records Office).

Page 169. The Appropriation List recording that Loveless was sent to the Domain Farm (C.S.O. 1/16103, Archives Office of Tasmania, Hobart).

Page 169. The Tasmanian defended Governor Arthur's conduct, and praised his refusal to work Loveless in irons on the roads, in an article of 16.9.1836.

Page 170. Loveless's laconic comment about the effects of transportation is recorded in *The Victims of Whiggery*.

Pages 170. His comments about the hut and the weather, ibid.

Page 170. His comments about being married to the three sisters, ibid.

Page 171. The magistrate's comments on releasing him with a reprimand, ibid. That Loveless was only reprimanded for 'neglect of duty' is also recorded in C.O.N. 31/28, Archives Office of Tasmania, Hobart.

Page 171. Loveless's description of Hobart as not inviting, and his comments on the abundance of peaches and grapes are from *The Victims of Whiggery*.

Page 173. His account of what happened to convicts Greenwood and Pocock, ibid.

Page 173. His meeting the survivor of the *George III*, ibid.

Page 174. Details of the loss of life on the *Neva*, and Governor Arthur's complaints about the missing despatches are contained in C.O. 280/58, Public Records Office.

Page 174. Loveless's conclusions about transportation are from *The Victims of Whiggery*.

Chapter 13: 'THE QUESTION OF THE DORCHESTER LABOURERS IS NOT FINALLY DISPOSED OF'

The chapter heading is the remark made by Lord John Russell to Melbourne in his letter of 9.10.1835 (*Early Correspondence of Lord John Russell, 1805–1840*).

Page 175. That Mr Baron Williams seemed to be regularly assigned to try men for administering illegal oaths was noted in the *True Sun*, 30.7.1834.

Page 175. The copy of the oath as administered by the unions was contained in Melbourne's letter to his law officers, 5.5.1834 (H.O. 49/7).

Page 176. Melbourne's comment on the damned boredom

of being Prime Minister is quoted from Lord David Cecil's *Melbourne*.

Page 176. Melbourne's leaving the King in a great state of excitement was reported in the *Sherborne, Dorchester and Taunton Journal,* 28.11.1835.

Page 176. The *Morning Chronicle*'s acid comments on Peel's ministry were reprinted in the *Sherborne, Dorchester and Taunton Journal,* 27.11.1835.

Page 179. The description of the fidgety Russell is quoted from *Lord John Russell* by A. Wyatt Tilby.

Pages 180 passim 185. The details of the debate of 25.6.1835, and the quotations from Wakley's speech are from *Parliamentary Debates*, vol. XXVIII.

Page 185. The London Dorchester Committee's analysis of the voting on Wakley's June 1835 motion was presented at the end of *The Victims of Whiggery*.

Page 185. The letter to Governor Arthur of 12.6.1835 (C.O. 408/10, Public Records Office); that to Sir Richard Bourke (C.O. 202/32, Public Records Office).

Page 187. The copy of Russell's letter to Glenelg was enclosed with a despatch to Governor Arthur of 8.7.1835 (C.O. 408/10, Public Records Office); that for Sir Richard Bourke (C.O. 202/32, Public Records Office).

Page 188. Russell stated that he was not disposed to do anything more for the Dorsetshire Labourers in his letter to Melbourne, 2.10.1835. It is quoted from the T.U.C. book.

Page 188. Melbourne's reply, considering that the matter had been settled, was written on 6.10.1835 and is taken from *Early Correspondence of Lord John Russell*, edited by Rollo Russell.

Page 188. Russell's next letter in which he stated that further facts had come to light, and that it required putting together two Acts of Parliament to prove the illegality, was written on 9.10.1835, ibid.

Page 188. Melbourne's reply, washing his hands of the matter, was written on 13.10.1835, ibid.

Page 188. Melbourne's suggestion that the wives might join their husbands was contained in his letter of 6.10.1835, ibid.

Page 189. The October 1835 letter from Glenelg to Governor Arthur (C.O. 408/12, Public Records Office); to Sir Richard Bourke (C.O. 202/32, Public Records Office).

Chapter 14: 'THE REAL DIFFICULTY RAISED BY THE ACT 2ND AND 3RD WILLIAM IV, C. 62'

The chapter heading is taken from Glenelg's letter to Governor Arthur, 8.7.1835 (C.O. 408/10, Public Records Office).

Pages 191–2. Loveless's account of his interviews with Mr Spode is from *The Victims of Whiggery*.

Page 191. His conversation with Governor Arthur, ibid.

Page 193. His exemption from every penal observance, dated 3.2.1936, is recorded in his convict record (C.O.N. 31/28, Archives Office of Tasmania, Hobart).

Page 194. A photostat of Governor Arthur's letter to Glenelg, 13.2.1836, in which he stated that Loveless was desirous of remaining in the colony is contained in the Dorset County Records Office, Dorchester.

Page 195. Major de Gillern's letters regarding his difficulties in obtaining denization papers (C.O. 280/56, Public Records Office).

Page 197. Sir Richard Bourke's memorandum, requesting information on the five men as quickly as possible, was written on 29.10.1835 (C.S.I.L. 35/9349, Archives Authority of New South Wales, Sydney).

Page 197. The Colonial Secretary's letter of 9.11.1835 to the Principal Superintendent of Convicts, transmitting the request (4/3681, Archives Authority of New South Wales, Sydney). ˙

Page 198. Sir Richard Bourke's memorandum of 13.1. 1836, ordering the men to be brought to Hyde Park Barracks (C.S.I.L. 36/509, Archives Authority of New South Wales, Sydney).

Page 198. The Superintendent's reply, 14.1.1836, explaining the reasons for the delay, ibid.

Page 198. The Colonial Secretary's instructions ordering the men to be brought to the barracks, 15.1.1836 (4/3682, Archives Authority of New South Wales, Sydney).

Page 199. Bourke's letter to Glenelg, 20.2.1836, explaining his actions regarding the five men (C.O. 201/252, Public Records Office).

Page 200. John Standfield's account of being marched through Sydney like a lot of wild beasts is from *A Narrative of the Sufferings* . . .

Page 201. James Brine's account of being put on board a ship for Norfolk Island, ibid.

Page 202. The Standfields' petition to Sir Richard Bourke (C.S.I.L. 36/2297, Archives Authority of New South Wales, Sydney).

Page 203. The Colonial Secretary's letter informing the Superintendent of Convicts that the Standfields were to be returned to Timothy Nowlan, 17.3.1836 (4/3682, Archives Authority of New South Wales, Sydney).

Page 204. Bourke's orders that the men were to be kept on the barrack list and not sent out to labour were transmitted by the Colonial Secretary on 15.2.1836 (4/3682, Archives Authority of New South Wales, Sydney).

Page 204. The Principal Superintendent's letter announcing that Hammett had arrived at the barracks from Woodlands (C.S.I.L. 36/3938, Archives Authority of New South Wales, Sydney).

Page 204. The Colonial Secretary's letter instructing that Hammett remain at the barracks until an opportunity arose for forwarding him to Port Macquarie (4/3682, Archives Authority of New South Wales, Sydney).

Page 205. Sir Richard Bourke's instructions that the men should receive the benefit of their pardons once the period fixed in the warrants had expired was written on 21.6.1836, and is quoted from H. V. Evatt's *Injustice within the Law.*

Page 205. That James Loveless was told he was fortunate not to have been hung was recorded in *A Narrative of the Sufferings* . . .

Chapter 15: 'HIS MAJESTY HAS BEEN PLEASED TO GRANT A FREE PARDON'

The chapter heading is Lord John Russell's announcement to the House of Commons on 14.3.1836 (*Parliamentary Debates,* vol. XXXII).

Pages 207–8. The information that an indictment had been prepared against the Duke of Cumberland appeared in the *Radical,* 3.4.1836.

Page 208. The comments about the Orange Lodges not being dissolved until after the Dorchester Labourer agitation appeared in the *Globe,* 24.12.1839.

Page 210. Lord John Russell's announcing the pardons with great satisfaction (*Parliamentary Debates,* vol. XXXII).

Page 211. The letter from the Tolpuddle wives and mother is quoted from the T.U.C. book.

Page 212. The despatches announcing the free pardons and the free passages if desired, to Sir Richard Bourke (C.O. 202/34, Public Records Office); to Governor Arthur (C.O. 408/12, Public Records Office).

Page 212. A copy of George Loveless's pardon is contained in H.O. 17/42.

Page 213. The accusation that the electors of Hobart were confined to a limited number of individuals was printed in a a pamphlet forwarded to the Colonial Office in London (C.O. 280/60, Public Records Office).

Page 214. The pamphlets showing the tyranny and oppression of Arthur's régime, ibid.

Page 215–16. George Loveless's words regarding the dilemma of his wife are from *The Victims of Whiggery*.

Page 216. Mr Spode's curt reply, ibid.

Page 216. The Colonial Secretary's argument that Loveless did nothing he was told, ibid.

Page 216. Loveless's plea that he was sent out a prisoner, etc., ibid.

Page 216. The Colonial Secretary's asking what he did want, ibid.

Page 216–17. The memorandum from Mr Spode regarding the free passage home, ibid.

Page 218. John Standfield's comment that nobody ever told them about their free pardons is from *A Narrative of the Sufferings* . . .

Page 219. Sir Richard Bourke's instructions to ascertain whether the men wanted their free passages home were transmitted by his Colonial Secretary to the Principal Superintendent of Convicts 18.11.1836 (4/3682, Archives Authority of New South Wales, Sydney).

Page 219. The Superintendent replied on 24.7.1837 (C.S.I.L. 37/6816, Archives Authority of New South Wales, Sydney).

Page 219–20. James Loveless recorded that he went to Sydney to learn the truth in *A Narrative of the Sufferings* . . .

Page 220. The fact that John Standfield wrote to inform Uncle James of the good news, ibid.

Page 221. Captain Robson's offer of £5 was transmitted by the Harbour Master to the Colonial Secretary, 23.8.1837, (C.S.I.L. 37/7954, Archives Authority of New South Wales, Sydney).

Page 222. The marginal note regarding the disposal of £5 was dated 30.8.1837, ibid.

Page 224. E. J. Eyre applied for a replacement convict on 1.5.1836 (C.S.I.L. 36/4314); instructions to supply him with one, in place of Hammett, were issued by the Colonial Secretary, 23.5.1836 (4/3682, Archives Authority of New South Wales, Sydney).

Chapter 16: 'THE POOR DORSETSHIRE LABOURERS RESTORED TO THEIR COTTAGES'

The chapter heading has been adapted from a paragraph that appeared in the *Standard*, 28.3.1834. The original ran thus: 'Let those who have sinned in ignorance have the benefit of ignorance; let the six poor Dorsetshire labourers be restored to their cottages.'

Page 229. His companions not being able to ascertain Hammett's residence was reported in the *Plymouth, Devonport and Stonehouse Herald*, 24.3.1838.

Page 229. That he had chosen to remain in the colony was reported in the *Devonport Telegraph and Plymouth Chronicle*, 24.3.1838.

Page 230. That the reading of *The Victims of Whiggery* excited much interest was recorded in the *Plymouth, Devonport and Stonehouse Herald*, 24.3.1838.

Page 230. That the procession could be viewed as proof of the people's advancement was reported in the *Plymouth Weekly Journal*, 19.4.1838.

Page 231. The wording of the banner – 'The Queen's Guards – The People' – was reported in the *Devonport Independent*, 21.4.1838.

Page 231. Details of the tunes played by the farriers' band are from the *Morning Chronicle*, 17.4.1838.

Page 231. The extraordinary nature of Doctor Wade's grace was recorded in the *Globe*, 17.4.1838.

Page 232. The description of the five men as unaffected labourers, ibid.

Page 236. The wording of the placard appeared in the *Dorset County Chronicle*, 15.11.1838.

Page 236. That the attendance figures barely exceeded 1,500, ibid.

Page 236. The ranting nature of the speeches, ibid.

Page 237. That Standfield received three cheers, ibid.

Page 237. The speaker's reference to the bloody Whigs and the purchase of the farms, ibid.

Page 237. Details of the resolution electing George Loveless as the Dorset delegate to the Chartist convention, ibid.

Pages 237. The *Dorset County Chronicle*'s observations on the meeting, ibid.

Page 237–8. James Frampton's letter to the Home Office, with marginal comment (H.O. 40/36).

Chapter 17: 'THEY THAT SOW IN TEARS SHALL REAP IN JOY'

The chapter heading is from Samuel Hammett's *Morning Light*. This was the waking thought for March 15th, the day the grand jury found the True Bill in 1834.

Pages 240. The marriage entry of James Brine and Elizabeth Standfield is extant in the Greensted parish records.

Page 241. The article on the Tolpuddle men and the Chartism in Essex appeared in the *Morning Post*, 17.12.1839. It was reprinted, almost in toto, in the *Essex Standard*, 20.12.1839.

Page 242. The indignant letter from the Conservative magistrate was printed in the *Morning Post*, 28.12.1839.

Page 243–4. Hammett's Memorial to Sir George Gipps (C.S.I.L. 39/2147, Archives Authority of Sydney, New South Wales).

Page 244. Sir George Gipps' memorandum regarding Hammett's passage was written on 20.2.1839. (C.S.I.L. 39/2147, Archives Authority of Sydney, New South Wales).

Page 244. The letter of 27.2.1839 confirming Hammett's

passage (C.S.I.L. 39/2497, Archives Authority of Sydney, New South Wales).

Pages 246. Advertisements for the Farewell Benefit, giving details of the price of seats and the entertainment to be presented, appeared in *Cleave's Penny Gazette* on 28.9 and 5.10.1839.

Pages 246–8. A full report of the actual Benefit, from which the quotations have been taken, appeared in *Cleave's Penny Gazette*, 19.10.1839. The T.U.C. book mentions the Benefit but gives the date as September 22nd, 1839. The book was well researched in the English sections (although no sources are given), so I can offer no explanation for this error of date. I have combed every contemporary 1839 London newspaper; there was only one Benefit for the Dorchester Labourers and it was on October 8th, not September 22nd, 1839.

Page 249. The 1841 census returns for Tolpuddle (H.O. 107/286).

Page 249. Regarding Hammett's third marriage, the remarks of William Hammett appeared in The *Scotsman*, 9.7.1934. The local genealogist who informed me of his conversation with Hammett's relative was Mr L. O. Bealing of Bournemouth.

Page 250. The report of the presentation appeared in the *Bee-Hive*, 20.3.1875.

Page 250. The description of Hammett as a simple old man, shrinking from the limelight, appeared in the *Dorset County Express*, 23.3.1875.

Page 251. The hymn composed for the occasion, ibid.

Page 251. The chairman's reference to the necessity for forming unions, ibid.

Pages 251–2. The reason for the meetings, to honour George Loveless and Hammett, ibid.

Page 252. The reference to the clergy alienating themselves from their flock, ibid.

Pages 252. The text of the illuminated address, ibid.

Page 253. Hammett's words of thanks, ibid.

Page 254. The information that Mrs Roberts believed her grandfather to have been a quiet saint was given to me by the Reverend R. D. Moore.

Pages 255–6. Samuel Hammett's copy of *Morning Light – A Waking Thought for Every Day of the Year* is in the T.U.C. library at Congress House, London. I am grateful to the Librarian for bringing it to my attention.

Chapter 18: 'THE LAND BIG ENOUGH TO MAKE A LARK A SOD'

The chapter heading is my transposition of the lines from a contemporary Canadian folk poem:

> We've got a tidy place, the saints be praised
> As nice a farm as ever brogan trod –
> A hundred acres – us as never owned
> Land big enough to make a lark a sod.

Page 258. I have been unable to trace *Christian Songs*, the pamphlet written by H. Brine. Neither the British Museum nor the master files of the Toronto public libraries were able to help. However, it is quoted with great authority in the T.U.C. book, and in various Canadian handouts, so I am sure it exists somewhere.

Page 260. The information to emigrants to Canada as to what they should take with them (C.O. 384/30, Public Records Office).

Page 262. The throwing into the Atlantic of dead passengers 'one after t'other' is quoted from *Building the Canadian Nation* by George W. Brown.

Page 262. The statement made in the Canadian Legislature about the emigrants arriving in a state of destitution is from *Papers Relative to the British Emigration to the British Provinces in North America, 1847.*

Page 262. Charity Brine's birth date was given as 28.1.1844, in a brief piece at the time of her death in the *Daily Express*, 3.8.1935.

Page 262–3. With reference to the birth dates of the Standfield and Brine children, and the years of emigration, Mr Allen Talbot of London, Ontario, kindly sent me photostats of family trees compiled by descendants. On examining these it became obvious that, if they were correct, the families could not all have emigrated in 1844. Mr Talbot then obtained for me copies of the 1851 and 1861 Ontario census returns which proved the family trees to be correct, and the separate emigration of the families.

Page 264. My information on William Loveless, who emigrated from Dorset in 1828, was obtained by Mr Allen Talbot who interviewed a descendant in June 1970, in St George, near Hamilton, Ontario. William Loveless landed in New York, and travelled to Scarborough via Niagara Falls (one of the possible routes suggested for George Loveless reaching Hamilton). He was a coachman to Lord Simcoe, the Lieutenant-Governor of Upper Canada.

Page 264–5. The discovery of George Loveless's first recorded home, lot 11 of the 12th concession of London Township, was made by Mr Leslie R. Gray in June 1970 and relayed to me. It had previously been believed that Loveless settled originally near Siloam, but Mr Gray was checking land records in Toronto when he found an unlisted deed recording the purchase of the land in the 12th concession by Loveless from Francis Walden in 1847, which meant that his first known home was near Bryanston.

Page 265. The brass-barrelled blunderbuss belonging to James Brine was in 1971 in the possession of Mr Allen Talbot of London, Ontario.

Page 266. The first recorded home of the Standfields in lot 8 of the 11th concession, not far from Bryanston, was relayed to me by Mr Allen Talbot from the Toronto land records.

Page 266. It was Governor Head who said that the people of Upper Canada detested democracy, in fact in 1836, but the sentiments had been true for many years. His words are quoted from *The Firebrand* by William Kilbourn.

Page 266. The descriptions of Mackenzie as the O'Connell of Canada, and being unable to keep a secret, ibid.

Page 269. The poem is quoted from *Building the Canadian Nation* by George W. Brown.

Page 271. Regarding the discovery of Diana and Thomas Standfield's grave, it was Mr Allen Talbot who undertook the task of sifting through the lists of plot owners and the original lay-out of Siloam cemetery. He has printed the story of his detective work in *In Memory of the Tolpuddle Martyrs.*

Page 272. The facts about the removal and reburial of James Loveless, ibid.

Page 273. Regarding the various plots of land owned by George Loveless and his sons, Mr Leslie R. Gray sent me the information which he had obtained from the land records in Toronto.

Epilogue: 'FREEDOM! GORGEOUS IS THE DAWN'

The chapter heading is the first line of a poem printed by *The Pioneer,* 15.3.1834.

> *Freedom! gorgeous is the dawn*
> *Of the brightly coming morn*
> *Radiantly approaching now*
> *Flushing every manly brow*
> *With a hue, from which decay*
> *Coldly glancing, wings away*
> *Like a baffled bird of prey.*

Page 276. The comments on the fearful immorality, unnatural crimes and the names by which convicts were known are from the report of the Select Committee on Transportation, 1837.

Page 277. Governor Arthur's comments, ibid.

Page 277–8. The comments on the destruction of the *York* and the hopes for the convicts' future appeared in *Illustrated London News*, 8.4.1854.

Page 281. The information about the piece of lead inscribed 'J. Hammett – 1862' came from the Tolpuddle Martyrs Memorial Trust, via the Reverend R. D. Moore.

Page 282. The arrival in Tolpuddle of 'char-à-bancs', brakes and motors was reported in the *Dorset County Chronicle*, 30.5.1912.

Page 282. The details of the Tolpuddle prosecution as obscure was recorded in the *Bee-Hive*, 27.3.1875.

Page 285. Lloyd George's remark that he would rather be descended from James Hammett than William the Conqueror was reported in the *News Chronicle*, 9.7.1934.

Page 285. The voice from the crowd replying, 'So will yours, Sir' was reported in *The Scotsman*, 9.7.1934.

Page 285–6. Lloyd George's remarks about the landless peasantry were reported in the *Salisbury Times*, 13.7.1934.

Pages 288–9. The author was present at the 150th anniversary gathering in Tolpuddle on 1 July, 1984.

Page 291. George Loveless's words are from *The Victims of Whiggery*.

Bibliography

MANUSCRIPT MATERIAL

Home Office and Colonial Office Papers. Public Records Office, London.

Calendar of Prisoners for the Dorchester Assizes. Dorset County Records Office, Dorchester.

Place Papers. British Museum.

Convict Records, Governors Minutes and Colonial Secretary In and Out Letters. Archives Authority of New South Wales, Sydney.

Convict Records. Archives Office of Tasmania, Hobart.

STATE PAPERS (*England*)

Third Report for the Committee on the Laws Relating to Penitentiary Houses 1812.

Select Committee on Transportation 1837.

Report from the Select Committee on Transportation 1838.

Papers Relative to the British Emigration to the British Provinces in North America. Part I, 1847.

Parliamentary Debates. Third Series (1830–91), vols. XXII, XXIII, XXVIII, XXX, XXXI, XXXII.

NEWSPAPERS AND JOURNALS

National

Bee-Hive.
Cleave's Penny Gazette of Variety.
Cobbett's Political Register.
Dispatch.
Globe.
Law Magazine, vol. XI, 1834.

Morning Chronicle.
Morning Herald.
Morning Post.
The Pioneer.
The Republican.
Standard.
The Times.
True Sun.

Provincial

Devonport Independent.
Devonport Telegraph and Plymouth Chronicle.
Dorset County Chronicle and Somersetshire Gazette.
Dorset County Express.
Plymouth, Devonport and Stonehouse Herald.
Plymouth Weekly Journal.
Sherborne, Dorchester and Taunton Journal.

Overseas

Australian.
Colonial Times, Tasmania.
The Tasmanian.

CONTEMPORARY BOOKS AND PAMPHLETS

Anon. *Life and Times of Daniel O'Connell.* Dublin, 1846.
Bulwer, William Henry Lytton. *Private Memoir of the Late Lord Melbourne.* London, 1848.
James, Revd. Charles J. *A Voice of Friendly Warning Addressed to the Labouring Classes who have been and are tempted to become Members of an Illegal Union.* London, 1835.
Loveless, George. *The Victims of Whiggery; being a statement of the persecutions experienced by the Dorchester Labourers; their trial, banishment, etc. Also reflections upon the present system of transportation. With an account of Van Diemen's Land, its customs, produce, and inhabitants, dedicated (without permission)*

to Lords Melbourne, Grey, Russell, Brougham and Judge Williams. London, 1837.

Loveless, George. *The Church Shown Up (Letter to the Revd. Henry Walter, Vicar of Haselbury Bryant, Dorsetshire)*. London, 1838.

Loveless, James (and Brine, Jas., Standfield, Thomas and John). *A Narrative of the Sufferings of Jas. Loveless, Jas. Brine and Thomas and John Standfield. Four of the Dorchester Labourers. Displaying the Horrors of Transportation. Written by Themselves. With a Brief Description of New South Wales by George Loveless*. London, 1838.

Torrens, R. *Wages and Combinations*. London, 1834.

Tufnell, Henry. *Character, Object and Effects of Trades Unions*. London, 1834.

Vaux, James Hardy. *Memoirs*. London, 1827.

LATER NINETEENTH-CENTURY WORKS

Arch, Joseph. *The Story of His Life*. London: Hutchinson, 1898.

Clarke, Marcus. *History of Australia*. Melbourne, 1877.

Frampton, Mary. *Journal*. London: Sampson, Low, Marston, Searle and Rivington, 1885.

Lovett, William. *The Life and Struggles of W. Lovett*. London, 1876. New edition under the title *Life and Struggles of William Lovett*. London: MacGibbon & Kee, 1967.

Sanders, Lloyd C. (editor). *Lord Melbourne Papers*. London: Longmans, 1889.

Sprigge, Sir Samuel Squire. *The Life and Times of Thomas Wakley*. London: Longmans, 1897.

Walpole, Sir Spencer. *The Life of Lord John Russell*. London: Longmans, 1889.

TWENTIETH-CENTURY WORKS

Bateson, Charles. *Convict Ships*. Glasgow: Brown Son and Ferguson, 1959.

Brown, George W. *Building the Canadian Nation*. Toronto: Dent (Canada), 1942.

Brown, George W. *Canada in the Making*. London: Dent, 1953.

Cecil, Lord David. *Melbourne*. London: Constable, 1965.

Citrine, Walter (editor). *The Martyrs of Tolpuddle*. London: T.U.C., 1934.

Cole, G. D. H. *Short History of the British Working Class Movement*. London: Allen & Unwin, 1948.

Cole, G. D. H. *Attempts at General Union*. London: Macmillan, 1953.

Cowan, Helen I. *British Emigration to British North America*. Toronto: University Library, 1928.

Dunbabin, Thomas. *The Making of Australia*. London: A. & C. Black, 1922.

Evatt, Herbert Vere. *Injustice within the Law*. Sydney: Law Book Co. of Australia, 1937.

Forsyth, William Douglass. *Governor Arthur's Convict System. Van Diemen's Land, 1824–36*. London: Longmans, 1935.

Groves, Reg. *Sharpen the Sickle. The History of the Farm Workers' Union*. London: Porcupine Press, 1949.

Hammond, J. L. and Barbara. *The Village Labourer, 1760–1832*. London: Longmans, 1911 (paperback edition, Longmans, 1966.)

Hobsbawm, E. J. and Rudé, George. *Captain Swing*. London: Lawrence & Wishart, 1969.

Kerr, Barbara. *Bound to the Soil*. London: John Baker, 1968.

Kilbourn, William. *The Firebrand*. London: Jonathan Cape, 1958.

Lewis, D. B. Wyndham. *Four Favourites*. London: Evans, 1948.

O'Faolain, Sean. *King of the Beggars. A Life of Daniel O'Connell, the Irish Liberator, in a Study of the Rise of Modern Irish Democracy, 1775–1847*. London: Nelson, 1938.

Pate, William (editor). *Victoria History of Dorset*. London: Constable, 1908.

Rashleigh, Ralph. *The Adventures of Ralph Rashleigh. A Penal Exile in Australia, 1825–1844*. London: Jonathan Cape, 1929.

Rattenbury, Owen. *Flame of Freedom. The Romantic Story of the Tolpuddle Martyrs*. London: Epworth Press, 1931.

Russell, Rollo (editor). *Early Correspondence of Lord John Russell, 1805–1840*. London: T. Fisher, Unwin, 1913.

Tilby, A. Wyatt. *Lord John Russell*. London: Cassell, 1930.

Wearmouth, Robert F. *Methodism and the Working Class Movements of England 1800–1850*. London: Epworth Press, 1937.

Webb, Sydney and Beatrice. *The History of Trade Unionism*. Revised edition extended to 1920. London: Longmans, 1920.

MONOGRAPHS AND ARTICLES

Landon, Fred. *The Tolpuddle Martyrs Settled Near London*. Text of a C.B.C. network broadcast.

Okeden, W. H. Parry. *The Agricultural Riots in Dorset*. Dorset Natural History and Archaeological Society, vol. LII, 1930.

Talbot, Allen G. *In Memory of the Tolpuddle Martyrs*. Ontario Historical Society, 1970.

Walker, W. Maitland. *An Impartial Appreciation of the Tolpuddle Martyrs*. Dorset Natural History and Archaeological Society, vol. LV, 1933.

Index

334